7AM

DOSTOYEVSKY'S CRITIQUE OF THE WEST

THE QUEST FOR THE EARTHLY PARADISE

BRUCE K. WARD

While most commentators reflect on the spiritual side of Dostoyevsky's writings, not as much attention has been given to his concern with the crisis of the modern West. His allusions to almost every aspect of Western civilization—including the political, economic, and social dimensions—are present in his literary works and abound in his secondary writings.

This book points the way to a proper understanding of the apparent contradiction between Dostoyevsky's concern with the highest reaches of human spirituality and at the same time with the most detailed developments in domestic and international politics. It posits that the apparent polarization of "religious" thought and "political" analysis of the West are held together for Dostoyevsky in his search for the best human order. Ward demonstrates not only that Dostoyevsky's observations about the West constitute a coherent critique intimately related to the deepest aspects of his thought, but also that these can be rendered more systematic and explicit and thus more accessible to those who are interested.

What results is an incisive and intriguing account of both the religious and the political thought of Dostoyevsky. It also fulfills the purpose of helping to clarify what Dostoyevsky can teach us about the modern situation of the Western world and about the problem of human order in general, for, as the author states, "it was Dostoyevsky's great virtue as a thinker always to see the pressing issues of his particular time and place in the light of the 'everlasting' problems."

Bruce K. Ward teaches in the Department of Religious Studies at Thorneloe College of Laurentian University, Sudbury, Ontario.

DOSTOYEVSKY'S CRITIQUE OF THE WEST

The Quest for the Earthly Paradise

Bruce K. Ward

Wilfrid Laurier University Press

Canadian Cataloguing in Publication Data

Ward, Bruce Kinsey.
    Dostoyevsky's critique of the West

Bibliography: p.
Includes index.
ISBN 0-88920-190-0

1. Dostoyevsky, Fyodor, 1821-1881 — Criticism
and interpretation.   I. Title.

PG3328.W37 1986   891.73′3   C86-094610-X

WILFRID LAURIER UNIVERSITY PRESS
Waterloo, Ontario, Canada   N2L 3C5

86 87 88 89 4 3 2 1

Cover design by David Antscherl

Printed in Canada

for
Norma

Il ne nous reste plus d'ailleurs qu'à renaître ou à mourir.
—Albert Camus, *L'Homme révolté*

CONTENTS

ACKNOWLEDGMENTS

Contrary to the usual impression, the writing of a book is not a solitary enterprise. This is especially evident to me when I consider all those who have helped to bring my study of Dostoyevsky to fruition, first as a doctoral dissertation in Religious Studies, and now as a book. I would like to acknowledge, first, my debt to Dr. George Grant, who encouraged me to read Dostoyevsky in the light of the perennial problems. I am grateful also for the assistance provided by the following people at McMaster University: Dr. John Robertson, Dr. Louis Shein, and Dr. Ian Weeks, in the early stages of the work; Dr. Robert Johnston, who offered helpful advice concerning its publication; Dr. Louis Greenspan, who read a later version of the manuscript and made suggestions for its improvement; and Dr. George Thomas, who kindly consented to check the manuscript for accuracy of translation and transliteration. The book owes much as well to the comments made by the anonymous readers for the Canadian Federation for the Humanities. I extend my thanks also to Mrs. Ruth MacDonald, who typed various revisions of this book with unfailing good humour and accuracy. Any errors of fact, omissions, or doubtful judgments that remain are of course my responsibility alone.

This book has been published with the help of a grant from the Canadian Federation for the Humanities, using funds provided by the Social Sciences and Humanities Research Council of Canada. I gratefully acknowledge this assistance. I am grateful also to Thorneloe College of Laurentian University for the financial assistance it has provided for travel when required in the final stages of publication.

Finally, I thank my wife Norma for her support and understanding, from the beginning to the end. This book is dedicated to her.

Sudbury, Ontario   B. K. W.
July 1986

NOTES ON TRANSLATION, TRANSLITERATION, AND REFERENCES

Dostoyevsky's novels, stories, and articles are now largely available in English translation, as are most of his rough notebooks. Since this book is intended to make his thought about the West more accessible to Westerners, including those who might not be expert in the Russian language, I have referred throughout to the English translations of his writings where these exist. (There is no English translation of Dostoyevsky's complete correspondence, and my references to his letters are therefore by date. In addition to the Russian edition of his complete correspondence there is, however, a reliable French edition about which information is provided in the bibliography). The interested reader will therefore be able to find most quotations or references within the context of a translated work. The translations have been checked against the original Russian, and altered where necessary for the sake of accuracy. For those readers who wish to consult the original Russian texts (or other translations), I have provided the following information in parentheses: for passages from the novels and stories—uppercase roman and arabic, and lowercase roman numerals for part, chapter, and section respectively; and for passages from *The Diary of a Writer*—the month and year. All quotations from Russian or other foreign texts are my own translations, unless otherwise indicated.

There is no one universally accepted system of transliterating Russian words. I have followed the system used by D. S. Mirsky in his *History of Russian Literature*. This system seems most effectively to convey the proper pronunciation of Russian words to those unacquainted with the language. I have departed from it only in two instances: where Mirsky would use *ë*, I use *yo* (as in Alyosha), and where Russian words have a generally accepted English spelling (e.g., troika), I retain the usual spelling.

For the sake of convenience, Dostoyevsky's writings are referred to by title alone. Complete bibliographic information concerning these works is provided in the bibliography. Those titles containing more than two words are abbreviated in the following manner:

The House of the Dead	HD
Winter Notes on Summer Impressions	WNSI
Notes from Underground	NU
Crime and Punishment	CP
The Notebooks for Crime and Punishment	NCP
The Notebooks for The Idiot	NI
The Notebooks for The Possessed	NP
The Notebooks for A Raw Youth	NRY
The Brothers Karamazov	BK
The Notebooks for The Brothers Karamazov	NBK
The Diary of a Writer	DW
The Dream of a Ridiculous Man	DRM
The Pushkin Speech	PS
Occasional Writings	OW
Dostoïevski et l'Europe en 1873	DE
The Unpublished Dostoevsky	UD

INTRODUCTION

The apprehension of a fundamental crisis in Western civilization has become pervasive in our century of war, terror, and tyranny. Anxiety for the health and even the existence of Western civilization is no longer limited, as it was in the previous century, to those rare voices which we now consider prophetic. Indeed the pervasive sense of crisis becomes itself an ingredient of the crisis as the modern West increasingly betrays a lack of belief in its own future, despite its apparently boundless technological power. Yet the general recognition of a Western crisis—a crisis which is also global, insofar as Western civilization has spread throughout the world—does not entail consensus concerning its nature. There is even little agreement about whether the crisis is fundamentally outward—a question of the political, economic, social, and ecological dislocations besetting modern technological society—or whether it must be understood as an inward crisis. For those who adopt the latter view, the material problems which threaten modern civilization are really symptomatic of a more fundamental problem of the spirit. This approach assumes that the diverse elements of a civilization are bound together into an ultimate unity, and that this unity is to be perceived in the light of what is prior in human life. The recognition among more thoughtful observers of a crisis of the spirit does not, however, entail agreement concerning the reasons for it. Still less does this recognition entail agreement about the means or even the possibility of bringing about a renaissance of the West. The lack of clarity concerning these questions presents a formidable task, a task which requires close attention to those thinkers who might be able to illuminate the crisis of Western modernity. One such thinker is Fyodor Dostoyevsky.

Dostoyevsky's concern with the West is evident throughout his writings. The most cursory reading of his major novels yields an abundance of allusions to almost every aspect of Western civilization. And in his secondary writings—his journalistic articles, unpublished notebooks, and correspondence—the question of the West figures prominently and more completely than in his art. According to his own testimony, his preoccupation with the West commenced when, as a child in Moscow, he listened "agape

1

with ecstasy and terror'' to his mother's readings of the Gothic horror tales of Hoffman and Radcliffe.[1] It was still evident in his last public address, a speech in commemoration of the Russian poet Pushkin, which he delivered in 1880. Dostoyevsky's concern with the West was not a mere whim incidental to his more fundamental work as a literary artist, but occupied a place at the very heart of his life and his writings. The centrality of his interest in the question of the West is demonstrated, if somewhat negatively, by the fact that this interest sometimes impelled him to contravene the strict aesthetic requirements of his art. Prince Myshkin's speech about the Western crisis, at one of the most critical moments in *The Idiot*,[2] must be regarded as an aesthetic impropriety. Yet one of the perfect achievements of Dostoyevsky's art—''The Grand Inquisitor'' in *The Brothers Karamazov*—is inextricably associated with the question of the West.

The basis of Dostoyeysky's preoccupation with the fate of Western civilization was his avowed conviction that the West was his ''second fatherland.''[3] This avowal implies two things: first, that as a son of Western civilization he knows this civilization intimately, and this knowledge is bound up with a certain reverence and love; second, that he is not completely a part of the West, that he is sufficiently detached to be a clear-sighted observer of Western civilization. Dostoyevsky thought that he could both understand the fundamental aspirations of the West and separate himself from these aspirations. It is this claim that underlies his contemplation of the Western crisis.

The same claim has been made by some modern Western thinkers (most notably Nietzsche). In Dostoyevsky's case, however, there is less doubt that there really is a significant distance between himself and the West which he observes. Because of the Westernizing reforms of Peter the Great, this distance is not as great as that centuries-old distance between Muscovite Russia and Europe and, more profoundly, between the Greek East and the Latin West. It is great enough, however, that Dostoyevsky was to repeat emphatically, and probably with justification, that a Russian is *not* a European. Is, then, the distance between Russia and the West so great that Dostoyevsky would have been incapable of grasping the Western crisis in all its depth? This raises the questions of the validity of his observations about the West and the acceptability of these observations to Westerners. Yet these questions are premature, for the observations themselves have yet to receive serious consideration in the West. Despite Dostoyevsky's evident preoccupation with the meaning and destiny of Western civilization, his critique of the West has not yet been adequately elucidated.

This is not to say that Dostoyevsky's engrossed encounter with the civilization of the West has been ignored. His knowledge of the Western cultural heritage, particularly its literature, and the influence of this knowledge upon

1 *WNSI*, p. 36 (1).
2 See *The Idiot*, pp. 585-88 (IV,7).
3 *DW*, p. 581 (Jan. 1877).

his own art have been explored at length. Yet this thorough examination of Dostoyevsky's relation as an artist to the culture of the West has coincided with a general disregard for his enucleation of the crisis of that culture. This disregard is certainly not attributable to any reluctance to consider Dostoyevsky a serious thinker. The novel was in nineteenth-century Russia far more than literature; it was the primary vehicle for the expression of philosophical, religious, political, and even economic teachings. The early Russian assessment of Dostoyevsky as a pre-eminent thinker has long been accepted in the West. The scholarly analysis of his artistic technique has thus proceeded in conjunction with expositions of his religious thought. The Western acknowledgment of Dostoyevsky's religious thought has not, however, been extended to his critique of the West. Where the two are found together, which they often are, the religious thought is separated from the associated observations about the Western crisis. "The Grand Inquisitor," for example, is generally acclaimed as writing of the highest intellectual and artistic order, but this acclaim generally disregards the fact that it is set in the West and its principal character is a Westerner. Even when this fact is recognized, it is not considered integral to our understanding of the more profound themes of "The Grand Inquisitor." Although Dostoyevsky is regarded as a teacher of the first order about the crisis of the human spirit, this does not apply to his teaching about the crisis of the human spirit *in the West*.[4]

There appear to be two primary obstacles to serious consideration of Dostoyevsky's observations about the West. First, there is the suspected possibility that his knowledge of Western civilization is limited to its aesthetic phenomena, that his grasp of Western art is not matched by his grasp of the more fundamental bases of Western civilization. Apart from the dubiousness of thus divorcing Western art from Western civilization as a whole, it must be emphasized that Dostoyevsky's knowledge of the West was not restricted to its artistic heritage. There is evidence that from his youth his reading included Western works of history, politics, philosophy, theology, and even economics. (These were generally read in the original French or German.)[5] The modern West was indeed opened up to him by the art of Schiller, Beethoven, Hugo, Balzac, and Dickens; but he also came to know it through his study of Rousseau, Kant, and Hegel. He was in close touch as well with some of the greatest nineteenth-century Russian interpreters of Western thought.[6] This

4 See, for instance, H. de Lubac, *The Drama of Atheist Humanism* (New York, 1963), pp. 227, 230; André Gide, *Dostoevsky* (Norfolk, Conn., 1949), pp. 87-98; A. de Jonge, *Dostoevsky and the Age of Intensity* (London, 1975), p. 69.

5 This evidence is provided implicitly by the allusions to such works which abound throughout Dostoyevsky's writings. It is provided explicitly by his correspondence and the testimony of his wife, friends, and acquaintances. Two studies of Dostoyevsky which consider this question in detail are J. Frank, *Dostoevsky, the Seeds of Revolt 1821-1849* (Princeton, 1976); L. Grossman, *Dostoevsky* (London, 1974). This question is treated at some length in the first chapter of the present study.

6 These included Alexander Herzen, Vissarion Belinsky, Vladimir Solovyov, and Nicholas Strakhov.

knowledge of Western thought was supplemented by a remarkably detailed acquaintance with Western practice. Dostoyevsky's occupation as an editor of various journals—which were as much political as literary in content—gave him occasion to familiarize himself with the most minute developments in Western politics, domestic and international. And this familiarity was made more tangible by prolonged travel and residence in Europe itself.[7] Any final judgment concerning the quality of Dostoyevsky's grasp of the significant constituents of modern Western civilization presupposes the adequate exposition of his critique of the West. The available biographical evidence permits the assertion here, however, that his acquaintance with the non-artistic aspects of Western civilization was not merely a scanty and superficial one gleaned from inferior sources.

The second obstacle to serious consideration of Dostoyevsky's teaching about the West is the suspicion that this teaching is incompatible with his best thought. Insofar as his observations about the crisis of the West are political, they would appear to bear no genuine relation to his more profound religious thought. His teaching about the West thus tends to be related to the political prejudice which characterized him as a nineteenth-century Russian nationalist rather than to the religious thought which speaks to all people.[8] Once again, such a view can finally be judged only after thoughtful consideration of what Dostoyevsky has to say about the West. Yet it can be remarked here that this distinction, which he never made, between his political observations about the West and his religious thought presumes a clearer understanding of his writings than he himself possessed. It presumes also that his penetrating insight into the most difficult questions of human life did not extend to the relatively simpler matter of his own Russian chauvinism. Presumptions such as these may well constitute an obstacle to the complete understanding of his whole thought.

Vladimir Solovyov, a close friend of Dostoyevsky and one of Russia's most important philosophers, wrote: "The general meaning of Dostoyevsky's entire activity, the meaning of Dostoyevsky, as a social figure consists in the resolution of this two-fold question: about the highest ideal of social order and the genuine way to the actualization of this ideal."[9] This expression of the fundamental "meaning of Dostoyevsky" has not received sufficient attention

---

7 For a detailed account of the itinerary of Dostoyevsky's travels in Europe, see G. Aucouturier and C. Menuet, *Album Dostoïevski* (Paris, 1975). For a detailed account of his years in Europe, see the reminiscences of his wife, Anna Dostoyevsky, *Reminiscences* (New York, 1975), chap. 4.

8 For the most extreme expression of this view, see I. Howe, *Politics and the Novel* (London, 1961), pp. 54-55. But essentially the same view of Dostoyevsky's observations about the West is expressed by commentators who are much more sympathetic to his thought as a whole. See, for instance, H. de Lubac, *The Drama of Atheist Humanism* (New York, (1963), p. 184; A. de Jonge, *Dostoevsky and the Age of Intensity* (London, 1975), p. 64; V. Ivanov, *Freedom and the Tragic Life, a Study in Dostoevsky* (New York, 1971), p. 155.

9 V. Solovyov, "Tri rechi v pamyat Dostoyevskago," *Sobranie sochinenii* (Brussels, 1966), III-IV, p. 193.

in the West. Yet it may point the way to a proper understanding of the apparent contradiction between Dostoyevsky's concern with the highest reaches of human spirituality and at the same time with the most detailed developments in domestic and international politics. This study is informed above all by the idea that the two poles of this "contradiction" between Dostoyevsky's religious thought and his political analysis of the West are held together in the question of the best human order. It is this question that informs both his elucidation of the Western crisis and his recommendation for overcoming it.

In understanding the problem of the best human order as both a political and a religious problem, Dostoyevsky is in accord with those whose thought has most decisively shaped Western modernity. He is in accord, for instance, with Hobbes, who felt the necessity of justifying his resolution of the problem of order not only on the basis of the scientifically verifiable *ius naturale*, but also according to a novel interpretation of Scripture; with Rousseau, who declared that the "true statesman" must admire the order established by Judaic law, and who himself wished to guarantee the sanctity of the social contract with the dogmas of civil religion; and with Nietzsche, for whom the struggle against liberal-socialist *décadence* entailed an attack on the Judaeo-Christian religious heritage of the West.[10] Yet Dostoyevsky cannot easily be located within the modern Western intellectual tradition defined by thinkers such as these. As we shall see, he is at one with Rousseau in his rejection of that English-speaking liberalism rooted in Hobbes which encourages the politicians of the modern world to "speak of nothing but commerce and money." Yet he is also at one with Nietzsche in his interpretation of the continental liberal-socialist tradition fathered by Rousseau as an attempt to bring "heaven down to earth," which inconsistently wants to retain Christian moral principles (such as equality) while doing away with the transcendent basis of these principles.[11] Such a tendency towards the immanentization of the Christian faith culminated for Dostoyevsky, as for Nietzsche, in the philosophy of Hegel.[12] It is a mistake, however, to identify Dostoyevsky with that European reaction against Hegelian liberal-socialism which found its definitive expression in Nietzsche, for Nietzsche's rejection of the concept of equality and indeed his thought as a whole is, from Dostoyevsky's perspective, already implicit within Hegel. (On one of the most pressing issues of contemporary political philosophy, then, Dostoyevsky would be with those who fear that the realization of the Hegelian universal and socially homogeneous state would imply the realization of a global tyranny.)[13]

10 See T. Hobbes, *Leviathan* (New York, 1962), part III; J-J. Rousseau, *Du Contrat social et autres oeuvres politiques* (Paris, 1975), pp. 263, 334-35; F. Nietzsche, *Beyond Good and Evil* (New York, 1966), 202.
11 *BK*, p. 27 (I,5).
12 For my use of the term "immanentization" here, see E. Voegelin, *Science, Politics and Gnosticism* (Chicago, 1968), pp. 88-92.
13 See L. Strauss, *On Tyranny* (New York, 1968); G. Grant, *Technology and Empire* (Toronto, 1969), "Tyranny and Wisdom."

But it would also be wrong to place Dostoyevsky too hastily with those who reject Hegel's attempt to reconcile heaven and earth by affirming the unqualified transcendence of heaven. Dostoyevsky felt himself very close to those who hunger and thirst for justice on earth. His rejection of the universal and homogeneous state does not entail the rejection of the aspiration to a universal order of freedom, equality, and brotherhood. The problem of human order is, for him, not encompassed within the mutually exclusive choices of *either* the immanentization of the *summum bonum* of biblical revelation and Greek philosophy *or* the emphatic assertion of its utter transcendence. Perhaps Dostoyevsky's most significant contribution to the thoughtful consideration of the Western crisis of order is his observation that this misconceived "either-or" arises out of a distortion of the religious teaching originally bequeathed to the West, and that for the same reason the resolution of the dichotomy must be sought within the original teaching. This is not to claim that Dostoyevsky himself does more than point the way towards this resolution.

A proper assessment of Dostoyevsky's contribution presupposes clarity about his analysis of the crisis of modernity. The primary intention of this study is to expound as clearly as possible Dostoyevsky's teaching concerning the West, demonstrating that his observations constitute a coherent critique which is intertwined with the deepest aspects of his thought. This intention is not based on any assumption of a capacity to express his critique of the West better than he himself expressed it. It is assumed, however, that his teaching about the West can be rendered more systematic and explicit, and hence more accessible to those who are interested—for this critique is only implicit in Dostoyevsky's own work. Indeed his many observations about the West are scattered in a seemingly random and unconnected fashion throughout his writings. Perhaps the requirements of art made a more systematic presentation extremely difficult, if not impossible. Even the prose articles directly concerned with the West, which appear in the various journals edited by him, are characterized by a feuilletonistic style quite unlike the more orderly style of a treatise or essay. My attempt to render Dostoyevsky's critique of the West more accessible will therefore employ a mode of organization and style which was not his own (although there is evidence that he himself was interested in giving his critique a more systematic form).[14]

This exposition will not constitute merely a judicious rearrangement of the observations about the West scattered throughout Dostoyevsky's writings. Such a passive approach to his thought is precluded by the medium in which it is expressed. Although much of his teaching about the West is present in his journalistic prose, the height of this teaching is expressed in his art. It is

---

14 See, for instance, his letter of 16 Aug. 1880 to K. P. Pobedonostsev: "I am always compelled to express certain thoughts only in the basic idea, which always greatly needs a further development and argumentation." This study undertakes to provide such "further development and argumentation."

expressed through fictional characters, none of whom is obviously his spokesman. Indeed his art as a whole can be regarded as an arena in which different teachings come into conflict, without the presence of a final arbiter.[15] The elucidation of his critique of the West therefore requires an active interpretation of his writings, an interpretation which must be careful, however, not to ascribe to Dostoyevsky teachings which do not belong to him.[16] It is hoped that the fulfillment of the primary intention of this study will serve the larger purpose of helping to clarify what Dostoyevsky can teach us about the situation in which the modern West finds itself and, beyond this, about the permanent problem of human order—for it was Dostoyevsky's great virtue as a thinker always to see the pressing issues of his particular time and place in the light of the everlasting problems.[17]

The crisis of the West first appeared to Dostoyevsky through the mediation of Russian Westernism. His enucleation of Russian Westernism determines his approach to the West itself, and is therefore the most appropriate introduction to his critique of the West. Our subsequent examination of this critique will take us from his consideration of the problem of order in the modern West, to his exposure of the inner meaning of the "final Western social formula," and finally to his judgment of the foundations of Western civilization.

15 For an illuminating discussion of Dostoyevsky's "polyphonic" artistry, see M. Bakhtin, *Problems of Dostoevsky's Poetics* (Ann Arbor, 1973), chap. 3.
16 It can, fortunately, be ascertained from the careful study of Dostoyevsky's correspondence, prose articles, and rough notes what he himself thought about the diverse teachings present in his art. Therefore it is possible to know his ultimate intentions (although the question must still be left open whether the art always faithfully reflects the intentions of the artist).
17 See *BK*, p. 295 (V,5).

ONE

RUSSIAN WESTERNISM: ITS HISTORICAL DEVELOPMENT

The problem of Russia and the West is rooted, according to Dostoyevsky, in the peculiar "historical evolution" of Russian society. His own consuming interest in Russian history was directed towards the manner in which "Europe has been reflected in us at different times, and, together with its civilization, has gradually imposed itself on us as a guest...."[1] Although his consideration of Russian Westernism as an historical phenomenon never achieved the systematic form which he once intended for it,[2] observations about the history of Europe's reflection in Russia are present throughout his writings. These observations constitute the basis of this chapter's historical introduction to Russian Westernism, an introduction which reflects Dostoyevsky's own idea of what should be known about the history of this movement.

The Early History of Russian Westernism

Russian Westernism had its effective beginning in the reign of Peter the Great (1696-1725); it was, according to Dostoyevsky, the "consequence of Peter the Great."[3] To Westerners Peter has been a compelling but ambiguous figure;

---

1 *WNSI*, p. 57 (3); *PS*, p. 72 (The "Pushkin Speech" was first published in the Aug. 1880 edition of *The Diary of a Writer*. My references hereafter will be to the English translation by S. Koteliansky and J. Middleton Murry, found in *The Dream of a Queer Fellow and The Pushkin Speech* [London, 1960]. This translation includes the "Pushkin Speech" itself and Dostoyevsky's response to the criticism of M. Gradovsky [chapters II and III of the Aug. 1880 edition of *The Diary of a Writer*]).

2 Dostoyevsky states his intention to write a long article "on Russia's relations to Western Europe, and on the upper classes of Russian society" in a letter of 16 Aug. 1867 to the poet, Apollon Maykov.

3 *NP*, p. 357.

boundlessly energetic, endowed with a versatile practical talent amounting to genius, deeply appreciative of Western technology, he was at the same time given to unpredictable, even grotesque behaviour, a semi-barbarian who never learned to write properly, a tyrant who obsessively strove to impose Western forms of life on his subjects with results that appeared highly dubious to Westerners. While for Westerners Peter represents a somewhat outlandish though important figure in Russian history, for Russians he has always constituted an overbearing problem imperiously demanding a solution. Dostoyevsky's abiding concern with the meaning of Peter is evident from the regularity with which references to him appear throughout his writings. He thought that Peter was a "genius" of immense will and boundless openness to new ideas, but he also regarded him as a "monster." He did not pretend to understand the man whose personality, "in spite of all the historical interpretations and research of recent times, is still a great mystery. . . ."[4] Yet it was not the extraordinary character that preoccupied Dostoyevsky so much as the influence that Peter exerted on Russia's historical destiny by turning it decisively towards the West.

According to Dostoyevsky, Peter's turn to the West was prompted initially by very limited utilitarian motives, particularly of a military nature.[5] These limited motives, however, led to a more general desire to construct a Russian state modelled after the emerging European nation-states. For Peter the transformation of Russia into a European state required a rationalized military machine and an efficient administrative apparatus, requirements which presupposed a large number of men trained in Western military and administrative techniques. In addition to the educational institutions which would impart the required technical knowledge to Russian students, Peter was in need of a reliable source from which to draw these students. The need for a constant supply of men prepared to devote their energies to the new state was a prerequisite that induced Peter to take measures which effectively transformed the Russian gentry into a permanent military and civil service.[6] In seventeenth-century Muscovy the gentry had owed only military service to the state, and only in times of emergency, but with Peter's reform all gentry and their sons were henceforth compelled to register with the state for a term of service which began in boyhood and extended through most of their lives. With the institution of the Table of Ranks in 1721, rank according to birth was subordinated to rank according to state service, so that this service became the basis of noble status itself.[7]

The state's need for capable servants did not leave the Russian peasantry untouched. Peter's new military establishment and grandiose public works

---

4 *OW*, pp. 62-63; *UD*, II, p. 61.

5 *PS*, p. 57.

6 *UD*, II, p. 79.

7 For further details on the emergence of the "service gentry" during Peter's reign, see
  M. Raeff, *Origins of the Russian Intelligentsia* (New York, 1966).

required masses of docile workers, who were recruited from the peasantry. Furthermore, the extraordinarily heavy poll tax introduced to finance his reforms effectively deprived the peasantry of any possibility of financial independence. Serfdom for the vast majority of the Russian peasantry was, in Dostoyevsky's words, the "veritable golden heritage of Peter's reform."[8]

Although the gentry and their serfs both felt the harsh impersonal power of the new state, subordination involved different implications for each group. Beyond the obvious difference of socio-economic circumstances, there was a more important difference which originated in the general tendency of Peter's reforms. The service caste Peter created was required to serve a state that was attempting to become Western, and the successful outcome of this attempt depended on the degree to which the service caste itself could adopt Western methods. Not content to educate the Russian nobility in Western military and administrative technique, Peter forced them to adopt the Western way of life, even in its most trivial details. The story of Peter attacking the beards of his highest officials with a razor following his first trip to Europe is merely one instance of the more bizarre aspect of his compulsion to emulate the West.[9] According to Peter's personal caprice, and the needs of the Petrine state, the gentry supplemented their Western technical education with a European appearance: wigs, beardless chins, and German and French clothes. The wholesale Europeanization of the gentry was not extended to the mass of the people who, although certainly harnessed to the requirements of the new state, were not compelled to become Frenchmen or Germans. The Westernization of Russia directly affected only the noble population, and the majority of the people were left with their traditions intact. This had great significance for Dostoyevsky:

The people were exempt from the ... reform from the very beginning; they were given up for hopeless. They were even allowed to keep wearing their beards.... The people weren't considered essential at the time, but were looked upon as raw material, and as payers of the poll tax. Sure, they were closely guarded, but as to their internal, proper life, it was left to them in its entirety....[10]

As the gentry came increasingly to accept their Westernization, the people regarded them and the process of Westernization with a growing hostility, which Dostoyevsky interprets as an unconscious protest on behalf of their "Russian own, and against its suppression."[11] The gentry, at first under compulsion and then voluntarily, had become uprooted from a set of traditions which still held the majority of their countrymen: "the entire upper class of Russia ended up by being transformed into Germans, and, uprooted, got to love everything German and to hate and despise everything of their

8 *NP*, p. 215. For a detailed study of the growth of serfdom, during and after Peter's reign, see J. Blum, *Lord and Peasant in Russia* (New York, 1965).

9 M. T. Florinsky, *Russia: A History and an Interpretation* (New York, 1966), I, p. 397.

10 *NP*, p. 146.

11 *DW*, p. 352 (June 1876).

own. . . ."[12] The gulf between the gentry and the Russian people came to be so impassable that Dostoyevsky characterizes it as a "schism."[13] Russian Westernism thus owed to Peter the Great its most significant characteristic— its restriction to an upper-class minority uprooted from the living Russian traditions.

For Dostoyevsky the next significant stage in the history of Russian Westernism was the effort of Catherine the Great (1762-1796) to put herself in the forefront of the European Enlightenment. Dostoyevsky calls her a "genius" in playing the "game" of Westernization.[14] Whereas Peter's turn to the West was determined by the strongly utilitarian bent of his nature, Catherine's Westernism could be said to have been determined by her vanity. Peter was anxious to learn from Europe; Catherine was more anxious that Europe should think well of Russia, and especially of her. She wanted all of Europe to acknowledge the truth of the declaration in her "Instruction" of 1767: "Russia is a European State." Not content with the favourable opinion of the rulers of Enlightenment Europe, Catherine sought the accolades of the *philosophes* themselves. Her initial success in this enterprise was demonstrated, for instance, by the high-flown praise which she elicited from Voltaire, who assured her that she was *"la première personne de l'univers,"* his *"passion dominante,"* and that Diderot, d'Alembert, and he were "setting up altars" to her.[15]

Nevertheless, Catherine remained content with the mere appearance of "enlightened monarchy." The "Instruction," which was a faithful theoretical expression of the political teaching of the Enlightenment, had no practical effect beyond bringing tears to the eyes of admiring *philosophes*.[16] After the French Revolution Catherine's flirtation with the Enlightenment was much less pronounced as she came to fear that the mere presence of French ideas

12 *NP*, p. 146. It should be noted that the Russian word *nemets*, meaning "German," was also used to denote "foreigner" in general.

13 Ibid., p. 115.

14 *UD*, II, p. 77. As I have emphasized, this chapter's account of the historical development of Russian Westernism is based on Dostoyevsky's *own* idea of its significant stages, stages which he identifies closely with particular rulers. There were, of course, several reigning monarchs between Peter the Great and Catherine the Great: Catherine I (1725-1727), Peter II (1727-1730), Anne (1730-1740), Ivan VI (1740-1741), Elizabeth (1741-1762) and Peter III (1762). The almost complete absence of references to these rulers in Dostoyevsky's writings would indicate that for him, as for most historians, they are of considerably less significance to Russian history. The same is true of Paul I (1796-1801), between Catherine the Great and Alexander I. A detailed account of these reigns can be found in V. O. Kluchevsky, *A History of Russia* (New York, 1960), vols. 4 and 5.

15 W. F. Reddaway, ed. *Documents of Catherine the Great: the Correspondence with Voltaire and the "Instruction" of 1767 in the English Text of 1768* (Cambridge, 1931), pp. 119, 67, 13. For a good account of Catherine's playing of the "game" of Enlightenment, see N. Riasanovsky, *A Parting of the Ways: Government and the Educated Public in Russia, 1801-1855* (Oxford, 1976), chap. 1.

16 "the *philosophes* wept as they read these laws, laws so beautiful that it was the duty of all sovereigns of the world to take them as their example." F. de Labriolle, "Le 'prosvescenie' russe et les lumières en France (1760-1789)," *Revue des études slaves*, vol. 45 (1966), pp. 75-91.

could encourage a similar revolution in Russia. The ambiguity of Catherine's dedication to the progressivist thought of the Enlightenment was reflected also in the Russian gentry. These "grandfathers" of Russian Westernism are pictured by Dostoyevsky as comic figures whose "enlightenment" is little more than a good-natured sham:

We donned silk stockings and wigs and hung little swords on ourselves, and lo and behold, we were Europeans. This did no harm; it was even fun. In actual fact, everything remained as before.... We dealt with the house-serfs just as before; we treated our families just as patriarchally as before; out in the stable we flogged the small land-owner who lived nearby if he was rude to us, just as before; and we kowtowed just as obsequiously before higher-placed personages.... In a word, all these gentlemen were a simple, hearty bunch; they never enquired how, when, or why; they took bribes, they beat, they stole, they kowtowed with feeling, and peacefully and abundantly lived out their time "in scrupulous childish depravity."...

Some of them were probably great rogues; they had their own ideas about all the European influences coming from above. All this phantasmagoria and masquerading, all these French surtouts, cuffs, wigs, little swords, all those fat, clumsy legs stuck into silk stockings, all those soldier boys in German wigs and boots—it was all, I think, downright knavery, lackies tricking their masters, such that even the people sometimes noticed and saw through it.[17]

In Dostoyevsky's view, the Russian Enlightenment under Catherine was a façade, although it was so adroitly contrived that Europe was fooled temporarily. Catherine nevertheless did begin the process of informing the Russian turn to the West with a distinct intellectual content. And it was during her reign that the first tentative efforts towards an independent Russian intellectual culture, modelled after that of the West, were made by a few notable members of the Russian upper class such as Alexander Radishchev, who achieved notoriety for his attack on serfdom in *A Journey from St. Petersburg to Moscow* (Catherine's "enlightened" convictions did not prevent her from exiling Radishchev to Siberia). France, Germany, Britain, and Italy all contributed to the intellectual content of the Russian Enlightenment, but France was clearly the most important (although several Russians studied the writings of the French intellectuals at German universities).[18] The writings of Diderot, d'Alembert, d'Holbach, Helvétius, and especially Voltaire and Rousseau, were widely discussed.[19] Enlightenment thought may have been approached by the Russian Westernism of Catherine's era in a generally haphazard, superficial manner, but it did become widely diffused throughout the Russian gentry. In the next important stage in the historical development of Russian

17 *WNSI*, pp. 61-63 (3).
18 Alexander Radishchev (generally acknowledged as the first Russian "radical"), for instance, was exposed to the thought of Helvétius, d'Holbach, Rousseau and Mably at the University of Leipzig.
19 See *DW*, p. 289 (April 1876). A thorough discussion of Rousseau's influence in eighteenth-century Russia is to be found in N. Riasanovsky, *A Parting of the Ways: Government and the Educated Public in Russia, 1801-1855* (Oxford, 1976), pp. 29-33.

Westernism, that of the Decembrist era, this thought was to take much firmer root.

Alexander the First (1801-1825) was known to be sympathetic to the modern Western ideas which were pervasive among educated Russians by the beginning of the nineteenth century. One of his first acts after his accession was the appointment of a special committee to draw up a constitution for Russia. However, the outbreak of war with Napoleon in 1812 marked the end of Alexander's sympathy for the liberal state, which he identified with Napoleon. The effect on the Russian nobility of the war with Napoleon was curious. Although Alexander turned away from the idea of the liberal state, the gentry that commanded the Russian armies desired it even more intensely after their victory. While marching through France, they had been affected by the still potent liberal fervour of the Napoleonic era, and their susceptibility to this heady atmosphere was apparently compatible with a newly found Russian patriotism. Alexander's failure to satisfy their aspirations frustrated them, and they began to form secret societies for the overthrow of the government. Alexander's death and the confusion over his succession provided the opportunity for the attempted *coup d'état* of December 14, 1825. The Decembrist insurrection, though it was a dismal failure, is of great symbolic significance to Dostoyevsky.

Even if the rebellion had been less ineptly undertaken and had succeeded, the Decembrists, in Dostoyevsky's view, "would have disappeared without having managed to hold on for two or three days."[20] Their attempt to establish a liberal constitutional regime in Russia could never have been more than a futile gesture, for they had made no serious effort to enlist the support of the Russian people as a whole. Their failure to do so reflected that relationship between the Westernized gentry and the Russian people, which is of such great concern to Dostoyevsky in his reflections on the historical development of Russian Westernism. In Dostoyevsky's view, the attitude of the Decembrists towards the Russian people differed little from that of their fathers during the final consolidation of serfdom under Catherine. Dostoyevsky was aware that Pestel, the leading figure of the Decembrist movement (whom he calls a "rascal"),[21] had called for the abolition of serfdom, but he maintains that the serfs would have been emancipated without their land:

I bet you that the Decembrists would have definitely freed the Russian people, and without delay, but also definitely without their land—for which the people would have definitely and without delay twisted off their heads . . . . What then? Why, even without their heads they wouldn't have been able to understand a thing, notwithstanding the fact that it was precisely their heads which, more than anything else, impeded their understanding.[22]

20 *UD*, II, p. 77.
21 Ibid., p. 77. Pestel came from a German family, professed the Lutheran faith, and usually wrote in French.
22 *NP*, p. 115.

The separation of the Decembrists from the Russian people was even greater than that of the "grandfathers" who were "less foreign" to the peasant.[23] The "grandfathers" had been divorced from the people by social and economic circumstance; the "fathers" were becoming divorced from the people by the force of ideas as well as by the force of external circumstance (and were thus becoming an "intelligentsia"). Pestel's manifesto and Muravyov's proposed constitution were indicative of the degree to which the Decembrists had gone beyond the "grandfathers" in appropriating that tradition of French liberal thought which was given political expression in the Constitution of 1793.[24] The prime legacy of the Decembrist generation, then, was a more profound gulf between the Westernized gentry and the people, as well as between the gentry and the monarchy. Dostoyevsky, however, apparently thought more highly of the upper class of Alexander's reign than of Catherine's, for his assessment of the Decembrists is tinged with a regret for the futile passing of so much selfless and energetic ability: "with the disappearance of the Decembrists—the as it were pure element of the Russian gentry disappeared."[25]

With the passing of the Decembrist generation, Dostoyevsky's reflections focus upon his own generation of Russian Westernism. At this point his consideration of the history of Russian Westernism merges with his consideration of his own history, for he believed that the significant stages in the development of Russian Westernism after the Decembrist era were reflected in his own life.

Dostoyevsky and the Russian Westernism of the 1830s and 1840s

Russian Romanticism

Dostoyevsky always emphasized that he was brought up in a "pious Russian family" in which he was exposed to the Gospel "almost from the cradle."[26] His grandfather and his uncle were Orthodox priests, and the deep piety of his parents (which is evident in their correspondence) was expressed in the care they took for the religious instruction of their children. His mother taught him to read from an eighteenth-century religious primer entitled "104 Sacred Stories from the Old and New Testaments," and as soon as he had learned to read he began to receive formal religious instruction from an Orthodox deacon, a skillful teacher (according to the recollection of his brother Andrey) whose lessons and stories, based on the Bible, had a deep effect on his young

---

23 *WNSI*, p. 62 (3).
24 For an account of the thinking of the Decembrists, with lengthy extracts from their own writings, see M. Raeff, *The Decembrist Movement* (Englewood Cliffs, N.J., 1966).
25 *UD*, II, p. 77.
26 *DW*, p. 152 (1873).

student.[27] Dostoyevsky was also in early childhood exposed to the visible heart of Russian Orthodoxy: "every visit to the Kremlin and the Moscow cathedrals was, to me, something solemn."[28] Although he spent most of his adult life in the city built by Peter the Great, his earliest childhood impressions were of Moscow, the city which he later came to regard as the true spiritual centre of Russia.[29] These early Moscow impressions were supplemented by annual visits to the Holy Trinity monastery (located just outside the city) which was founded by St. Sergius, one of the most venerated of Russian Orthodox saints. Later in his life, when considering the possibility of the Russian monastery as a setting for a novel, Dostoyevsky wrote to a friend: "I am an expert in this world, and I have known the Russian monastery from childhood."[30] Little can be learned from his autobiographical reflections of the theological content of these early religious influences, but Dostoyevsky clearly regarded his religious upbringing as thoroughly Orthodox.

Although the influence of Russian Orthodoxy in Dostoyevsky's upbringing may have been atypical of the Russian gentry, he too was exposed at an early age to Western culture.[31] He recalls, for instance, that he had yearned to travel to Europe since his childhood, when he used to "spend the long winter evenings before going to bed listening (for I could not yet read), agape with ecstasy and terror, as my parents read aloud to me from the novels of Anne Radcliffe."[32] Dostoyevsky's secular education was largely European in content: he was learning French by reading Voltaire (*La Henriade*) at the same time as he was receiving Orthodox religious instruction from the deacon. His early contact with Europe was mediated through the writings of Russian Westernism, especially Karamzin's *Letters of a Russian Traveller*. This account of Karamzin's wanderings through Europe is replete with praise for Europe and European progress, although this praise is somewhat qualified by an uneasiness about the final consequences of the French Revolution.[33] Russian writers were read and discussed a great deal in the Dostoyevsky household but, other than Karamzin, Pushkin, and Gogol, the Russian writers

27 For an excellent, detailed account of Dostoyevsky's family background and early life, see
   J. Frank, *Dostoevsky, the Seeds of Revolt 1821-1849* (Princeton, 1976). See also
   L. Grossman, *Dostoevsky* (London, 1974).
28 *DW*, p. 152 (1873).
29 Ibid., pp. 314-15 (May 1876).
30 Letter of 24 March 1870. St. Sergius, a leading figure in the successful Russian revolt against Mongol rule in 1380, embodied that combination of Christian faith and Russian patriotism which was so characteristic of Muscovite Russia.
31 The influence of Russian Orthodoxy was almost entirely absent in the upbringing of, for instance, Herzen, Tolstoy, and Turgenev. In their early instruction Western secular writings, and even Western Christianity, far outweighed any Orthodox influence. See, for instance, A. Herzen, *The Memoirs of Alexander Herzen* (London, 1968), I, chaps. 2 and 3.
32 *WNSI*, p. 36 (1).
33 It was presumably through this book that Dostoyevsky was first acquainted with the moral thought of Kant. During the course of his travels Karamzin met Kant; and Kant obligingly summed up the principal teachings of the *Critique of Practical Reason* for his Russian visitor. See N. Karamzin, *Letters of a Russian Traveller, 1789-90* (New York, 1957), pp. 40-41.

whom he read as a boy were to have little influence on him. He quickly passed from them to the European literature which they tended to imitate.

Schiller and Scott were the European writers who made the deepest impression on him. He himself attests to the influence they exercised on his spiritual life when, late in his life, he was asked by a correspondent to recommend proper reading for a young girl:

When I was ten years old, I saw at Moscow a performance of *"Die Räuber"* . . . and I can only say that the deep impression which that performance made upon me has worked most fruitfully ever since on my whole mental development. At twelve I read right through Walter Scott during the summer holidays. . . . I got from it many fine and noble impressions, which gave my soul much power of resistance against others which were seductive, violent, and corrupting.[34]

In his adolescent years, Dostoyevsky was introduced to the writings of Victor Hugo, Balzac, and George Sand (serialized in a periodical to which his father subscribed), and by the time his father sent him to the Engineering Academy in St. Petersburg (in 1838), his appetite for European literature had become insatiable. The requirements of a training in military engineering placed a constraint on this appetite, but did not diminish it in the least. It was during his years at the Engineering Academy that he read and assimilated a vast and varied amount of European literature. In a letter he wrote to his brother Michael from the Engineering Academy, he discusses, for instance, Homer, Shakespeare, Hoffmann, Schiller, Byron, Hugo, Racine, and Corneille.[35]

Dostoyevsky came to understand and direct his consuming love of literature within the intellectual framework provided by the Russian Romanticism of the 1830s. The transition from the Westernism of the Decembrists to that of the Russian Romantics was occurring even as the Decembrists were planning their insurrection. A group of young Russian intellectuals, styling itself the "Society of the Lovers of Wisdom," was formed in 1823. Although most of the members of this circle had older friends and relatives among the Decembrists, they were not interested in political questions. Indeed, so anxious were they to eschew political concerns that after the failure of the Decembrists they voluntarily disbanded for fear that the government might misconstrue the nature of their meetings, which were concerned almost exclusively with the reading and discussion of modern German philosophers such as Kant, Fichte, and Schelling. The primacy of Schelling among these is eloquently explained by one of the members of the society, Prince Odoyevsky:

At the beginning of the 19th century, Schelling was for us what Christopher Columbus had been for the 15th century; he revealed to man a hitherto unknown dimension of his own being, his soul, his spirit . . . . Like Christopher Columbus he had found what he had been searching for; like him, he had awakened unrealizable

34 Letter of 18 Aug. 1880.
35 Letter of 1 Jan. 1840.

hopes; like him, he had indicated a new direction for human activity! Everyone threw himself towards this admirable, splendid new world. . . .[36]

Schellingian metaphysics became, for many Westernized Russians, a new religion directing them away from the world of appearance towards an Absolute which could be experienced by the individual only after a long and lonely inward journey.

This interpretation of Schelling encouraged the disregard for sociopolitical questions and the emphasis upon individual salvation which characterized Russian Westernism throughout the 1830s. The magnitude of Schelling's influence at this time, and the way in which he was read, was to some extent attributable to the position in which Russian Westernism found itself in the repressive aftermath of the Decembrist insurrection. The resolution of the crisis in favour of Alexander's brother Nicholas brought to the throne a man understandably suspicious of Western thought and prepared to place severe constraints upon it. Although its socio-economic circumstances changed little during Nicholas I's reign (1825-1855), Russian Westernism as an intellectual movement was forced underground. Any thinking which was independent of the teaching of "Official Nationality" was restricted to the ubiquitous "circles," which were such a characteristic feature of Russian social life in this period. Dostoyevsky described the more serious circles:

> In some "circles," though, the members conduct heated debates about matters of importance. A number of well-educated and well-meaning persons gather with enthusiasm, fiercely banish all innocent amusements, such as gossip or preference . . . and with quite incomprehensible animation discuss all sorts of important subjects. Finally, having discussed, talked about and solved a number of problems of general importance and having reached a unanimous decision, the entire "circle" lapses into a state of irritation, into a kind of unpleasant state of limpness.[37]

This description of a typical serious circle exposes the limitation which was so fundamental to Russian Westernism after the failure of the Decembrist revolt—the absence of any relation between thought and practice. To the sincere followers of Schelling, his thought held out the promise of an experience of an inner truth which bore no relation to the manifest imperfections of Russian social and political life. To the insincere hangers-on, it justified and concealed a propensity for affectation and a lazy complacency.

Schelling's thought apparently did not become a religion for Dostoyevsky to the extent that it did for so many Westernized Russians during the 1830s. It is likely, then, that his involvement with Russian Romanticism was limited to his concern with formulating a theoretical idea of the literary activity which was engaging him ever more deeply. He was thus particularly interested in Schelling's teaching that knowledge should ultimately be identified with an apprehension attained through mystical intuition rather than

36 A. Koyré, *La philosophie et le problème national en Russie au début du XIX siècle* (Paris, 1929), p. 40.
37 *OW*, p. 12.

through speculative reason. To the aspiring young novelist this implied that "the poet, in the moment of inspiration, comprehends God, and consequently does the philosopher's work."[38] Russian Schellingianism did not make positive political demands on its adherents and, in Dostoyevsky's case, it was apparently compatible with Christianity, which he continued to profess in the late 1830s.[39] Perhaps for these reasons he did not regard the influence of Romanticism as the decisive factor in his transformation into a "European liberal," a transformation which, he declared later, occurred during his youthful years in St. Petersburg (1836-1849). He always attributed the decisive influence in this transformation to his meeting in 1845 with Vissarion Belinsky—the founder of Russian literary criticism and one of the dominant figures in the history of Russian Westernism. Dostoyevsky recounts the highlights of his relationship with Belinsky in two articles written much later in his life, "Old People" and "One of the Contemporaneous Falsehoods" (from *The Diary of a Writer*, 1873). These articles, although autobiographical, are clearly intended to portray a relationship of symbolic significance for the history of Russian Westernism.[40] In "Old People" Dostoyevsky asserts that by 1847 he had "passionately embraced" the teaching of Belinsky.

The Influence of "Furious Vissarion"

Although he wrote as a literary critic, Belinsky's passion for philosophical speculation was so great that it prompted his acquaintances to call him "furious Vissarion." In his *Literary Reminiscences* Turgenev recalls Belinsky's indignation at the suggestion that a day-long argument be interrupted for a meal: "We haven't yet decided the question of the existence of God . . . and you want to eat!"[41] This love of speculation was combined with a temperament wholly unsuited to careful reflection: his highly emotional and enthusiastic nature prompted him to take immediately to heart new ideas without fully understanding them. According to Dostoyevsky, "Belinsky was not a reflective person, but all his life he was always a boundlessly enthusiastic individual."[42] Belinsky himself was aware of the danger of the "fanaticism" implicit

---

38 Letter of 31 Oct. 1838.

39 See J. Frank, *Dostoevsky, the Seeds of Revolt 1821-1849* (Princeton, 1976), p. 98. During his years at the Engineering Academy (1838-1843) Dostoyevsky, according to the recollection of a fellow student, was "very religious, and zealously performed all the obligations of the Orthodox Christian faith. . . . All this struck his comrades so much that they dubbed him the monk Photius."

40 The significance of Dostoyevsky's relationship with Belinsky for his subsequent thought and life has generally not been sufficiently emphasized. For two detailed studies of this relationship, see I. Dolenc, *Dostoevsky and Christ* (Toronto, 1978) and J. Frank, *Dostoevsky, the Seeds of Revolt 1831-1849* (Princeton, 1976). Frank's treatment of the relationship is particularly thorough and thoughtful, as is his entire study of the various intellectual influences which acted upon Dostoyevsky prior to 1849. The account which follows of Belinsky's influence on the young Dostoyevsky is indebted to Frank's study.

41 I. Turgenev, *Turgenev's Literary Reminiscences* (London, 1958), p. 110.

42 *DW*, p. 6 (1873).

in that impetuosity which propelled him from one intellectual conversion to another.[43] However, this same quality made him a powerful teacher and propagator of ideas. By the sheer force of his personality he became the dominant intellectual figure in the Russian Westernism of the 1840s. The "furious" manner in which he approached philosophy is manifest in the remarkable intellectual odyssey which he had experienced by the time Dostoyevsky met him.

In the 1830s, like most of his Westernized contemporaries, Belinsky professed himself to be a follower of Schelling. Towards the end of the decade, however, Schelling's ascendancy over Russian thinking was being replaced by that of Hegel, whose thought was promulgated by eminent intellectuals such as Turgenev, Bakunin, Stankevich, Granovsky, and Herzen—all of whom, at one time or another, took courses from Hegel's students (Gans, Ranke, Werder) in Germany. The Russians turned to Hegel's thought with an extraordinary fervour to which Herzen attests in his memoirs:

> They discussed these subjects incessantly; there was not a paragraph in the three parts of the *Logic*, in the two of the *Aesthetic*, the *Encyclopedia*, and so on, which had not been the topic of desperate disputes for several nights together. People who loved each other avoided each other for weeks at a time because they disagreed about the definition of "all-embracing spirit," or had taken as a personal insult an opinion on "the absolute personality and its existence in-itself." Every insignificant pamphlet published in Berlin or other provincial or district towns of German philosophy was ordered and read to tatters and smudges, and the leaves fell out in a few days, if only there was a mention of Hegel in it.[44]

This passion for Hegel was coupled with an impatient desire to understand and assimilate his thought immediately. Initially he was interpreted in a manner which was most natural for educated Russians at this time. Insofar as the political writings and the political implications of his thought were studied at all, they were understood in a way which reinforced the tendency of Russian Westernists to ignore political and social problems and to concentrate on the inner contemplation of truth (as revealed in the *Logic*).[45] Bakunin's interpretation of Hegel's well-known dictum concerning the "rationality of the real" and the "reality of the rational" is indicative of the way in which Hegel was read. Bakunin simply identified the "real" with all that one meets in the world, seeing no distinction in Hegel between authentic reality and the given historical situation. Disregarding the role of negation in Hegel's notion of historical development, Bakunin apotheosized Nicholas' socio-political order. Belinsky, who did not know German, relied largely on Bakunin for his

---

43 V. G. Belinsky, *Selected Philosophical Works* (Moscow, 1948), p. 150. For a detailed and colourful description of Belinsky, see A. Herzen, *The Memoirs of Alexander Herzen* (London, 1968), II, pp. 402-44. See also Turgenev's recollection of Belinsky in *Turgenev's Literary Reminiscences* (London, 1958).

44 A. Herzen, *The Memoirs of Alexander Herzen* (London, 1968), II, p. 398.

45 For an excellent account of Russian Hegelianism, see G. Planty-Bonjour, *Hegel et la pensée philosophique en Russie, 1830-1917* (The Hague, 1974).

knowledge of Hegel. The derivative nature of his Hegelianism did not affect the ardour with which it was embraced, and Belinsky made his contribution to Bakunin's praise of the Russian government. A contemporary bore witness to this remarkable period in the lives of Bakunin and Belinsky:

The arrival of Bakunin in Petersburg in the winter of 1840 gave Belinsky great joy. Bakunin visited us almost every day and, full of monarchical ecstasy according to Hegel, related to us various anecdotes concerning the emperor, which had been passed on to him. . . . To doubt the genius of Nikolay Pavlovich [the Emperor Nicholas] was considered a sign of ignorance. All this seemed a little strange to me; still, I too, following the authority of Belinsky and Bakunin, directed myself toward reverent admiration of the Monarch.[46]

Belinsky's period of "reconciliation with reality," however, ended as abruptly and fervently as it had begun. His reassessment of Hegel in the early 1840s was determined primarily by his deep concern with a problem which constituted the principal intellectual preoccupation of Russian Westernism throughout the nineteenth century—the problem of Russia's proper relationship with the West.

The question of Russia and the West is deeply rooted in Russian history. Russia's relatively late entry into Christendom in the tenth century originally prompted an anxiety about the place of Russians among other Christian peoples, which was allayed somewhat by contemplation of Christ's parable of the labourers in the vineyard (Matthew 20). The next major expression of the question was prompted by the rise of Moscow as the political centre of Orthodoxy after the fall of Constantinople in 1453. The monk Filofey's teaching that Moscow was the last and greatest temporal centre of Christianity—the "Third Rome"—demonstrated an enormous growth in the self-confidence of the Russian church since the tenth century. The problem of Russia's proper place among the world's peoples received its first great secular expression in Nicholas Karamzin's *The History of the Russian State*, written in the early nineteenth century. Under the influence of French Enlightenment thinkers, Karamzin interpreted Russian history as the progressive evolution of the Russian state. His emphasis on the state rather than the church had as its corollary an emphasis on the problematic relationship of Russia to the states of modern Europe, rather than to the Eastern or Western churches. After the appearance of Hegel's thought in Russia, the question of the role their nation was to play on the stage of world history became a constant subject of discussion and debate among educated Russians of every description. A lack of certainty about the proper nature of Russia's relation to the West, however, was responsible for a deep division within Russian Westernism.

This division was rooted in the common conviction, derived from Hegel's thought, that European civilization had reached its apogee and, at the same time, was coming to an end. The depressing thought that the progressive unfolding of the Spirit in history had hitherto overlooked Russia was banished

46 P. V. Annenkov, *Literaturnye vospominaniya* (Leningrad, 1928), p. 506.

by the expectation, encouraged by Hegel himself, that the Spirit, which had come to the end of its manifestation in Europe, might find a new incarnation for itself further West, in North America, or to the East, in Russia. The Russian Westernists regarded the United States with curiosity, but with little respect, and certainly not as a likely centre of a renewed Western civilization. Herzen's dismissal of the United States as "the last, well-produced edition of the same feudal-Christian text and, what is more, in a crude English transla-tion"[47] expressed the common view of educated Russians, who were con-vinced that the Russian people, by virtue of their greater proximity to Europe, their lack of identification with only one part of Europe, and above all their greater spiritual depth, were the more likely bearers of a renewed civilization. This agreement within Russian Westernism, however, provided the framework for the Slavophile-Westernist controversy which dominated intel-lectual life after 1840. Herzen's well-known dictum is particularly apt: "like Janus, or the two-headed eagle, they and we looked in different directions while one heart throbbed within us."[48]

The Slavophiles thought that the fulfillment of Russia's historical destiny depended on the recognition and fostering of the unique spirit of the Russian people, although they themselves were very much the product of the Russian turn to the West, for they received the initial impulse for much of their thought—especially the concept of the unique "spirit of a people"—from Schelling and Hegel. However, as they came to realize that the content of the unique spirit of the Russian people was, first and foremost, Orthodox Chris-tianity, their thinking came increasingly to reflect the teaching of the Greek Church Fathers. Although the Slavophiles went to "some German Peterschule, sitting over a German book and repeating its everlasting German lesson,"[49] this initial German schooling ended in an attempt to return to the theology of the Greek Fathers, and by means of this theology to respond to the important questions raised for Russians by Western modernity. This tendency was especially true of the two most eminent proponents of the Slavophile position: Alexey Khomyakov and Ivan Kireyevsky. The Westernists, on the contrary, maintained that it was the very lack of uniqueness or "exclusive-ness" of the Russian people in relation to Europe which made them peculiarly receptive to Western civilization. They argued that this receptivity destined the Russian people to provide a fresh and more abundant soil for what was best in Europe, which they identified with the thought and practice arising out of the French Revolution. Belinsky was among this group.

For Belinsky the whole problem of Russia and the West had become contained within the particular issue of Russia's relation to the dynamic socio-political situation of Europe during the decade preceding the revolutions of 1848. This issue entailed a more sober appraisal of that "surrounding

47 A. Herzen, *From the Other Shore* (New York, 1963), p. 78.
48 A. Herzen, *The Memoirs of Alexander Herzen* (London, 1968), II, p. 549.
49 *The Devils*, pp. 50-51 (I,9).

reality" which he had thitherto ignored in favour of the "charming inner world of German contemplation."[50] Ironically, Belinsky's new interest in historical reality coincided with a renunciation of Hegel, or at least of the image of Hegel to which he and Bakunin had paid homage. Belinsky's character gave an added impetus to this renunciation: he was not naturally given to contemplation, and the impetuosity of his temperament, as well as a deep sensitivity to human suffering, would have made it difficult for him to content himself for long with meditation on the sublimity of Hegel's logical categories. By 1842 Belinsky was convinced that socialism was the final and best fruit of Western civilization and that it would take up its new abode in a youthful, energetic Russia. He thus became allied with Herzen who declared that "the free and rational development of Russian national life coincides with the aspirations of Western socialism."[51] Socialism had become for Belinsky, in his own words, "the idea of ideas, the being of beings, the question of questions, the alpha and omega of belief and knowledge."[52] The socialism to which he turned with such fervour was that French "utopian" socialism of Pierre Leroux, Louis Blanc, George Sand, Saint-Simon, and Fourier, whose writings had been making their way into Russia at an increasing rate after 1840. It was under the influence of these French socialists that Belinsky penned his famous retort to Hegel on behalf of those whose suffering cannot be alleviated by reference to the "cunning of reason":

No thank you, Egor Fedorych [Hegel], with all due respect to your philosophical cap; let me inform you, with all respect for your philosophical philistinism, that if I did succeed in reaching the top of the evolution ladder, I would demand even there an account from you of all the victims of the conditions of life and history, of all the victims of accident, superstition, the Inquisition, Philip II, etc., etc.,: otherwise I will throw myself headlong from the top rung. I will not have happiness if you gave it to me *gratis* unless I feel assured about every one of my blood brothers, the bone of my bone and flesh of my flesh. Disharmony is said to be a condition of harmony: that may be very profitable and pleasant for megalomaniacs, but certainly not for those whose fates are destined to express the idea of disharmony.[53]

The sort of socialism Belinsky professed after 1842 permitted Russian Westernists to direct a growing urge for practical activity in a way which would not be totally incompatible with their previous lofty, unworldly aspirations. Activity in this world would be for the sake of a transformed world of freedom, equality, and brotherhood. This vision of a new world, first articulated in Christianity, had finally achieved political expression in the French Revolution, but had yet to achieve a complete social realization.[54] In the

50 V. G. Belinsky, *Selected Philosophical Works* (Moscow, 1948), p. 161.
51 See, for instance, A. Herzen, *The Memoirs of Alexander Herzen* (London, 1968), II, p. 530. See also Herzen's more extended treatment of this question in "The Russian People and Socialism," *Selected Philosophical Works* (Moscow, 1956).
52 V. G. Belinsky, *Selected Philosophical Works* (Moscow, 1948), p. 159.
53 Ibid., pp. 149-50.
54 For the most characteristic expression of Belinsky's "New Christianity," see his "Letter to Gogol," *Selected Philosophical Works* (Moscow, 1948), pp. 503-12.

article entitled "One of the Contemporaneous Falsehoods," Dostoyevsky
notes the religious aura in which French socialism lived among the Russians:

at that time the affair was conceived in a most rosy and paradisiacally moral light.
Verily, socialism in its embryo used to be compared by some of its ring-leaders
with Christianity and was regarded as a mere corrective to, and improvement of,
the latter, in conformity with the tendencies of the age and civilization.[55]

Belinsky did much in his writing to propagate the "New Christianity" of
Pierre Leroux, George Sand, Louis Blanc, Saint-Simon, and Fourier. His own
allegiance to this socialism, however, proved to be ultimately and uncharac-
teristically ambiguous. In "One of the Contemporaneous Falsehoods," Dostoyevsky depicts Belinsky as a fervent advocate of French socialism, and he
remarks elsewhere that at this time Belinsky bowed before France "with a
reverence approaching weirdness."[56] However, "Old People" reveals a different Belinsky, a Belinsky who felt "duty-bound to destroy the teaching of
Christ, to call it fallacious and ignorant philanthropy, doomed by modern
science and economic tenets." And he impugned not only the teaching of
Christ, but Christ himself:

there remained the radiant personality of Christ himself... the beatific image of
God-man, its moral inaccessibility, its wonderful and miraculous beauty. But in his
incessant, unquenchable transport, Belinsky did not stop even before this insurmountable obstacle....
   "Believe me that your Christ, if he were born in our time, would be a most
imperceptible and ordinary man; in the presence of contemporary science and contemporary propellers of mankind, he would be effaced!"

He later accedes, however, to the suggestion of an interlocutor that if Christ
returned to earth he would join the socialists. This ambivalence concerning
the relation of Christ to socialism is highlighted by the list of thinkers to whom
Dostoyevsky ascribes the greatest influence over Belinsky at this time:

These propellers of mankind, whom Christ was designed to join, were then the
French: George Sand, the now altogether forgotten Cabet, Pierre Leroux and
Proudhon, who was then only beginning his activities. As far as I remember, at
that time Belinsky respected these four most.—Fourier had already lost much of his
prestige.—They were being discussed through whole evenings. There was also a
German before whom Belinsky bowed with great deference, namely, Feuerbach.
(Belinsky, who all his life was unable to master any foreign language, pronounced
the name of Feuerbach as "Fierbach.") Strauss was spoken of with great reverence.

It is clear from Dostoyevsky's account that Belinsky's conversion to
French socialism was being rapidly undermined by the teaching of the left-

---

55 DW, p. 148 (1873).
56 WNSI, p. 46 (2). For the two quotations from "Old People," which follow, see DW,
   pp. 7-8 (1873).

Hegelians, especially Feuerbach and Strauss. It is not clear whether Belinsky was dubious of the compatibility between Christianity and socialism before he encountered the teaching of these German thinkers. The unsuitability of his temperament for compromise of any sort makes this likely. At any rate, the reading of Feuerbach's *The Essence of Christianity* and Strauss' *Life of Jesus* was decisive for him. By 1845 he was proclaiming the logical necessity of the relation between atheism and socialism—"he knew that the revolution must necessarily begin with atheism." Although Dostoyevsky does not refer specifically to the influence of Marx's thought on Belinsky, it was also apparently decisive. After reading Marx's essays, "On the Jewish Question" and "A Contribution to the Critique of Hegel's *Philosophy of Right*," Belinsky wrote to Herzen: "I have accepted the truth—and in the words 'god' and 'religion' I see darkness, gloom, shackles, and the knout; and now I love these two words as much as I love the four that follow them."[57]

Belinsky's increasingly "furious" commitment to the atheist humanism of Feuerbach and Marx was supplemented by a growing interest in the natural sciences (particularly the physiology of Emile Littré). Belinsky had become convinced that the scientific approach to human nature was ultimately the only proper one. Although he conceded that modern science may never be able to solve completely the "mystery" of the individual "personality," just as it cannot yet tell us precisely what electricity and magnetism are, he thought it at least possible that science might eventually be able to "trace the *physical* process of *moral* evolution."[58] It was apparently his hope that the scientific study of humanity would constitute the basis for the construction of the perfectly just society of "freedom, equality, and brotherhood." Belinsky dedicated himself to the construction of such a society for the sake of human happiness, though he was aware that people would probably have to be "forcibly . . . led to happiness."[59]

Belinsky's extraordinarily rapid shift from a Romanticism based on Schelling and Hegel to "utopian" socialism, and then from left-Hegelianism to some sort of "scientific" socialism represented, in a condensed form, the development which the mainstream of Russian Westernism was to undergo in the course of the nineteenth century. Two of the most illustrious names in the history of Russian Westernism underwent an intellectual development almost identical to Belinsky's. Under the influence of the German left-Hegelian Arnold Ruge, Bakunin made amends for his earlier disregard of Hegel's idea of negation. His energetic application of the principle that "the passion for destruction is also a creative passion" made him as famous (and as dubious) a Russian ambassador to Europe in the nineteenth century as Peter the Great had been in the eighteenth. Herzen's reading of Hegel was characterized by greater caution, consistency, and intellectual acumen than that exhibited by

57 V. G. Belinsky, *Selected Philosophical Works* (Moscow, 1948), p. xxxvi.
58 Ibid., pp. 368-69.
59 Ibid., p. 111.

any Russian Hegelian of the nineteenth century.[60] This reading, nevertheless, led him very quickly to the left-Hegelianism expressed in his conviction that Hegel's thought is the "algebra of revolution." And Herzen's growing interest in the natural sciences, especially after the defeat suffered by European socialism in 1848, led him increasingly to combine his socialist hopes for a future golden age with a rigorous scientific realism. For Dostoyevsky, it is clearly Belinsky above all who embodies the tendency in Russian Westernism which was manifest in all three. The picture he presents of Belinsky initiating him into "European liberalism" signifies the intellectual influence of Belinsky on a generation of Russian youth.

This influence, however, was to be realized posthumously. Belinsky's tempestuous intellectual transformations were not shared by the majority of his Westernist contemporaries of the 1840s. Indeed, the rapid movement of Belinsky, Herzen, and Bakunin towards an atheist humanism resulted in another division within Russian Westernism which became apparent shortly after the Slavophile-Westernist split. The chief issue of this new controversy is clearly indicated in the argument that took place in 1845 between Herzen and Granovsky over the immortality of the soul.[61] Timofey Granovsky is described by Dostoyevsky in an article entitled "Idealists—Cynics" in *The Diary of a Writer* (July-August, 1876): "Granovsky was the purest of all men of those days; he was irreproachable and beautiful. An idealist of the Forties—in the loftiest sense—he possessed the most individually peculiar and original nuance among our progressives...." An extremely influential professor of European history at the University of Moscow, he was chiefly responsible, through his public lectures during the 1840s, for propagating Hegel's thought in Russia. His interpretation of Hegel remained consistently and stubbornly independent of the later left-Hegelianism of Belinsky, Herzen, and Bakunin, which saw in Hegel a thinker unwilling to face the revolutionary implications of his own thought. Granovsky's reluctance to give up some sort of belief in God led him to understand Hegel's thought as disclosing an Absolute which ultimately transcends the world. He was, in Dostoyevsky's words, a preacher of "the beautiful and the lofty." Yet he was concerned also with injustice in this world, and in this regard he identified Hegel's Absolute with the Christian God whose providence guides free individuals towards the accomplishment of their moral destiny—that is, life within a humane society of freedom, equality, and brotherhood.[62] Granovsky's thinking was typical of the majority of Westernists of the 1840s, but within a decade Belinsky's

---

60 This is evident in Herzen's "Letters on the Study of Nature," a series of articles on the history of philosophy which Dostoyevsky read and greatly admired later in his life. See A. Herzen, *Selected Philosophical Works* (Moscow, 1956).

61 See A. Herzen, *The Memoirs of Alexander Herzen* (London, 1968), II, p. 586.

62 "No one did more to introduce into the consciousness of society the idea of universal history as a progressive movement towards humaneness." N. Riasanovsky, *A Parting of Ways: Government and the Educated Public in Russia, 1801-1855* (Oxford, 1976), p. 223. For the quotation from "Idealists-Cynics," see *DW*, p. 379 (July-Aug. 1876).

scientific socialism was to eclipse completely the attempt to combine some sort of belief in God with an interpretation of history as a progress towards a perfect society of freedom, equality, and brotherhood. Already by the early 1850s Granovsky himself seemed to sense that he had lost his prominent place in Russian intellectual life and, despondent, he spent most of his time gambling at cards.

Did Dostoyevsky, unlike the majority of Russian Westernists (represented by Granovsky), "passionately" embrace *all* of Belinsky's teaching after their first meeting in 1845? In "Old People" Dostoyevsky does not say what aspect of Belinsky's teaching he embraced, although it is in this same article that he is so careful to distinguish the principal phases of Belinsky's intellectual journey. In the second article concerning his "European liberalism" of the 1840s, "One of the Contemporaneous Falsehoods," Dostoyevsky does state clearly that Belinsky initiated him into the "New Christianity" of the French socialist thinkers:

Already in 1846 I had been initiated by Belinsky into the whole *truth* of that future "regenerated world" and into the whole *holiness* of the forthcoming communistic society. All these convictions about the immorality of the very foundations . . . of modern society, the immorality of religion, family, right of property; all these ideas about the elimination of nationalities in the name of the universal brotherhood of man, about the contempt for one's native country, as an obstacle to universal progress, and so on, and so forth—all these constituted such influences as we were unable to overcome and which, contrariwise, swayed our hearts and minds in the name of some magnanimity.[63]

In the article Dostoyevsky reinforces this statement when he characterizes his thinking during the 1840s as that of a "Petrashevetz."

M. V. Petrashevsky, founder of a circle which Dostoyevsky joined in 1848, was an ardent follower of Fourier, and his adherence to French socialism was generally shared by the members of his circle. Subsequent to the European upheaval of 1848, the highly theoretical and diffuse discussions of the circle became imbued with a new sense of practical urgency, and the members came increasingly to focus their attention directly on Russian political and social conditions. This practical concern expressed itself above all in the formulation of two objectives: the abolition of serfdom and the reform of the Russian legal system. It is notable that in the realm of practice the Russian "New Christians" had to resort to the familiar liberal goals of the Decembrists. They apparently found the writings of the French socialists of little aid in formulating clear practical objectives, as well as in deciding the best means of attaining these objectives. This question of means was the source of deep division in the circle. The once friendly and relaxed discussions concerning the intricate details of Fourier's "phalanstery" gave way to tense debates concerning the relative merits of peaceful propaganda among the people and of violent political agitation which would establish a political democracy or

63 *DW*, pp. 148-49 (1873).

even a temporary dictatorship. The presence of this dissension (as well as the ever-increasing number of new members) prompted the formation of several satellite circles centred around the original Petrashevsky circle. One such circle devoted itself entirely to the theoretical elaboration of Fourier's doctrines; another, the Palm-Durov circle, was composed of those who were more interested in literature than in Fourier; and a third, the Speshnev circle, was formed to promote a revolution in Russia by sowing discontent with the established order everywhere, beginning with the young people in the schools.

It is evident, then, that the word "Petrashevets" encompasses various possibilities. A reasonably precise idea of the sort of "Petrashevets" which Dostoyevsky was can be gleaned from the recollection of his acquaintances, as well as from his own testimony and that of his fellow prisoners during the government's investigation of the Petrashevsky circle.[64] All such testimony indicates that Dostoyevsky's "European liberalism" at this time reflected above all the teachings of French socialism. Dostoyevsky was apparently familiar with the writings of Saint-Simon and Fourier, as well as with historical accounts of the French Revolution by Thiers, Mignet, and Louis Blanc. He was known, moreover, to have borrowed the following books from Petrashevsky's library: Louis Blanc's *Histoire de dix ans*, which is concerned with the historical developments that led to the formulation of utopian socialism; a popularization of Fourierism by Paget, entitled *Introduction à l'étude de la science sociale*; and Etienne Cabet's *Le vrai Christianisme suivant Jésus Christ*. Although Dostoyevsky was later to remark that at this time he "believed in all the theories and Utopias,"[65] it is apparent that his dedication to the theories of French socialism was markedly less than that of Petrashevsky himself. In his testimony before the investigating tribunal, Dostoyevsky admitted his sympathy for the intentions of French socialism and his admiration for the intelligence and fervent love of humanity manifest in its theorists. But he also asserted that the application of any of their proposed theoretical social systems would be impossible and undesirable, and not only in Russia but also in France. The circumstances of this declaration may cast some doubt on it, but it is generally corroborated by the observations of other "Petrashevtsi" concerning Dostoyevsky's participation in the circle. One of these, A. Milyukov, later recalled:

We all studied the Socialists, but all were far from believing in the possibility of the practical realization of their plans. Dostoyevsky was among the sceptics. He read the Socialist writers assiduously, but regarded them critically. Agreeing that at

---

64 For a detailed account of the Petrashevsky circle, the nature of Dostoyevsky's participation in it, and his testimony before the investigating tribunal, see J. Drouilly, *La pensée politique et religieuse de Dostoïevski* (Paris, 1971); J. Frank, *Dostoevsky, the Seeds of Revolt 1821-1849* (Princeton, 1976); L. Grossman, *Dostoevsky* (London, 1974).

65 Letter of 24 March 1856.

the foundation of their doctrines there was a noble aim, he nonetheless considered them only as estimable visionaries.[66]

The fact that Dostoyevsky was a "Petrashevets" of the sort described—after Belinsky's death in 1848—would indicate that Belinsky did not initiate him into anything more radical than utopian socialism (though, as we have seen, even this initiation was not complete). Belinsky, however, certainly attempted to take him further. As Dostoyevsky recalls in "Old People," "I do not at all exaggerate his ardent attraction to me, at least during the first months of our acquaintance. I found him a passionate socialist, and, straight off the bat, he embarked upon atheism." Belinsky immediately "embarked upon atheism," but Dostoyevsky would not renounce the vaguely Christian ethos which apparently remained characteristic of his "European liberalism." In "Old People" he recalls Belinsky's consternation at this: " 'I am even touched to look at him', said Belinsky, suddenly interrupting his furious exclamations, turning to his friend and pointing at me. 'Every time I mention Christ his face changes its expression, as if he were ready to start weeping. . . .' "[67]

Dostoyevsky stubbornly persisted in his fervent admiration for the person of Christ, however understood; yet he also parted company with Belinsky for the same reason that Granovsky rejected Herzen's left-Hegelianism. This is evident from a brief ironic note which Belinsky addressed to Dostoyevsky shortly before the rift between Herzen and Granovsky over the immortality of the soul: "Dostoyevsky, my soul (immortal) longs to see you."[68] However vague and uncertain Dostoyevsky's conviction of the immortality of the soul may have been at this time, it clearly signified a refusal to acquiesce in Belinsky's atheism.

It is worth noting, moreover, that Belinsky's influence did not move Dostoyevsky to put his art directly at the service of the socialist cause. Although Belinsky hailed his first novel, *Poor Folk*, as "the first attempt at a social novel we've had," the young author resisted this sort of interpretation, even at the risk of forfeiting the acclaim which *Poor Folk* earned him.[69] It is clear from his writings during the 1840s (*Poor Folk, The Double, Mr. Prokharchin, The Landlady, White Nights, Netochka Nezvanova*) that Dostoyevsky did not think that a scientific reorganization of society could solve the problem of human suffering, which he portrayed so powerfully. Certainly he shared Belinsky's yearning for the overcoming of suffering and injustice; yet he would not reduce the ultimate "mystery of man," which is partially revealed to the artist's intuition, to the question of social organization.[70]

66 Found in R. Tarr, trad., *Dostoïevski vivant* (Paris, 1972), pp. 58-59.
67 *DW*, pp. 6-7 (1873).
68 See J. Frank, *Dostoevsky, the Seeds of Revolt 1821-1849* (Princeton, 1976), p. 196.
69 See Dostoyevsky's account of Belinsky's ecstatic reception of this first novel, *Poor Folk*, in *DW*, pp. 584-88 (Jan. 1877).
70 Letter of 16 Aug. 1839.

Belinsky thus took Dostoyevsky as far as the mainstream liberalism of the 1840s—represented by men such as Granovsky—and no further.

In "Old People" Dostoyevsky states that he embraced *all* of Belinsky's teaching. His liberalism did entail implications that may explain this exaggeration. He refers to these implications in "One of the Contemporaneous Falsehoods," where he compares his political activity during the 1840s with that of the young people who followed the revolutionary socialist, Nechayev, in the 1870s:

How do you know that the Petrashevtsi could not have become the Nechayevtsi, i.e., to have chosen the "Nechayev" path, *if things had turned that way?* . . . probably I could never have become a Nechayev, but a Nechayevets—for this I wouldn't vouch, but maybe I could have become one . . . in the days of my youth.[71]

As a member of the Speshnev circle Dostoyevsky was definitely a participant in a plot to print pamphlets designed to incite a violent insurrection of the Russian peasantry. The moving force of this plot, Nikolay Speshnev, was a remarkable figure who, like Belinsky, had traversed the road from "New Christianity" to an explicitly atheist socialism. The reasons for Dostoyevsky's participation in Speshnev's conspiracy are obscure, but it seems clear that this participation did not signify any accord with Speshnev's atheism.[72] Whatever his reasons, in retrospect Dostoyevsky saw that his liberalism, far from being incompatible with such practical activity, had actually rendered him peculiarly vulnerable to Speshnev's influence. He avows that he was "unable to struggle against it. And so, why do you think that even murder (à la Nechayev) would have stopped—of course, not all, but at least, some of us—in those fervid times, in the midst of doctrines fascinating one's soul?"

Thus in his autobiographical reflections on the development of Russian Westernism, Dostoyevsky deliberately associates his theoretical "European liberalism" with Belinsky's scientific socialism, and his practical participation in the Petrashevsky circle with the revolutionary socialism of Nechayev that gave concrete expression to Belinsky's declaration: "Men . . . must forcibly be led to happiness." His concern in making these associations is, not with strict autobiographical accuracy, but with indicating the basic direction of the historical development of Russian Westernism after 1840. The "European liberalism" of Dostoyevsky, which held the majority of Russian Westernists during the 1840s, was eventually to find its theoretical expression in the scientific socialism of Belinsky's last years and its practical expression in Nechayev's revolutionary socialism.

In 1849 Dostoyevsky's active participation in the Petrashevsky circle resulted in his arrest and sentence of penal servitude and exile in Siberia. This marked the beginning of a decade of experience that would profoundly alter

71 *DW*, p. 147 (1873).
72 For a detailed account of Speshnev, and of his influence over Dostoyevsky, see J. Frank, *Dostoevsky, the Seeds of Revolt 1821-1849* (Princeton, 1976), chap. 18.

his connection to Russian Westernism. In 1849 Dostoyevsky had been prepared to die for his liberal convictions. Ten years later he returned from Siberia to begin the critique of Russian Westernism which preoccupied him until his death. In one of his last autobiographical reflections he expresses the change wrought in him by saying that in Siberia "I received Christ into my soul once more, whom I knew in the home of my childhood, and whom I all but lost when in my turn I changed into 'a European Liberal'."[73]

The Christ whom Dostoyevsky came to know once again was the Christ of the Russian people rather than of the French socialists, for his experience in Siberia was, first, the experience of the Russian people. He wrote to his brother Mikhail towards the end of his exile: "I have learnt to know the Russian people as only a few know them. I am a little vain of it. I hope that such vanity is pardonable."[74] The men he came to know so well were criminals, but in his view they were representative of the Russian people, and even "exceptional men," perhaps "the most gifted, the strongest" of the Russian people.[75] For the first time he came to know directly the distance which the years after Peter the Great had placed between the Westernized gentry, including himself, and the bulk of the Russian people. He bears witness to it throughout *The House of the Dead*.[76] The "impassable" gulf was characterized, not only by indifference, but by an active abiding hatred of the people for the gentry. Dostoyevsky describes this attitude in a letter to his brother: "Their hatred for the nobility is boundless; they regard all of us who belong to it with hostility and enmity. They would have devoured us if they could. . . . A hundred and fifty foes never wearied of persecuting us—it was their joy, their diversion, their pastime . . . ."[77]

This experience posed a grave problem for his "European liberal" convictions. His liberalism was perhaps primarily responsible for his persistent effort to establish contact with these Russian representatives of oppressed humanity; but it was precisely this liberalism that made contact so problematic. He found it difficult to see and accept the Russian people as they actually were, rather than as he and his fellow Petrashevtsi had imagined them to be. But more significantly, his liberal convictions had all but eclipsed in him what the Russian people still held most dear—their religion. Dostoyevsky was surprised and impressed by the piety of his fellow prisoners. In *The House of the Dead* he describes the incredible transformation wrought during Christmas and Easter in the usually coarse, shameless, and cynical demeanour of these representatives of a people which Belinsky had characterized as "innately atheist":

[On Christmas Day] one heard nothing of the usual swearing and quarreling. Everyone realized that it was a great day and a holy festival. . . .

73 *PS*, p. 65.
74 Letter of 22 Feb. 1854.
75 *HD*, p. 351 (II,10).
76 See ibid., pp. 126-28 (I,6).
77 Letter of 22 Feb. 1854.

[At the Lenten service preceding Easter the] convicts prayed very earnestly and every one of them brought his poor farthing to the church . . . to buy a candle, or to put in the collection. . . . When with the chalice in his hands the priest read the words: ". . . accept me, O Lord, even as the thief", almost all of them bowed down to the ground with a clanking of chains, apparently applying the words literally to themselves.[78]

In the epilogue to *Crime and Punishment* Dostoyevsky reverses Belinsky's dictum by having the criminals from among the common people accuse the educated member of the gentry, Raskolnikov, of atheism. Whether they fully understood their meaning or not, the Russian people obviously cherished the customary observances of Christianity. Dostoyevsky thus found that his "European liberalism" excluded him from a sympathetic communion with the people for whose sake he had been imprisoned.

Yet Dostoyevsky's concern for communion with the Russian people was a secondary factor in his turn from liberalism to Christianity. More important was the awareness, prompted by his experience in Siberia, that his liberalism was simply unable to account for the "mystery of man." He was particularly overwhelmed by the mystery of human evil. A criminal named Orlov, who had murdered children in cold blood, both fascinated and horrified Dostoyevsky: "I can confidently say that I have never in my life met a man of such strength, of so iron a will as he. . . . His was unmistakably the case of a complete triumph over the flesh."[79] Dostoyevsky could not accept that this man's evil, in which was exhibited a "complete triumph" over the flesh, was attributable to a corrupt or unjust social structure. The vision of the flowering of human goodness in a society of "freedom, equality, and brotherhood" based on reason appeared woefully inadequate in the face of Orlov's contemptuous laughter. Dostoyevsky discerned in Christianity, however, an appreciation of the mystery of evil which was lacking in his liberalism. Finding the rational liberal account of human nature insufficient in the face of actual experience, Dostoyevsky began to turn towards the Christian tradition,[80] and simultaneously towards the Russian people who were the bearers of that tradition. (It should be noted that his concrete experience was constantly regarded in light of the New Testament, the only reading available to him for the first few years in Siberia.) As he wrote to his brother, this turning was the most significant transformation "undergone by my soul, my faith, my mind, and my heart in those . . . years."[81] He clearly regarded it as the final significant alteration of his convictions, for his autobiographical reflections end with his release from the Siberian prison where he "received Christ into his soul once

78 *HD*, pp. 170-77, 273 (I,10; II,5).

79 Ibid., pp. 86-87 (I,4).

80 In a letter written to his brother after five years in Siberia (dated 22 Feb. 1854), he asked for the writings of the Church Fathers; and it can be assumed that he received them while still in exile.

81 Letter of 22 Feb. 1854.

more.''[82] For Dostoyevsky this return to Christianity did not entail a renunciation so much as a redemption of his former "European liberalism."

When Dostoyevsky returned to the intellectual life of St. Petersburg in 1860 he found that the debates within the Russian intelligentsia (especially the Slavophile-Westernist controversy) were no longer confined to the polite conversation of the circles. The intellectual life of Russia now lived, with much less restraint, in the plethora of journals which appeared in the early, relatively unrepressive years of Alexander II's reign (1855-1881). There was as well a significant inner change in the Russian intellectual world. The Slavophiles had lost their greatest thinkers, Khomyakov and Kireyevsky. In Dostoyevsky's view, the thought of these men had been transformed by their more shallow disciples into a tiresome litany expressing an impotent yearning for the pre-Petrine past and a self-righteous indignation at everything new in the present. Slavophilism had degenerated into a futile conservatism of the Moscow gentry, and was no longer equal to the struggle with its Westernist opponents.[83] These opponents, too, had changed. The journal, *The Contemporary*, which had been a forum for Belinsky during the 1840s was, in the 1860s, in the hands of thinkers such as Dobrolyubov and Chernyshevsky, who were the mentors of a new generation of Westernists. The majority of this generation was well along the road that Belinsky had travelled so rapidly during the 1840s.

Dostoyevsky adopted an independent and conciliatory stance in relation to the Slavophile-Westernist controversy. This mediatory position is evinced in the articles written shortly after his return from Siberia for his own journal, *Time*. In these articles he defends the Slavophile return to the Christianity of the Russian people against the enlightened and cosmopolitan atheism of the Westernists. And he defends the passion for truth and universality of the Westernists against the complacent and inward-looking religious nationalism of the Slavophiles. Dostoyevsky never abandoned his mediatory position between the two movements. In one of his last public statements, the *Pushkin Speech* of 1880, he called for a reconciliation between the Westernists and the Slavophiles, asserting that their controversy was a "great misunderstanding."[84] He was able to call for a reconciliation because he never wholly identified himself with either movement, but always distinguished between what he affirmed and rejected in both. He was a Slavophile insofar as Slavophilism affirmed the truth of Christianity and the Russian people as

82 Although Dostoyevsky's thought certainly did not remain static after his return from Siberia, it did evince a remarkable consistency. After 1860 his thought about the most important questions does indeed undergo development, but it shows no evidence of significant alteration. For this reason my exposition of his thought throughout the remainder of this study will draw from the entire range of his post-1860 writings, without undue concern for chronology. See, in this regard, G. Kabat, *Ideology and Imagination* (New York, 1978), p. x.
83 See *OW*, p. 216.
84 *PS*, p. 57.

bearers of this truth. He was a Westernist insofar as Westernism moved towards the truth of the universal human community. Both of these positions will concern us in this study. But we must turn now to Dostoyevsky's exposition of the fundamental idea underlying Russian Westernism.

TWO

THE THEORY AND PRACTICE OF THE "GREAT IDEA" OF ORDER

Uprootedness and Human Order

In his rough notes for *The Devils* Dostoyevsky states that the problem of Russian Westernism, and the chief concern of the novel, "amounts to no more than the question as to what ought to be considered 'truth'."[1] He always associated a thought with a thinker, and therefore any elucidation of the "truth" spoken by Russian Westernism had to be concerned with two questions: *what* is being said and *who* is speaking. Dostoyevsky's response to the second question could be expressed in one word—the "uprooted."

Dostoyevsky's observations about the historical development of Russian Westernism focus on the process whereby the Russian upper class came to be uprooted from its native soil. And it is this theme of uprootedness which informs his view of the historical process initiated by Peter the Great: "Where did this society come from? Oh, you, historians of ours, celebrating the two-hundredth jubilee [birthday of Peter the Great]; tell me . . . whatever caused or contributed to the uprooting from the soil."[2] The "uprooting from the soil" has different levels of meaning for Dostoyevsky. Most literally, it signifies the gradual separation of the upper class of Russia from the land, a separation that had its origin in Peter's transformation of a landed gentry into a mobile public

---

1 *NP*, p. 408. It should be noted that the Russian title of the novel, *Besy*, can be translated into English as *The Devils*, or, less literally, *The Possessed*. The English translation referred to in this study uses the former title, while the translation of the notebooks for the novel uses the latter.

2 *UD*, II, p. 5. See also *PS*, p. 44. The Russian word by which Dostoyevsky designates the "uprooted" is *bespochvenniki*—"those without the soil."

service class and that culminated in the general exodus of the gentry from the land following the abolition of serfdom in 1861. Uncertain and frightened by the liberation of the serfs, many of the gentry sold their land and lived off the revenues in St. Petersburg and Moscow, or abroad in Europe. Dostoyevsky feared for the future health of a society in which the character of land-ownership had become so unstable.[3] Yet he was more deeply concerned with a less literal and more fundamental aspect of the "uprooting from the soil"— the separation of the upper class from the Russian people. For nearly a century before the emancipation of the serfs the nobility had been effectively divorced from the people by the influence of modern Western education. In Dostoyev-sky's view, uprooting from the land entails separation from the most appro-priate material framework for the preservation of tradition; but uprooting from the people entails separation from the actual bearer of tradition. And the loss of tradition is, for Dostoyevsky, the loss of the chief source of personal and social order. The theme of uprootedness thus leads to the more fundamental question of order.

The problem of order (*poryadok*) and disorder (*besporyadok*) is a central theme not only of *The Adolescent* (which Dostoyevsky had considered calling "Disorder"), but of all his major writings, literary and journalistic.[4] Indeed, the concept of order constitutes one of those guiding ideas or keys which can be invaluable to the interpreter in unlocking a body of thought as complex and many-sided as Dostoyevsky's. Above all, it is a concept that reveals the unity of thought underlying the diverse aspects of Dostoyevsky's writing. For example, the apparent gulf between Dostoyevsky's psychological analyses in the novels and his political analysis of, for instance, Austrian foreign policy in the Balkans (in *The Diary of a Writer*) can be bridged if approached in the light of his concern with human order, in both its personal and social dimen-sions. Yet to emphasize the unity of thought that a concept like order gives to his writing is not to claim that Dostoyevsky was an explicitly systematic thinker. The concept of order itself is nowhere directly elucidated by him and its meaning can be inferred only by careful examination of its use throughout his writings.

To Dostoyevsky the *sine qua non* of human order is the possession of an idea of life. In this context the word "idea" (*ideya* or *mysl*) signifies that framework of unquestioned presuppositions about the nature of things within which one thinks and acts. Human order, then, depends upon an idea of the ultimate meaning or purpose of existence—an idea which is not consciously

3 See the article entitled "Former Agriculturists—Future Diplomats" in the May-June 1877 edition of *The Diary of a Writer*.

4 See A. R. MacAndrew's introduction to *The Adolescent*, p. v. For Dostoyevsky's explicit reference to the problem of order, see, for instance, *The Adolescent*, p. 563 (IV,13,iii). It should be noted here that the Russian title for the novel, *Podrostok*, can be translated as *The Adolescent* or *A Raw Youth*. As in the case of *Besy*, the English translation of the novel referred to in this study uses one title, while the translation of the notebooks uses the other.

perceived as "idea" but is simply and unquestioningly accepted as "reality" itself. In the ordered human being this fundamental, though largely implicit, idea of life seeks and finds outward expression in the concrete world. The human need for order is thus a two-fold need for an idea of the ultimate meaning of life, and a way of living out one's daily life in accord with this idea. The primacy of this need makes the presence of order necessary for the preservation of life itself.[5]

For Dostoyevsky the most complete human order is characterized by the coincidence of personal and social meaning. He writes, for instance, of the "spontaneous" life which was possible for human beings in the "primitive patriarchal communities." In these ancient communities "about which legends have been left" everyone obeyed implicitly those laws and customs having their source in an idea of life which was "the collective idea of humanity, the masses, *everyone*."[6] "Spontaneous" life or "living life" was possible in these ancient communities because individuals were wholly integrated into the unity of the common life, and everything around them confirmed rather than threatened their idea of their final destiny and their active living out of this idea. The identity of private and public meaning precluded any tension between the order of the individual and that of society. Dostoyevsky's statements concerning the societies of the ancient world are of importance at this point primarily because they furnish the theoretical criterion according to which he assesses various degrees of order. For him the satisfaction of the human need for order is more or less complete as there is a more or less powerfully present idea of life that is at once personal and social, private and public.

In Dostoyevsky the concept of order is intimately associated with that of religion, because historically religion has been the primary vehicle of order for humanity. It is religion that has provided those great ideas by which entire peoples have lived, and it is these religious ideas that have preceded and determined the appearance of the socio-political traditions of peoples: "always so soon as a new religion began, a new nationality was also created immediately." The Jewish nationality, for instance, came into being only after the promulgation of the Law of Moses, and the Moslem nationalities only after the appearance of the Koran.[7] For Dostoyevsky (as for Hegel) the character of a people is fundamentally determined by its conception of God. This notion is expressed forcefully through Shatov in *The Devils*: "The purpose of the whole evolution of a nation, in every people and at every period of

---

5 See *PS*, pp. 83-84. Dostoyevsky's expression of the primacy of the need for an idea of the meaning of life is found, for instance, in these words of the Grand Inquisitor: "the mystery of human life is not only in living, but in knowing why one lives. Without a clear idea of what to live for man will not consent to live...." *BK*, p. 298 (V,5). Cf. Nietzsche's teaching concerning the necessity of a "horizon" for "health, strength, and productivity." F. Nietzsche, *The Use and Abuse of History* (New York, 1957), p. 7.

6 These references to the order of ancient communities are found in the rough notes for an article (never published) entitled "Socialism and Christianity" in *UD*, I, pp. 95-96.

7 *PS*, pp. 83-84.

its existence, is solely the pursuit of God, their God, their very own God, and faith in Him as the only true one. God is the synthetic personality of the whole people, taken from its beginning to its end."[8] The "uprooting from the soil" therefore entails separation from the religious consciousness of the people, which in turn implies the deprivation of the usual source of order for human beings.[9]

For Dostoyevsky the chief consequence, the real significance, of the "uprooting from the soil" is the attempt of the uprooted to live their lives outside the order once provided by their religious tradition. The growing separation of the upper class from the Russian people after Peter's reforms coincided with an increasing tendency to see in the Christian religious tradition of the people "nothing but dead formalism, segregation, ritualism, and ... even prejudice and hypocrisy...."[10] The radical rejection of the order provided by a religion that had become dead for them rendered the Westernized nobility highly vulnerable to the disease of disorder. Just as order is the prerequisite of "living life" or "spontaneous" life, so the absence of order, or disorder, is the basis of a diseased life: "man in this condition feels bad, is sad, loses the source of living life, doesn't know spontaneous sensations and is conscious of everything."[11] The notion of disease is more than a metaphor in Dostoyevsky's thought. Its function is similar to that of the category of *nosos*, "disease of the soul," which Plato applied to those "in every age" who suffer from spiritual disorientation.[12] Although Dostoyevsky was particularly concerned with the diagnosis and description of the *nosos* afflicting uprooted Russians of the nineteenth century, this concern resulted in an analysis of disorder which is important to every age.

In his study of the disease of disorder, Dostoyevsky chronicles the external social consequences of the loss of a common idea of the meaning of human existence. His deep interest in contemporary Russian social life is evinced by his almost obsessive reading of the newspapers and his attempts to

8 *The Devils*, pp. 256-58 (II,1,vii). Cf. G. W. F. Hegel, *The Philosophy of History* (New York, 1956), p. 50.
9 A clarification should be made in regard to the meaning of "religion" in the preceding discussion. I employ the term "religion" according to its most probable etymological origin as any mode of belief and practice which "binds together" the lives of people giving to those lives their meaning and purpose. (See G. Grant, *Technology and Empire* [Toronto, 1969], p. 46). This broad understanding of religion, which would incorporate the various traditional religions of the world, as well as certain modern secular "religions" (such as scientism, positivism, and communism), is in keeping with the conception of religion expressed by Dostoyevsky through Shatov. It is this general understanding of religion which informs much of what is to follow concerning Dostoyevsky's teaching about human order. Yet as we shall see at a later point in this study, such a broad conception of religion, useful though it may be for Dostoyevsky's analysis of the problem of order, is ultimately insufficient for him. He must finally raise the question of the truth or falsity of a given religion, and of the "idea" in which it is rooted; for in his view, the human need for order can only be genuinely satisfied by a *true* idea of life.
10 *DW*, p. 630 (March 1877).
11 *UD*, I, pp. 95-96.
12 Plato, *Laws* 888b-c.

observe, at first hand, any significant social phenomenon.[13] Although Dostoyevsky attached great significance to social phenomena such as suicide, alcoholism, aversion to work, and the disintegration of the family, he was most concerned with the symptom of disorder he regarded as more fundamental than these—the appearance in society of the "underground" type of man.

Dostoyevsky considered that his own "glory" lay in his discovery of the "underground," which had been overlooked by those who shared his concern with the more superficial and easily identifiable consequences of uprootedness. He speaks of this discovery in his rough notes for *The Adolescent* where, with other Russian artists such as Tolstoy in mind, he reveals something of the intent of his art and justifies its peculiarly dissonant quality:

They are passing by. They don't notice. There are no *citizens*, and nobody wants to make an effort and force himself to think and to notice things. I haven't been able to tear myself away, and all the shouts of our critics, . . . who say that I am not depicting real life, haven't dissuaded me. Our society has no *foundations*, it hasn't worked out any rules of life, because there really hasn't been any life either. . . . Our most talented writers, who have been describing, in highly artistic form, the life of our upper middle class . . . thought that they were describing the life of the majority; in my opinion, what they were describing were the lives of some exceptions . . . .

And what about the underground and *Notes from the Underground*? I am proud to have presented, for the first time, the real image of the Russian *majority* and to have exposed, for the first time, its misshapen and tragic aspects . . . .

"Underground, underground, *poet of the underground*," our feuilletonists have been repeating over and over again, as if this were something derogatory to me. Silly fools, it is my glory, for that's where the truth lies. . . .

The reason for the underground is the destruction of our belief in certain general rules. "*Nothing is sacred.*"

Unfinished people (as a consequence of the Petrine reforms *in general*) . . . .[14]

The speech and actions of the protagonist of *Notes from Underground* have been subject to a variety of interpretations; but as his opening words indicate ("I'm a sick man"), the underground-man should be understood above all as the embodiment of the disease of disorder. The ennui, the vague yet persistent anxiety, the sense of alienation, the degrading and self-destructive impulses which this "modern intellectual" chronicles himself

13 Even when abroad, in Europe, Dostoyevsky made a point of searching out libraries which subscribed to Russian as well as European newspapers, and spent a part of every day perusing them. See A. Dostoyevsky, *Reminiscences* (New York, 1975), pp. 153, 157. Dostoyevsky regarded his journalistic activity, especially *The Diary of a Writer*, as, among other things, a way of acquainting himself "down to the smallest detail . . . with everything—current no less than historical events—relating to that reality" which he attempted to "show forth" in his novels (see his letter of 9 April 1876 to Mrs. Altaschevsky). Dostoyevsky is possibly the greatest observer and recorder of the social consequences of the uprootedness engendered by the Westernization of Russia, and his writing is an invaluable source for those interested in the social consequences of uprootedness wherever it occurs.

14 *NRY*, pp. 424-26.

with such "lucidity of perception" are all symptomatic of a profound personal disorder. For the "lucidity of perception," or "heightened consciousness," which the underground-man regards as the cause of his paralysing illness is tantamount to the absence of an idea of life sufficiently clear and powerful to govern his consciousness and bring his contradictory impulses into some sort of order. As a man without an idea it is not difficult for the underground-man to "see through" the ideas which have given meaning to the lives of others. In his view, he is merely guilty of being more intelligent than "real, normal" human beings who live enveloped within the comforting bounds of a more or less narrow horizon of meaning. And yet an admixture of envy is apparent in his contempt for the "normal." He possesses too much "lucidity of perception" not to be aware of his own longing to be "clearly characterized," to be "a real, positive person."[15] The underground-man regards his disorder as a fact from which he even derives a voluptuous pleasure, but also as an affliction from which he yearns to be delivered. He loves his suffering, but this knowledge itself is a source of suffering. Out of his awareness that "we've all lost touch with life and we're all cripples to some degree," he is still able to yearn for "real" life.[16] His longing for real life or living life is a desire for order, despite his doubt concerning the possibility of any human order.[17] It is precisely this tension between the "awareness of a better life" and the "impossibility of attaining it" that constitutes for Dostoyevsky the tragedy of the underground.[18]

The longing of the uprooted for order is, first, the longing for an idea, or truth, which could serve as the source of order. Of his generation of Russian Westernism, Dostoyevsky writes: "To sacrifice one's self, to sacrifice everything for truth—that is the national trait of this generation. . . . For the whole problem amounts to . . . the question as to what ought to be considered 'truth'."[19] This longing for truth seemed to be faced with the absence of a common guiding idea. The thirst for ideas to the point of self-sacrifice and the absence of an inherited intellectual concord can combine in a positive or

15 *NU*, pp. 90, 93-101, 104-105 (I,1-6).

16 Ibid., pp. 202-203 (II,10).

17 For an expression of this doubt, see ibid., p. 110 (I,7).

18 *NRY*, p. 425.

19 *NP*, p. 408. Dostoyevsky here uses "truth" (*pravda*) in the same sense as he uses "idea" in relation to the human need for order. The emphasis on this being a "truth" which serves as the source of order is indicated in the Russian language by the fact that *pravda* also means "justice." Dostoyevsky does not use the word *istina*, which denotes theoretical truth only.

All Dostoyevsky's uprooted characters seek an idea to which they can give themselves. Although their interpretations of truth vary in depth and clarity, as well as in content, they demonstrate a similar selflessness in the degree to which they give themselves up to an idea once they have found one. Indeed, they come to embody their truths. In his attempt to give artistic form to this situation, characterized by the absence of a binding idea and the consequent proliferation of ideas dependent on diverse "personal consciousnesses," Dostoyevsky employed a literary technique which can be termed "polyphonic." See M. Bakhtin, *Problems of Dostoevsky's Poetics* (Ann Arbor, 1973).

negative manner. Dostoyevsky's presentiment of the destructive consequences of such a combination is memorably expressed in Raskolnikov's
dream in the epilogue to *Crime and Punishment*:

He dreamt that the whole world was ravaged by an unknown and terrible plague
that had spread across Europe from the depths of Asia. All except a few chosen ones
were doomed to perish. New kinds of germs—microscopic creatures which lodged
in the bodies of men—made their appearance. But these creatures were spirits endowed with reason and will. People who became infected with them at once became mad and violent. . . . They were in a state of constant alarm. They did not
understand each other. Each of them believed that the truth only resided in him,
and was miserable looking at the others, and smote his breast, wept, and wrung his
hands. They did not know whom to put on trial or how to pass judgement; they
could not agree what was good or what was evil. They did not know whom to accuse or whom to acquit. Men killed each other in a kind of senseless fury. . . . In
the cities the tocsin was sounded all day long: they called everyone together, but no
one knew who had summoned them or why they had been summoned, and all were
in a state of great alarm.[20]

Whether prophetic or not, this depiction of complete disorder is merely a
dream, a possibility. While the crisis provoked by the modern "uprooting
from the soil" presents a great danger to human beings, it presents at the same
time an unprecedented opportunity for a new and perhaps definitive solution
to the problem of human order. For the whole problem amounts to "the
question as to what ought to be considered 'truth'." This brings us to the
question of *what* idea of truth is being spoken in Russian Westernism.

The "Great Idea": The Westernism of the 1840s

By the 1840s the dominance of European ideas and the intellectual confusion
of the then completely uprooted Russian gentry had reached a zenith. In *The
Diary of a Writer* Dostoyevsky emphasizes the difficulty of discerning a
common idea within the chaotic milieu of second-hand European thought:

In fact, nothing in the world was ever as obscure, vague, uncertain, and indefinable
as that "*cycle of ideas*" which we managed to accumulate in the course of the two
centuries of our Europeanism; essentially, it is not a cycle, but a chaos of fragments of sentiments, of alien unintelligible ideas, inferences, habits, but particularly
words, words, words . . . .[21]

Nonetheless, as we have seen in the preceding chapter, Dostoyevsky purported to discern an intellectual coherence in Russian Westernism which
belied the immediate impression of chaos. Although in his view many Russian
Westernists perceived in Western teachings "nothing but a right to infamy,"[22]

20 *CP*, p. 555 (VII,2).
21 *DW*, p. 886 (Nov. 1877).
22 Ibid., p. 271 (March 1876).

the better among them had been captivated by a teaching which seemed to promise an end to their confused longing for order. The conception of a new order is first to be discerned in that liberalism of the 1840s which Dostoyevsky embodies in Stepan Verkhovensky in *The Devils* and Andrey Versilov in *The Adolescent*.

In his rough notes for *The Devils*, Dostoyevsky indicates that he means Stepan Verkhovensky to embody the "pure and idealistic Westernizer in his full splendour." It is also clear from these notes that Verkhovensky is modelled chiefly after the historian Granovsky who, in Dostoyevsky's view, was the most outstanding figure in the mainstream of the Westernism of the 1840s.[23] Verkhovensky, too, has become painfully aware of his obsolescence with the passing of the 1840s, and he contents himself in his retirement with cards, drink, and the "amiable, jolly, typically Russian liberal chatter" of a provincial circle of which he is the honoured mentor. The "liberal idealist" is a celebrity in the small provincial town; his name is spoken in the same breath as those of Belinsky, Granovsky, and Herzen. Judging from his activities towards the end of the 1840s, his notoriety is apparently well deserved: while a history professor at the university he crushed the Slavophiles with his brilliant thesis on the civic and Hanseatic significance of the German town of Hanau between 1413 and 1428; he courted the wrath of Nicholas' Third Section by his propagation of the ideas of George Sand; and he began a work of research into the causes of the "extraordinary moral nobility of certain knights of a certain epoch, or something of the kind." Verkhovensky's career as an influential Westernizer came to an abrupt end when Nicholas' secret police seized an unintelligible but evidently dangerously liberal poetic play, written while he was studying in Berlin and circulated in manuscript "among two literary *dilettanti* and one student." Before the government could exile him, he exiled himself. Although he surrenders to a self-pitying nostalgia for the time of his past greatness, Verkhovensky does not give up his faith in the "great idea" which inspired him then.[24] Although the personal portrait which Dostoyevsky draws of the liberal idealist is, according to his own admission, a caricature of Granovsky,[25] the thinking which he ascribes to Verkhovensky accurately reflects the teaching of the most prominent Westernizer of the 1840s.

Due to its "muddled" nature,[26] Verkhovensky's liberal idealism does not lend itself to systematic exposition. Nevertheless, in the course of the novel he gives utterance, in a random way, to the thinking of Granovsky and his followers; the intellectual configuration of his various utterances can be viewed as that amalgam of Russian Romanticism and French socialism

23 *NP*, p. 82. Throughout his rough notes for the novel Dostoyevsky actually refers to Stepan Verkhovensky as "Granovsky." See also *DW*, p. 379 (July-Aug. 1876).
24 *The Devils*, pp. 47, 27, 23, 24, 39-40 (I,1,ix,ii,i,vi).
25 *NP*, p. 131.
26 Ibid., p. 249.

which is typical of the mainstream of 1840s Westernism,[27] and which constitutes the external intellectual framework encompassing that great idea Verkhovensky serves. But what precisely is the content of this idea which he has "long revered as sacred"?[28] In order to come to this idea we must attend to the cardinal fact of uprootedness, which for Dostoyevsky most fundamentally conditions Russian Westernism and, hence, Stepan Verkhovensky.

The Russian upper classes did not effectively resist their uprooting, but their acquiescence in this process was involuntary. Although it later became voluntary, their co-operation was a matter of expedience, marked primarily by opportunism, or servility before the power of the Petersburg state. In the liberal Westernism of the 1840s, however, the denial of roots became a matter of principle. The central element of Verkhovensky's muddled idealism is his theoretical denial of the Russian particularity. He concedes his inability to argue with Shatov's accusation that his liberalism is "antinational . . . nurturing a personal hatred toward Russia," and he does not deny Shatov's contention that he despises his native country. Moreover, he seems to assent to Shatov's characterization of Russian Westernism as a denial of nationality on principle. He is quite willing to concede "the uselessness and absurdity of the expression 'mother country'." Although he claims to love the Russian people, Verkhovensky is not willing to grant any respect to the particular traditions which constitute their identity. In this regard he cites Belinsky, whose love for the people certainly did not induce him to "seek salvation in Lenten oil or turnips with peas!"[29] Dostoyevsky intimates in *The Diary of a Writer* that in this rejection of Russia there is an irreducible element of physical hatred—hatred for "her climate, her fields, her forests, her status, her liberated peasants, [her] history . . . for everything." He thought that this instinctive hatred of the uprooted for the rootedness which is no longer theirs was especially characteristic of the more vulgar Russian Westernists. His chief concern, however, was with that denial of Russia "on moral grounds" which was so characteristic of the finest representatives of the Westernism of the 1840s.[30] Stepan Verkhovensky's rejection of the Russian nationality on principle is for him a moral act, for it is in accord with the great idea to which he is devoted.

Dostoyevsky, however, never attributes to Verkhovensky a clear statement of this great idea. Verkhovensky's rejection of the Russian tradition appears to depend on his assumption of his own moral superiority, and of those like him, over those who are still bound by their traditions. He declares that "the nobleman is everything, for the elements of civilization and leadership are concentrated in him."[31] He is the bearer of civilization, and this constitutes his superiority and hence right to leadership over those who are

27 See *The Devils*, pp. 27, 37, 41, 48, 50, 51, 73, 343-45, 367, 633 (I,1,ii,v,vii,ix,2,iv; II,5,iii,6,iv; III,7,i).
28 Ibid., pp. 39-40 (I,1,vi).
29 *NP*, pp. 114-15, 378, 85; *The Devils*, pp. 39, 52 (I,1,vi,ix).
30 *DW*, p. 711 (May-June 1877).
31 *NP*, p. 178.

still rooted in the Russian soil. His unreflective acceptance of his own superiority, though amusing, is not very instructive, for the nature of the "civilization" which he embodies is far from clear. It can hardly consist in the ability to intersperse his conversation with French aphorisms, nor even in an easy familiarity with the most recent European ideas. Such second-hand Europeanism may have satisfied the more vulgar majority of Russian liberals, but Stepan Verkhovensky is a "pure and idealistic Westernizer in his full splendour."

The civilization to which Verkhovensky aspires is something more than a faithful mimicry of Europe. Although he does not, in the various expressions of his liberal idealism, delineate the content of his civilization in a positive manner, some idea of it may be inferred from the negative emphasis of his assumption of superiority. Since Verkhovensky apparently derives a sense of moral superiority from his lack of attachment to any particular nationality, his notion of civilization must exclude attachment to a particular rootedness because it is obsolete, "useless," and "absurd." Uprootedness is accorded its recognition and justification in the idea of a universal humanity, for it would seem that only those who are not bound within a particular order could truly participate in a universal civilization.

Further clarification of this idea of a universal order can be found in another of Dostoyevsky's liberal idealists of the 1840s—Andrey Versilov (in *The Adolescent*). It is probable that the portrayal of Versilov was inspired by Herzen, who is also a "*gentilhomme russe et citoyen du monde.*"[32] Versilov is a self-conscious liberal idealist who lacks the purity, but also the muddled naiveté, of Stepan Verkhovensky. Versilov, too, denies nationality on principle, but his affirmation of the universal man is much more explicit than Verkhovensky's. He maintains that the aspiration of the Russian gentry towards universality cannot be entirely understood as yet another instance of borrowing from Europe, for the Russian "concern for the world" is not manifest to the same degree among Europeans:

They still cannot understand that in Europe. Europe has produced noble types of Frenchmen, Englishmen, and Germans, but it still knows almost nothing about the man of the future . . . .
[I]n order to serve mankind as a whole, and even just France for that matter, a Frenchman must remain thoroughly French. And the same goes for an Englishman or a German. Only a Russian—even in our time, that is, much earlier than the coming-to-be of universality—has fulfilled his deepest possibility, has become most Russian, only when he also feels completely European. And this is the most important difference between us and all the others, for we are different from the rest.[33]

The acknowledged capacity of uprooted Russians to enter easily into the spirit of other particularities—to be a Frenchman in France, a German in Germany, even a Hellene in ancient Greece—is, according to Versilov, evidence of a

---

32 See *DW*, pp. 5-6 (1873); *The Adolescent*, pp. 465-66 (III,7,ii); *NRY*, pp. 84, 88, 523.
33 *The Adolescent*, pp. 469-70 (III,7,iii).

capacity to prepare the advent of the universal "man of the future." This capacity is what distinguishes and ultimately justifies the existence of the uprooted Russian gentry—and, indeed, the existence of Russia itself:

> After generations and generations a certain cultural type has come into existence among us, a higher cultural type than has ever existed in the world before, a type filled with universal concern, a feeling for the whole world. This type is purely Russian, but since it is still confined to the upper cultural layers of the Russian nation, I have the honor of belonging to it. There are, perhaps, at the present time no more than a thousand representatives of that type . . . but, so far, Russia has existed in order to produce that thousand men . . . .
>   I'm a pioneer of that Russian idea.

The Russian idea, according to Versilov, is the idea which will reconcile all conflicting ideas and will serve as the foundation of a future order of "universal citizenship."[34] In the absence of an elucidation of its positive content, the Russian idea could be suspected of being synonymous with the absence of ideas, and the boasted reconciliation of all national ideas with the spreading of disorder among more rooted peoples. Such a surmise would have a natural plausibility in light of the evident uprootedness of the "chosen thousand." If the universalism of Russian liberals is not directed towards a positive new order, then it is merely a rationalization of disorder. In this case the finest representatives of Russian liberalism would merely lack the uncompromising integrity of the underground-man, who confesses his disorder. Dostoyevsky, however, thought that the great idea of the Russian liberals was much more than an eloquent, self-serving justification of their own uprootedness.

Since the uprooting of the Russian gentry coincided with their Europeanization, it was natural that they would interpret their own uprootedness in terms of European thought. Versilov tends to equate the capacity for universalism with the ability to feel "completely European." The Russians may possess the capacity for a universal concern to a greater degree than the Europeans, but it is to Europe that Versilov turns for guidance in defining and directing this concern. Most Russian Westernists, as we have seen, turned to the promise of a universal order contained in the European liberal-socialist tradition, which Dostoyevsky designates the "Geneva" idea.[35] When he speaks of the Geneva idea, Dostoyevsky is referring to the entire stream of thought which found its original inspiration in Rousseau. Above all he is thinking of the slogan of the French Revolution—"freedom, equality, and brotherhood"—and of the theoretical elaboration which was subsequently given to it. Broadly speaking, this would include French liberalism, the French socialism which appeared almost at the same time, and the German philosophical commentary on these movements. More specifically,

34 Ibid., pp. 469-70, 483 (III,7,iii,9,i). The "Russian idea" is characterized by Versilov as the *vseprimirenie idey*—literally, the "all-reconciliation" or "all-harmonization" of ideas.
35 This designation is especially prevalent in *The Adolescent* (for instance, pp. 104, 212 [I,6,ii; II,1,iv]).

"Geneva" thinkers would include such figures as Rousseau, Saint-Just, Saint-Simon, Fourier, Kant, Hegel, Feuerbach, and Marx.[36] Dostoyevsky's account of the impact of these thinkers on Russian intellectual life has already been considered. Other than the general intellectual context established by this account, his elucidation of the Geneva teaching ignores questions of intellectual history, such as which European thinker should be associated with particular aspects of this teaching. However, our concern here is not with intellectual history, but with Dostoyevsky's understanding of the essence of the Geneva idea the Russian Westernists of the 1840s borrowed from continental Europe.

The Geneva Idea: Freedom

Versilov defines the Geneva idea as "virtue without Christ,"[37] a meaning that is illumined in Versilov's thought and practice and, less clearly, in Stepan Verkhovensky's. In his most explicit analysis of Versilov, in the rough notes for *The Adolescent*, Dostoyevsky describes him as a man who has been deprived of the order provided by religion. Versilov is "convinced of the loss and of the stupidity of every ideal." Although he once attempted to force himself to believe in Christ, this attempt failed and "his whole faith went to pieces." Unable to recover the order of traditional religion, Versilov is compelled to rely on nothing but his own "conscious will" and to acknowledge his freedom from any order which precedes it.[38]

Although Versilov seems to think that freedom is inconceivable apart from the conscious will, he does not define clearly the relationship between the two. It is clear, however, that he does not understand freedom as the emancipation of capricious desire—doing what one pleases when one pleases—nor does he understand it as a more rational emancipation of desire. On the contrary, for Versilov freedom is intimately associated with morality and is thus set against natural desire. Versilov has lost his faith, but there still remains to him the "moral feeling of duty." This feeling of duty enjoins him to "strive for self-perfection and good actions *under any circumstances* ... regardless of any loss of faith." He does not give way to despair, but decides instead to start "straight from himself" in his quest for moral perfection. Sure of the connection between freedom and morality, he believes that he will "get somewhere, and that something will be revealed to him along the way."[39]

---

36 It must be noted, however, that the French and German socialists can be included only insofar as their socialism is "humanistic" or "utopian," rather than strictly "scientific." "Scientific" socialism lies outside Dostoyevsky's "Geneva" designation, although, as we shall see, he considers the two to be intimately related.

37 *The Adolescent*, p. 212 (II,1,iv).

38 *NRY*, p. 344. "Conscious will" in the Russian is *soznatelnaya volya*. *Soznatelnaya* also means "conscientious," and thus the phrase could perhaps be rendered as "conscience." *Volya* means not only "will," but also "freedom," with an overtone of "not forced" or "without limits." See A. B. Gibson, *The Religion of Dostoevsky* (London, 1973). pp. 47, 81.

39 *NRY*, p. 344.

The Geneva Idea: Equality and Brotherhood

Versilov's Geneva thought does not end with the rather austere notion of the moral striving of individual freedom. According to this notion, whatever their natural and conventional inequalities, all human beings are equal in the most decisive respect—the possession of a conscious will, and hence the capacity for moral goodness. The fundamental equality of all individuals implies the possibility of an elusive, yet enticing vision of brotherhood, which captivates Versilov. It is a vision of a perfect human society, a veritable earthly paradise or "Golden Age" in which people are, not only perfectly moral, but also perfectly happy.[40] Versilov's association of this vision with ancient Greece may signify a yearning to return to the "spontaneous" life of the ancient patriarchal community. But the complete order of the ancient world excluded the individual freedom which the uprooted Versilov cannot deny, even if he wishes to. In the thinking of Versilov, Dostoyevsky reveals a contradiction at the heart of the Geneva idea. It upholds individual freedom and at the same time it yearns for social unity; it associates moral goodness with an austere striving of the conscious will and yet it yearns for a fulfilled natural happiness. But Versilov does not resign himself to this contradiction. He transfers his vision of an earthly paradise from the Greece of "three thousand years or so" in the past to a future time, when "all the battles have been fought and the struggle is over."[41] For Versilov, the future contains the hope of a social order in which the contradiction between individual freedom and social unity, and between morality and happiness, will be resolved.

Versilov points hopefully to a possible mediator of the contradiction—love—which he thinks becomes effective in the world only when people are emancipated from the restraints of traditional religion. Versilov apparently thinks that love can become effective only independently of traditional religion because traditional religion is divisive. Even Christianity, with its aspiration to universality, makes a general distinction between believer and unbeliever, if not between Greek and Jew. Those who do not live within any religious tradition are free for a love "encompassing all mankind." Versilov asserts, moreover, that love can be fully realized only when people acknowledge that their final destiny is an earthly one. Then the love hitherto lavished on God will be freed for the earth:

With the great concept of immortality gone, they have to replace it with something, and the immense reserves of love that before were lavished on Him who *was* immortality are now directed toward nature, the world, fellow men, every blade of grass. The more clearly they come to realize how transitory and finite their own existence is, the more ardently they grow to love the earth and life, and that special love is different from anything they've felt before. They start noticing and discovering in nature moments and secrets that they never suspected until then, because now they look at it with different eyes, with the eyes of a lover looking at his be-

40 *The Adolescent*, p. 467 (III,7,iii).
41 Ibid., p. 471 (III,7,iii).

loved. On awaking, they rush to kiss one another in their haste to love, constantly aware that the number of their days is limited and that there is nothing left for them when these days are spent. They work for one another and each of them gives up all he has, and this giving is happiness in itself... everyone is anxious for the life and happiness of everyone else.[42]

With this flowering of love the paradisaical social order becomes possible. Free individuals who stand over against nature will be reconciled to it through love. And free individuals who stand over against society will be reconciled to it through love. Love for others would induce individuals to give themselves to society, and this same love would prompt society to devote itself to the good of the individual, because "everyone is anxious for the life and happiness of everyone else."[43]

Although Versilov's vision thus depends on the presence of a powerful love which can arise only when the yearning for immortality is renounced, his fantasy ends with Heine's vision of "Christ on the Baltic Sea." Apparently he cannot help suspecting that humanity "couldn't manage without Him altogether." This allusion to Christ may be merely a tacit acknowledgment of the indebtedness of Geneva thinking to Christianity. "Virtue without Christ" would thus be a radical rejection of Christianity, and at the same time an affirmation of its work in preparing the way for the triumph of the Geneva interpretation of freedom, equality, and brotherhood.

The great idea which Russian liberalism borrowed from the West to give content to its universal aspiration is this idea of a universal brotherhood of free and equal individuals who have renounced a yearning for eternity for the sake of an earthly destiny. This idea of universal union is the "virtue without Christ" which, according to Versilov, is the "idea underlying today's civilization."[44] It should be clear from Dostoyevsky's account of the great idea that he regards it as a political idea only in the broadest sense of the word. Russian liberalism, in his view, is concerned not with constitutional reform or with the establishment of a democratic regime, but with the attainment of a social order which will fulfill humanity's ultimate destiny.[45]

---

42 Ibid., pp. 472-73 (III,7,ii,iii).
43 Ibid., p. 472 (III,7,iii).
44 Ibid., p. 212 (II,1,iv). Dostoyevsky's emphasis on the atheism of Geneva thought is significant. He clearly considers the interpretation given to Western liberal-socialist thought by Russians such as Herzen, Bakunin, and Belinsky to reflect the essence of that thought. Although Granovsky represented the majority of Russian Westernists of the 1840s, his attempt to cling to the concepts of God and immortality signifies, in Dostoyevsky's view, a failure to face the consequences of his liberalism. In the context of Russian intellectual history, Geneva thought could be regarded as that amalgam of Romanticism and utopian socialism characteristic of Granovsky, but with the explicit statement of the atheism which Dostoyevsky thought to be inherent in this amalgam. At this point in our study, however, we can merely note, without elaboration, Dostoyevsky's contention that the thought having its source in Rousseau essentially conceives man's final destiny to be earthly.
45 Cf. Herzen's statement that "the future is outside politics" in *From the Other Shore* (Cleveland, 1956), p. 89.

Through Versilov, Dostoyevsky presents not only his understanding of the essence of Geneva thought, which had captivated the best Russian Westernists of the 1840s, but also the ambiguity which he discerned at its centre, in the all-important notion of love. Versilov's dream of a love which will flow forth when people have turned to the earth is presented with all the powerful beauty of poetry. However, it is a dream which is not illumined by careful thought. Versilov cannot imagine people "turning into ungrateful and stupid animals" in the absence of God,[46] but he can offer little in the way of a theoretical defence of this conviction. At one point in the rough notes for the novel, Dostoyevsky does have him offering an argument concerning the incompatibility of belief in God with the full flowering of humanity's potential: "If we believe in God, our respect for human reason must needs disappear, and from a disappearance of respect for human reason, also our respect for the image of man, which gave birth to reason, and consequently, also our respect for human dignity must disappear, and so our respect for one another . . . ."[47] When Versilov expounds his ecstatic vision of the earthly paradise in more prosaic language he speaks, not of love, but of respect for the dignity of human reason. For Dostoyevsky this is an extremely significant characteristic of Geneva thought. When the Geneva vision is expressed with sobriety by its adherents, love tends to give way to reason as its basis. It is not surprising that reason should be of central importance in Geneva thought because it is reason that criticized the traditional morality, thereby freeing people for a morality based on their own conscious wills—that is, for a rational morality. Dostoyevsky implies, however, that for Geneva thought not only does reason emancipate humanity for the universal union of free and equal individuals; it tends also to be the ultimate foundation of this union.[48]

The tendency towards the displacement of love by reason in Geneva thought is not surprising in light of the unreliability of love. Versilov finds that love is as uncertain in practice as in theory. Immediately after his confession of that dream of human harmony which filled him with the "sensation of universal love encompassing all mankind," he reveals the great difficulty he has had attempting to love just one human being—his common-law wife, Sofia. Perhaps as a consequence of his own failure at an actual love—"I have felt universal love, but I don't love Mother"[49]—Versilov himself casts doubts on the quality of his general love of humanity. He declares that it is impossible to love people as they actually are, that "man is physically unable to love his neighbour." And yet his most ardent hope requires that he "must" be able to love humanity. Versilov suggests a way in which this contradiction can be overcome: love of humanity should be considered to be the love of an idea of

46 *The Adolescent*, p. 472 (III,7,iii).
47 *NRY*, p. 509.
48 See, for instance, V. G. Belinsky, *Selected Philosophical Works* (Moscow, 1948), p. 165;
      A. Herzen, *The Memoirs of Alexander Herzen* (London, 1968), III, chap. 10.
49 *NRY*, p. 540.

human beings as they could be, rather than a love of human beings as they actually are. Otherwise, the concept of love of humanity is found to be "completely misleading." Thus a balance could be struck between contempt for actual human beings and love for them as they could be in the future. Until the advent of the future humanity, the best recourse is to follow the counsel of the Koran, according to which Allah bids the Prophet to look upon men as upon mice, do them good, and pass them by—"it may sound rather haughty, but it's the right way."[50]

Thus love of humanity, which is so fundamental to the great idea of Russian liberalism, shows itself to be highly problematic. This raises the question of whether the earthly paradise is realizable, a question accentuated by Versilov's remark that the hoped-for humanity of his dream "has never really existed and never will." Nevertheless, he believes ardently in his vocation as a herald of world citizenship and universal love. He is even willing to die for it.[51] It would seem that Versilov believes in the great idea and works towards its realization, while at the same time knowing that this work will probably never be accomplished. The gulf between the great idea and the possibility of its actualization appears to be impassable. And yet Versilov does not despair. That "moral feeling of duty," commanding him to strive for "good deeds" under any circumstances, banishes despair, if not the debilitating scepticism that continually threatens his vitality. He is still able to act, although the goal of his activity can only be a helpful guide (an "Idea" [*Idee*], in Kant's sense), and not a certainty.[52]

Dostoyevsky thus exposes a highly uncertain relation between thought and practice at the heart of Geneva thinking. The extent of this uncertainty determines the degree to which even the finest liberals are unable to overcome the disorder of the underground type. In them, disorder manifests itself, above all, as "ridiculousness." The startling contrast between Versilov's elevated moral aspirations and his mad, pathetic behaviour in the climactic scene of *The Adolescent* is one striking instance of this. Despite his great idea, he is unable to control himself, to exercise self-restraint, for there is "disorder inside" him. Stepan Verkhovensky's purer, more self-assured liberalism is also replete with ridiculousness. As he himself concedes, his actual behaviour almost always fail to measure up to the loftiness of his ideas: "*Et puis toujours des idées, et rien dans les faits.*"[53]

In Stepan Verkhovensky and Versilov, Dostoyevsky presents what he understood to be the essential content of the great idea which inspired the best Russian liberals of the 1840s. And, at the same time, he discloses in them a gulf between the idea and its realization. The question remains to what extent this gulf could be attributed more to the adherents of Geneva thought than to

50 *The Adolescent*, pp. 213-14 (II,1,iv).
51 Ibid., pp. 214, 565 (II,1,iv; IV,13,iii).
52 Cf. I. Kant, *On History* (New York, 1963), L. W. Beck's introduction, pp. xix-xx.
53 *The Adolescent*, p. 516 (IV,10,iv); *NRY*, pp. 456, 513, 126; *NP*, p. 392.

anything inherent in the thinking itself. In his rough notes for *The Devils* Dostoyevsky implies that the liberal idea could be regarded as a seed which, in the person of Stepan Verkhovensky, fell upon sand.[54] Perhaps Verkhovensky and Versilov cannot provide good soil for this seed because, as children of the age of transition,[55] their living-out of the idea is hampered by the remnants of the older tradition which they never succeed in discarding completely. Verkhovensky, for instance, still retains the traditional gentry fear of rebellion among the peasantry. And Versilov vacillates confusedly between his urge towards the order of the future and the traditional order personified by his wife Sofia. Such was to be the contention of those of the next generation of Russian Westernism, who maintained that the liberals of the 1840s were not sufficiently emancipated from the old traditions to permit the liberal idea to bridge the gap between dream and fulfillment. They regarded themselves as more fully liberated from the encumbrances of tradition, and hence a more suitable soil for the realization of the new order.

Further Development of the "Great Idea": The Westernism of the 1860s

The relationship between the Westernism of the 1840s and that of the 1860s became, with the publication of Turgenev's *Fathers and Sons* (1861), one of the central preoccupations of Russian thought. *The Devils* was Dostoyevsky's version of *Fathers and Sons*. In this novel, and in the rough notes for it, Dostoyevsky encourages the most explicit self-expression of the Russian Westernism of the 1860s found in his writings. It will thus be the principal source for our exposition of his understanding of what was subsequently spoken in response to the great idea of Russian liberalism.

Dostoyevsky thought that the Westernism of the 1860s exhibited contrary extremities. On one hand, he detected an appalling listlessness, a bored indifference to ideas of any kind and to life itself; on the other hand, he found evidence of boundless energy, combined with fervently held convictions. According to Dostoyevsky, the former tendency was characteristic of the sons of those vulgar liberals of the 1840s whose liberalism amounted to no more than a supercilious scoffing at tradition. Brought up without moral guidance, they were without any conviction that might have given shape and force to their lives. They were not even bequeathed the "outmoded" notion of filial duty and, in the absence of this notion, they sometimes aroused themselves from their lethargy sufficiently to hate and despise the fathers who had failed them in the most important respect.[56] The other sons, who were bequeathed the Geneva thinking of the finer representatives of 1840s liberalism, became

---

54 *NP*, p. 134.
55 *NRY*, p. 513.
56 *UD*, II, pp. 8, 66.

men of energy and principle. But they too came to despise their fathers. Their contempt stemmed from a clear perception of the "ridiculousness" of the previous generation. They were determined to avoid this ridiculousness themselves, and hence to overcome the gulf between thought and practice which they discerned at its root. The great idea was to be translated from words into action, to be liberated from the interminable discussions of drawing-rooms and universities which have no issue in the actual world. Versilov's uncertain dream was to be made certain.

Although the Petersburg state had always been greatly interested in Western technology, as an intellectual movement Russian Westernism had never embraced modern science to the extent that it had embraced modern Western philosophy, history, literature, and even theology. By the 1860s, however, educated Russians were beginning to pay homage to scientific knowledge with a fervour which more than compensated for their earlier lack of interest. The prestige of science in the West had become so great by the middle of the nineteenth century that a tendency to seek a scientific solution to the fundamental problems of human life became apparent. This tendency was so pervasive in Russia after 1860 that it was inevitable that the discoveries of modern science would be applied to the great idea which had beguiled Russian Westernism since the 1840s. The initial product of this application—scientific socialism—proved extremely attractive to a generation which was interested in making the great idea an actuality rather than the plaything of cultured intellectuals. Scientific socialism was given its first significant expression in the writings of N. G. Chernyshevsky, the most outstanding Russian representative of the movement prior to Lenin. Chernyshevsky's political novel, *What is to be Done?*, became the catechism of scientific socialism, and it is to this novel Stepan Verkhovensky turns in a desperate attempt to ascertain the aspirations of the younger generation.[57] *What is to be Done?* comes most explicitly under Dostoyevsky's scrutiny in *Notes from Underground*. Through the words of the underground-man, Dostoyevsky expresses his understanding of the essential teaching of scientific socialism.

According to Dostoyevsky, scientific socialism teaches that human nature can be fully understood in terms of the necessary laws which science formulates. If regarded entirely as a product of necessity—natural and social—the human being is comprehensible as the sum of various calculable desires. Eventually the scientist of human nature will "find a formula at the root of all our wishes and whims that will tell us what they depend on, what laws they are subject to, how they develop, what they are aiming at in such and such a case, and so on and so forth—that is, a real mathematical equation." When human desires have been identified, their relative strength assessed, and their origin (whether biological, psychological, or sociological) understood, it will be possible to organize them to ensure humanity's optimal satisfaction or happiness. This organization will be increasingly complete as

57 *The Devils*, p. 308 (II,4,ii).

scientific knowledge of human nature expands to the point at which it is possible finally to understand what actually governs what we now describe as our free will. And such an understanding will one day be achieved, for "it is contemptible and meaningless to maintain that there may exist laws of nature which man will never penetrate."

On the basis of a scientific understanding of human nature—that is, an understanding of people as they actually are rather than as they ought to be—the realization of a complete social order (the image of which, for Chernyshevsky, was London's Crystal Palace) is attainable. It will become merely a question of arranging relations among individuals so that the satisfaction of the desires of each tends to cement social unity rather than to disrupt it. If necessary, human desires can be changed so that they accord with the requirements of social organization. To the extent that this change can be effected with voluntary co-operation, it is necessary to re-educate people to a knowledge of their true interests, so that they may act according to rational self-interest. To the extent that human desires can be altered by scientifically manipulating the social and physio-psychological factors that determine them, it is necessary to transform the social environment (first abolishing irrational social institutions such as the Church and the family) and, if possible, human beings themselves.[58] In undertaking these tasks, scientific socialism is encouraged by the assurance of success: history itself is moving progressively towards the actualization of the perfect social order, and human agency is able merely to hasten or retard the progressive overcoming of the gulf between the great idea and its practical realization. For the sake of certainty, scientific socialism renders explicit a doctrine of historical progress which is much more subtle, and even ambiguous, in Geneva thinking.[59]

The "reasonableness" of world history makes it a powerful guarantee for the realization of the perfect social order. According to Dostoyevsky, it is the desire for such a guarantee which chiefly determines not only scientific socialism's turn to history but its attitude towards science itself. In his view, scientific socialism subordinates science to socialism. It regards the teaching of science as, above all, the most effective tool for putting into practice the liberal idea of an earthly paradise embodying freedom, equality, and brotherhood. The overriding concern is with the great idea, and science would be quickly renounced if it proved to be incompatible. As Stepan Verkhovensky remarks, scientific "realism" is a façade which conceals a more primary allegiance to "the sentimental and idealist side of socialism; its religious aspect, as it were; its poetry." The "science" of "scientific" socialism is that "half-science," unknown until the nineteenth century, before which "science

58 NU, pp. 151, 111, 108, 105, 115-16 (II,4; I,6-9). Cf. N. G. Chernyshevsky, What is to be Done? (New York, 1967), pp. 81-82, 83, 132-33, 265, 328.
59 NU, p. 114 (I,8); NP, p. 272. Cf. N. G. Chernyshevsky, What is to be Done? (New York, 1967), pp. 86, 145, 165, 354. For a detailed discussion of the relation of Chernyshevsky's thought to that of Marx, and of Lenin's commentary on both, see G. Planty-Bonjour, Hegel et la pensée philosophique en Russie 1830-1917 (The Hague, 1974).

itself trembles and surrenders in a shameful way."[60] It is only a half-science because the quest for knowledge is not motivated by the concern for truth, as in genuine science, but by the concern for social order. This concern even determines the particular scientific disciplines which are adopted by the Westernists of the 1860s. The natural and social sciences of physiology, anatomy, psychology, and sociology are of greatest interest to those whose primary concern is to organize human beings into a complete social order.[61]

According to Dostoyevsky's presentation of the Geneva idea, love was to mediate between the individual and the social union. As we have seen, however, the crucial but uncertain notion of love tended to give way to reason. This tendency was carried to its logical conclusion in the next generation. Unwilling to tolerate any gulf between the Geneva idea and its realization, the sons excluded love from any role in binding together the new order. Although the scientific socialists continue to invoke love of humanity as the ultimate justification of their social teaching, they rely entirely on reason—which they identify with modern science—as the means for its actualization.[62] Scientific socialism assumes that a scientific understanding of human beings as entirely subject to natural and social necessity could be the basis of an order in which people would be not only happy but also genuinely good. Yet this reliance on scientific necessity, as well as the concomitant conviction of historical inevitability, raises a crucial question: is the teaching that people will "have no choice but to become good"[63] compatible with the morality of the free individual which is so central to the Geneva idea? Versilov's morality is rooted in his own conscious will, and a good will cannot be legislated.[64] In Geneva thinking the concept of love promises to reconcile individual freedom with social unity; but in scientific socialism love of humanity is invoked to justify a realizable social unity which threatens to undermine the free individual. This one-sided emphasis on social unity was bound to evoke a protest within Russian Westernism on behalf of the individual.

Among the opponents of scientific socialism were those liberals of the 1840s who did not, like Karmazinov in *The Devils*, curry favour with the younger generation.[65] Stepan Verkhovensky, for instance, objects that in the

60 *The Devils*, pp. 89, 257 (I,2,viii; II,1,vii).
61 Dostoyevsky refers to the socialist lieutenant who "in his room . . . had placed on three stands in the form of three lecterns, the works of Vogt, Moleschott, and Buechner, and before each lectern he burned a wax church candle." *The Devils*, p. 349 (II,6,ii). The French physiologist, Claude Bernard, is also, for Dostoyevsky, representative of the "half-science" which was so influential in Russia after 1860. See *BK*, pp. 690-91 (XI,4). Dostoyevsky's concept of "half-science" is further illuminated by Eric Voegelin's critique of "scientism" in "The Origins of Scientism," *Social Research*, XV (1948), pp. 462-94.
62 "You won't need any kind of love then . . . but only knowledge, science." *NP*, p. 89. Cf. N. G. Chernyshevsky, *What is to be Done?* (New York, 1967), pp. 95, 229, 247, 271.
63 *NU*, p. 105 (I,7). Cf. S. Weil, *Oppression and Liberty* (London, 1958), pp. 173-74.
64 Cf. Kant's objection to any human "goodness" which is not the outcome of a "morally good disposition" in *On History* (New York, 1963), p. 21.
65 Karmazinov is meant to represent Turgenev. See Dostoyevsky's letter to A. Maykov, dated 16 Aug. 1867.

future Crystal Palace nobody will have any kind of personal guarantee against the collective. The moral basis of his concern with the place of the individual in scientific socialism is evident in his response to his son's assurance that in the new society personal charity will be rendered obsolete by the re-organization of relationships among people according to "strictly scientific natural definitions": "Why won't you leave the initiative to me! . . . Leave me a chance to satisfy a need of my heart, let me give freely when I feel compassion . . . . Leave me my personal freedom."[66] Verkhovensky thus insists that charity is good only if it proceeds from personal freedom. His defence of art against scientific socialism is even more impassioned than his defence of an autonomous morality. Morality and art, for Geneva thinking, are a sign of the need and the ability to strive for a destiny which is not equivalent to the fulfillment of natural desires—that is, they reveal humanity's freedom from nature. While scientific socialism subjects human beings to natural and social necessity, Verkhovensky insists on their need for beauty. The strength of this insistence threatens to lead him away from the Geneva idea altogether, and towards an aestheticism which is unconcerned with the problem of social order: "I maintain that Shakespeare and Raphael are higher than the emancipation of the serfs, higher than nationalism, higher than socialism, higher than the younger generation, higher than chemistry, higher even than almost all humanity, for they are the fruit of all mankind, and perhaps the highest fruition that can possibly exist."[67]

Verkhovensky, however, does not renounce his love of humanity. He remains loyal to the great idea, and even acknowledges that this idea is also the ultimate goal of scientific socialism. After reading Chernyshevsky's *What is to be Done?*, he concedes: "I agree that the author's fundamental idea is right . . . . It's just our idea—yes, ours! We were the first to plant it, nurture it, to get it ready." However, he then expresses his reservations concerning the younger generation's appropriation of the liberal idea:

"But, good Lord, how they have expressed it all, distorted, mutilated it!" he cried, rapping on the book with his fingers. "Were those the conclusions we wanted to draw? Who can recognize the original idea here?"[68]

Verkhovensky opposes, not the ultimate goal of scientific socialism, but that impatient desire to overcome the dissociation of thought and practice which prompts the sons to a dangerous reliance on modern science. In his view, it is "sheer stupidity" to expect to reach in a few days a goal which may require centuries to achieve. However, the liberal counsel of patient resignation to a gradual regeneration of humanity was construed by the sons as a rationalization of laziness or cowardice. The protest of the fathers against scientific socialism was dismissed as merely the posturing of "witty old fossils" or the

66 *NP*, pp. 138, 139, 142, 89, 189.
67 *The Devils*, p. 483 (III,1,iv).
68 Ibid., p. 308 (II,4,ii).

whining of "civic-minded old women."[69] It was from within the ranks of the sons themselves that the more powerful attack on scientific socialism was to emerge.

In Peter Verkhovensky, Dostoyevsky embodies a threat to scientific socialism which is much more radical than that of his "phrase-mongering" father. His portrayal of Peter Verkhovensky was inspired by a fascination with Sergey Nechayev, whose name is closely associated with Bakunin. Bakunin was a prophet of revolution, a dreamer of the 1840s who pursued his vision of an earthly paradise quixotically throughout Europe, while Nechayev, a realist of the 1860s, was a new breed of revolutionary—a technician of revolution whose genius for revolutionary organization was much admired by Lenin.[70] Although Russian scientific socialism early claimed Nechayev as its first martyr, Dostoyevsky discerned in his ruthless practice of socialist revolution a hidden possibility which threatened to undermine the very cause to which he devoted such unrelenting energy.

The desire of the youth of the 1860s to give practical expression to the liberal idea of an earthly paradise was not entirely satisfied by Chernyshevsky's scientific socialism. Even his prosaic realism appeared to some to be mere verbiage, more of the futile talk which had enveloped the liberal idea since its inception in the 1840s. Peter Verkhovensky maintains that there are now "better" things to read than *What is to be Done?*, and he dismisses Chernyshevsky as a "wind-bag."[71] Increasingly dissatisfied, even with the scientific assurance of the not-too-distant triumph of socialism, a growing number of young Russian socialists wished to advance the moment of triumph so they could witness it themselves. The hope for the future held out in Chernyshevsky's doctrine of historical progress inspired fierce impatience for activity rather than quietism. What Chernyshevsky promised for tomorrow, the youth of the 1860s was beginning to desire for today.

According to scientific socialism, history decrees the inevitable disappearance of the old order to make way for the new. According to Peter Verkhovensky's revolutionary socialism, this process could be hastened "by a blow of the axe."[72] The "blow of the axe" was to be very carefully directed, however. An overwhelming impatience may have determined the revolutionary intent, but this did not exclude the careful formulation of an elaborate plan of action. Dostoyevsky's portrayal of this plan corresponds closely to the actual writings and testimony of Nechayev and his followers. The essence of Peter Verkhovensky's doctrine of revolution is expressed in the phrase "organize destruction," which entails the undermining of religion, marriage, family, and private property—"the foundations of life as it exists now." To

---

69 *NP*, pp. 95, 97; *The Devils*, p. 344 (II,5,iii).
70 For further reading about Nechayev and the revolutionary socialist movement in Russia, see R. Payne, *The Terrorists* (New York, 1951); A. Yarmolinsky, *The Road to Revolution* (New York, 1962).
71 *The Devils*, p. 308 (II,4,ii); *NP*, p. 97.
72 *NP*, p. 272; *The Devils*, pp. 407-10 (II,7,ii).

this end, secret groups of five were to be organized in Russia with the task of enhancing the disorder already existing throughout Russia as a result of the uprooting process of Westernization. Verkhovensky's plan of action, to be carried out by each revolutionary cell, calls for "increasing the incidence of villainies, crimes, and suicides, so as to shake the morale of the people, to undermine faith in the stability of the existing order, and to get the criminal element among the people stirred up. Increase sin and debauchery, liquor. Distribute money."[73]

Dostoyevsky portrays with great artistry Verkhovensky's successful accomplishment of general social demoralization in the provincial capital which is the setting for *The Devils*. The measured prose of the first part of the novel, which is dominated by the liberal father living idly off the landed gentry, gives way, after the appearance of Peter Verkhovensky, to an increasingly frantic, disjointed narrative style which seems to have difficulty in keeping pace with the onrush of events—the sabotage of social functions, arson, murder, suicide, insurrection, sacrilege, mob violence, and administrative collapse. Peter Verkhovensky hopes that the ensuing social demoralization will lead to general insurrection. The Russian people, "crazed after a year of insurrection," will be thirsting for order at any price, to replace that which they have lost. The time will then be right for the establishment of "a social republic, communism and socialism."[74]

The advent of the socialist order is the ostensible justification of Peter Verkhovensky's doctrine of organized destruction. The revolutionary socialists are willing "to shed blood, because this blood will be the price of happiness." People who refuse the new order will be killed "and *so much the better*."[75] Verkhovensky, however, is concerned not with the new order itself, but only with preparations for its coming. Much to the consternation of the more earnest of his followers, who yearn to have their fondness for discussions about "the future social organization of mankind" indulged, he refuses to engage in speculation about the future earthly paradise. He protests that he has no idea what is going to happen after the revolution. The one essential thing is the activity of organized destruction, "and the rest is all so much idle talk."[76]

Peter Verkhovensky's exclusive emphasis on action is not due to an inability to think, or to an ignorance of socialist doctrine. Dostoyevsky intimates that Verkhovensky is thoroughly familiar with all the socialist writings, and that he is much more a theoretician than he pretends.[77] His emphatic call for action is based in a reasoning which may be more consistent than that of Chernyshevsky, for Verkhovensky is not as quick to subordinate the scientific

73 *NP*, pp. 361, 273, 100-101, 348-49. Cf. S. Nechayev's "Revolutionary Catechism" (co-authored by Bakunin) in R. Payne, *The Terrorists* (New York, 1951), pp. 21-27.
74 *NP*, p. 349.
75 Ibid., pp. 140, 349.
76 *The Devils*, p. 406 (II,7,ii); *NP*, pp. 273, 100.
77 *NP*, pp. 206, 350, 360-61, 99-100.

insight to the requirement of socialist order. He accepts the teaching that human beings are fully explicable according to natural laws discoverable by science,[78] but his rigorous adoption of materialism ultimately excludes the great idea of a perfect social order of freedom, equality, and brotherhood. Verkhovensky regards the future utopia of "phalansteries where people will be dancing and singing while mowing hay" as an idea "made up for fools only," though perhaps useful as "bait." He rejects the great idea as a sort of "Christianity without Christ."[79] And he does so, not because it distracts from the imperative of action, but because it is incompatible with theory. While emphasizing throughout his rough notes that Peter Verkhovensky is an "abstract" man, Dostoyevsky does not present an explicit account of the reasoning which leads him to turn away from scientific socialism. It is made clear, however, that for Verkhovensky the theoretician *par excellence* is the "grim and gloomy" Shigalyov, whom Verkhovensky regards as a genuis greater than, for instance, Fourier.[80] We must thus turn to the question of Shigalyov's "despair."

At a meeting of the revolutionary cell, Shigalyov offers a brief summary of his final "solution of the social formula." He maintains that his attempt to resolve the problem of social order is the first to be based uncompromisingly on science:

Having devoted all my energies to the study of the social organization of the society of the future which is to replace our present one, I have come to the conclusion
that all the inventors of social systems, from ancient times to our present year, have
been dreamers, story-tellers, fools who contradicted themselves and had no idea of
natural science or that strange animal called man. Plato, Rousseau, Fourier,
aluminum pillars, all that is only good for sparrows, and not for human society.
But as the future form of society is of the utmost importance now that we at last
are all ready to act, I am submitting to you my own system of world organization
so as to make any further thinking unnecessary.[81]

The source of Shigalyov's despair is his realization of the final incompatibility of science and socialism. In the light of his logical investigation of the facts of nature, Shigalyov finds himself compelled to renounce the great idea of a future order reconciling individual freedom and social unity; or rather, he subjects the great idea to a scientific reinterpretation. According to this reinterpretation, individual freedom becomes the prerogative of the strong minority (roughly one-tenth of humanity) who are worthy to exercise tyrannical rule over the remainder of humanity. Social unity belongs to the weak majority who have renounced their freedom. In the equality of slavery they are transformed into a herd, which by its unconditional obedience "will by a series of

78 *The Devils*, p. 286 (II,2,iv).
79 *NP*, pp. 91, 400.
80 *The Devils*, p. 418 (II,8).
81 Ibid., pp. 404-406 (II,7,ii).

regenerations attain a state of primeval innocence, something like the original paradise."[82]

There is something fantastically eccentric in Shigalyov's insistence that his social formula is the only certain theoretical foundation for an earthly paradise. But his "grim and gloomy" certainty nevertheless poses a formidable threat to both liberals and scientific socialists. Through Shigalyov, Dostoyevsky gives voice to the possibility that the gulf between thought and practice in the Geneva idea can be finally overcome only by an uncompromising alteration of the idea itself, so that it conforms with life as it actually is rather than as it ought to be. The place of reason in Geneva thinking is central, yet not absolute. But in scientific socialism reason is wholeheartedly adopted as the principal means whereby the great idea is to be realized; and finally, in Shigalyov's system, the means apparently undermines the great idea itself. It is noteworthy, however, that Shigalyov continues to invoke love of humanity as the ultimate justification of his social formula.

From the Critique of Russian Westernism to the Critique of the West

For Dostoyevsky, Shigalyov's social formula is the final word of Russian Westernism. Now that his presentation of the various voices of Russian Westernism—from the Geneva idea, through scientific and revolutionary socialism, to tyranny—is complete, it is possible to broach the question of Dostoyevsky's final understanding of what, most fundamentally, is spoken in Russian Westernism.

Although Dostoyevsky emphasizes the intellectual diversity of Russian Westernism, he tends to view it in terms of the division between the Westernism of the 1840s and the Westernism of the 1860s. And it would appear that his sympathies are with the former. The most severe indictments of the Westernism of the 1860s to be found in Dostoyevsky's writings (in *Notes from Underground* and *The Devils*) are actually voiced by liberals of the 1840s. Moreover, Stepan Verkhovensky and Versilov are not entirely unattractive characters. Their principal fault seems to be their inability to give practical effect to their noble dreams; but, according to Dostoyevsky's portrayal of their dilemma, it is at least doubtful that they themselves are entirely responsible for the gulf between thought and practice which characterizes them. It is noteworthy that Stepan Verkhovensky, who eloquently pronounces one of the most direct condemnations of the Westernism of the 1860s to be found in Dostoyevsky's writings, meets his death with a greatness of spirit which seems to belie the characterization of him throughout the greater part of the novel. Versilov too is partially redeemed at the close of *The Adolescent*. Yet

82 Ibid., p. 405 (II,7,ii).

these indications of Dostoyevsky's evident sympathy for his liberal characters—especially in relation to the often ugly face presented by the Westernism of the 1860s—do not constitute an exoneration of the Westernism of the 1840s. In the illumination of his approaching death, Stepan Verkhovensky recognizes the inner relation between his great idea and the Westernism of the 1860s. After listening to the words of the Gospel of Luke 8:32-36, this purest representative of Russian liberalism confesses his own responsibility for the chaos which is engulfing his "*sainte Russie*":

You see, that's just like our Russia. Those devils who go out of the sick man and enter the swine—those are all the sores, all the poisonous exhalations, all the impurities, all the big and little devils, that have accumulated in our great and beloved invalid, in our Russia, for centuries, for centuries!. . . and all those devils, all those impurities, all those abominations that were festering on the surface—all of them will themselves ask to enter into swine. And, indeed, they may have entered into them already! They are we, we and they, and Peter [Verkhovensky]—*et les autres avec lui*, and *perhaps I at the head of them all*, and we shall cast ourselves down, the raving and the possessed, from the cliff into the sea and shall all be drowned, and it serves us right, for that is all we are good for.[83]

Stepan Verkhovensky's confession is especially significant for it indicates that Dostoyevsky's understanding of the "truth" preached by Russian Westernism not only includes the liberalism of the 1840s, but focuses on it as the source of the later movements which apparently deny it. The analogy of the father-son relationship which is so central to Dostoyevsky's critique of Russian Westernism thus takes on its full importance. The mutual denial of father and son, vehement though it may be, cannot dissolve the bond which unites them; nor can it diminish the responsibility of the father for the fact that the son exists at all. This assigning of responsibility to the fathers is related most immediately to the question of education and upbringing. As we have noted, Dostoyevsky thought that a liberal upbringing played a significant role in rendering young people peculiarly susceptible to ideas of all sorts, including the most extreme. This susceptibility was enhanced by that urge for action, which Dostoyevsky thought characterized the Westernists of the 1860s. In the hands of these impatient young people, the delicate balance of the Geneva idea was upset by one-sided interpretations which lent themselves more easily to practical activity. Yet Verkhovensky's final confession says more than this. Whereas earlier he had blamed the sons for misguidedly distorting the great idea he serves, he finally perceives that, in essence, there has been no distortion. He acknowledges an intrinsic relation between the liberal idea and the extreme products of the Westernism of the 1860s.

For Dostoyevsky, the fundamental goal of Russian Westernism, uniting fathers and sons, is the earthly paradise founded on reason and justified by the appeal to love of humanity. As Versilov's earthly paradise is translated ever more single-mindedly from theory into practice, it gives way to Shigalyov's

83 Ibid., pp. 647-48 (III,7,ii). The italics are mine.

earthly paradise. The great idea of a universal union of free and equal human beings points to a union in which a few are free and the rest are equal only in their slavery. Dostoyevsky's critique of Russian Westernism was concerned with enucleating its great idea, and tracing the process of filiation whereby this idea issues in scientific socialism and, finally, in tyranny. By itself this critique must be considered incomplete, for it leaves two important questions unresolved. First, the theoretical necessity of the relationship between Shigalyov's tyranny and Geneva thought is not elucidated. Dostoyevsky does not reveal the logic whereby Shigalyov arrives at his cryptic social formula; he merely has him declare that such an undertaking would require ten evenings. A full response to this question perhaps presupposes the answer to a second, more immediate question: can Geneva thinking, which has its true home in the West, be adequately understood solely according to its expression within a Russian context?

Dostoyevsky himself emphasizes the differences between Russian and Western liberalism. He maintains that in the West liberalism is the mature product of a sustained, gradual, and painful effort of thought and practice and that, whatever its aspirations in theory, it is subject to the moderating influence of an historical tradition with which it is intimately associated. Russian liberalism, however, mechanically imports alien ideas which cost no effort, and which are subject to no moderating influence because they are adopted by people who are uprooted from all restraining traditions. Moreover, Dostoyevsky notes the tendency of Russian Westernism as a whole to take Western ideas to far greater extremes than Westerners themselves.[84] On the basis of distinctions such as these, it is possible that the direct relation between Geneva thinking and the various fruit which it bore in Russia—the ridiculousness of the liberals of the 1840s and the scientific and revolutionary socialism and intimations of tyranny of the 1860s—could be attributed to the shallowness of the Russian soil onto which the seed of the great idea fell, rather than to something inherent in the idea itself. It is surely possible, as has been asserted by an eminent Western scholar, that Russian tyranny in this century represents the triumph of a native "Oriental despotism" *over* the Geneva idea.[85] So long as this is a possibility, the liberal idea of freedom, equality, and brotherhood may still constitute the best conception of human order.

The demonstration of a relationship between tyranny and the Geneva idea would have to be considered inconclusive if confined to Russian Westernism. Dostoyevsky's critique of Russian Westernism points inevitably towards his critique of the West itself.

84 See, for instance, *The Idiot*, p. 587 (IV,7); *The Devils*, pp. 372-73 (II,6,v); *BK*, p. 274 (V,3).
85 L. Strauss, *The City and Man* (Chicago, 1964), p. 3.

THREE

THE "GREAT IDEA" IN THE MODERN WEST

The Breakdown of Traditional Western Order

The initial concern of Dostoyevsky's turn from ''Russian Europe'' to ''European Europe'' is the consideration of the historical outcome of the great idea within its originating civilization.[1] His examination of Geneva thought in its modern Western context presupposes a particular understanding of its place within Western civilization as a whole.

Believing that a civilization is founded, not merely on the ''need to get along,'' but ''always as a result of a great idea,''[2] Dostoyevsky identifies the foundation of the West as the great religious idea embodied in Latin Christianity. He thought that Roman Catholic civilization had reached its apogee in the twelfth century. The buffoon, Lebedev (in *The Idiot*), enumerates some of

---

1 It should be emphasized that this ''turn,'' though logically appropriate in my exposition of Dostoyevsky's critique of the West, is not explicitly made by Dostoyevsky himself. His consideration of the West is generally intertwined in his writings with his consideration of Russian Westernism. There are, however, writings or parts of writings in which he examines directly the problem of order in the West itself: for instance, *Winter Notes on Summer Impressions* (written in 1863, after his first trip to Europe); a series of articles on Europe which he wrote for the journal *Citizen* in 1873 (brought together and translated into French by J. Drouilly in *Dostoïevski et l'Europe en 1873*); articles appearing in *The Diary of a Writer* for 1876-1877, 1880 and 1881; and unpublished rough notes and drafts for articles (written during the 1860s and 1870s and now published in English as *The Unpublished Dostoevsky*). In addition to these non-literary writings there are in the novels (and in the rough notes for them) numerous observations about the West expressed through the various characters. (For Dostoyevsky's use of the terms ''Russian Europe'' and ''European Europe,'' see *WNSI*, p. 77).

2 *UD*, III, p. 152.

the horrors of famine and disease which attended life in twelfth-century Europe, and he then relates a bizarre anecdote about a man who was reduced by starvation to cannibalism. This medieval man supposedly consumed, in the course of his famine-ridden life, sixty monks (notoriously fleshier than lay people) and several lay infants; and rather than take his terrible secret with him to the grave he confessed his crime, in the certain knowledge that he thereby faced a dreadful retribution. Lebedev draws a highly significant conclusion from this act of voluntary confession:

The criminal ends up by going and laying information against himself with the clergy and by giving himself up to the authorities. Now one cannot help asking oneself what tortures awaited him in that age—the wheel, the stake, and the fire! Who induced him to go and inform against himself? Why not simply stop at the figure of sixty and keep the secret till his dying day? Why not simply leave the monks alone and live in penance as a hermit? Or why not, finally, become a monk himself? Well, here is the solution! There must have been something stronger than the stake.... There must have been an idea stronger than any calamity, famine, torture, plague, leprosy, and all that hell which mankind could not have endured without that idea that bound and guided men's hearts and fructified the waters of life!

Surveying the modern age, Lebedev observes that the people of the West are no longer held by an idea as forcefully as they were held by the Roman Catholic idea during the Middle Ages:

Show me anything resembling that force in our age of liars and railways—I'm sorry, I ought to have said in our age of liners and railways, but I said liars and railways because I'm drunk but just. Now, show me an idea that binds mankind together today with half the strength that it had in those centuries. And don't try to frighten me with your prosperity, your riches, the infrequency of famine, and the rapidity of the means of communication! There is more wealth, but less strength; the binding idea is no more; everything has become soft, everything is flabby, and everyone is flabby.[3]

Since the twelfth century the Roman Catholic order had become "moribund."[4] The "broadening of human thought" accomplished in the Renaissance of the fifteenth and sixteenth centuries engendered modern science, which was to achieve its first great successes in the "astronomical discoveries" of Copernicus, Kepler, and Galileo. The Roman Catholic order early came to regard modern science as a mortal enemy. This may have been proof of a remarkable prescience, for just over a century after the trial of Galileo in 1616, the *philosophes* of the Enlightenment were to preach "to the whole world that science had come and that they could get along without the Church...." The broadening of human thought in the Renaissance contributed also to the Protestant Reformation of the sixteenth century. The emphasis

---

3 *The Idiot*, pp. 416-17 (III,4). Lebedev is a buffoon, with a penchant for bizarre clowning. There is no doubt, however, that he here expresses Dostoyevsky's thought, though in his own inimitable manner.

4 Dostoyevsky uses this word in a letter of 31 Dec. 1867 to his friend, Apollon Maykov.

of Protestantism on the individual conscience as the ultimate guide of faith contributed immeasurably to that "disintegration of the masses into personalities" which is, for Dostoyevsky, the prime expression of civilizational disorder.[5] The undermining of Latin Christian order by the individualism and rationalism fostered by the Reformation, Renaissance, and Enlightenment culminated in the most significant event in the history of the modern West— the French Revolution:

"Profound silence reigned throughout Europe when Frederick the Great shut his eyes forever; but never did such a silence precede so great a storm!" . . .
   In fact, who in Europe in those days . . . could have foreseen—even in a remote manner—the things which would happen to men and to Europe in the course of the subsequent thirty years?[6]

Dostoyevsky thought that the French Revolution was both an end and a beginning for Western civilization. While completing the destruction of the traditional order, it held out the promise of a new order. The inspiring presence of a new idea of social order rendered even the work of revolutionary destruction systematic, and because of it the Revolution itself came to signify a negation for the sake of the positive fulfillment of humanity's most profound aspirations. The new idea of order was characterized in various ways: the order of science rather than superstition, of the state rather than the church, of the "rights of man" rather than feudal obligation. For Dostoyevsky these are partial characterizations of the fundamental "dream of a justice founded solely on the laws of reason," that is, an order based entirely on a human reason liberated from the fetters of tradition, and particularly religious tradition. The unqualified affirmation of the moral superiority of such an order, "for the first time . . . in the life of humanity," constituted the primary significance of the French Revolution.[7]

The French Revolution aspired to be a European revolution, and indeed a world revolution. While negating the Roman Catholic aspiration to universality, it offered the West its new, rational formulation of "universal unity." The defence of the Revolution against the monarchs of Europe soon passed over into an active proselytism, carried on largely by the remarkably successful citizen-army. Under Napoleon the principles of the French Revolution began "to change the whole face of Europe."[8] But Napoleon failed to unite Europe according to his interpretation of the principles of 1789, and his legacy appeared to put a union of any sort out of reach of the West. He had made it impossible once and for all for the West to return to the enfolding unity of medieval order, for his political and legal reforms had weakened irrevocably

5 See Dostoyevsky's letter of 15 May 1869 to Apollon Maykov outlining the salient features of the history of Russia and the West. The account of the disintegration of medieval civilization given in this paragraph is derived from Dostoyevsky's comments in *UD*, II, pp. 30, 151, and *DE*, p. 149.
6 *DW*, p. 723 (May-June 1877).
7 *DE*, p. 149.
8 *DW*, p. 724 (May-June 1877).

the remnants of the old feudal-Christian civilization. And his effort to realize a
new universality had actually fostered an intense particularism among the
Western peoples. This assertion of particularity had been a significant concomitant of the Reformation; it became more aggressive as it found theoretical
justification in the principles of 1789, and emotional justification in the un-
welcome presence of arrogant French troops. French imperialism, according
to Dostoyevsky, inspired a "new form of democracy," or "nationalism,"
which portends the almost endless fragmentation of the West.[9] The right of
particular peoples to self-determination may be theoretically compatible with
the universality of the "rights of man," but the fervid assertion of this right in
practice entailed consequences which did not bode well for the possibility of a
new Western unity. The French Revolution had thus apparently dissolved the
traditional bonds of European order without realizing its promise of a new
civilization.

Yet Dostoyevsky always insists upon the incalculable power of an idea to
alter the shape of human affairs: "The tiniest fire can give birth to a universal
conflagration. You have exactly the same thing with an idea—one fiery spot
in the deepest darkness (provided it is not extinguished)."[10] The fundamental
idea of the French Revolution had not been extinguished at Waterloo. Even
the zealous vigilance of the Holy Alliance could not prevent the formula of
"*liberté, égalité, fraternité*" from becoming ascendant in Western intellectual life. The theoretical elaboration which this formula had undergone, particularly in France and in Germany, constituted for Dostoyevsky one of the
supreme achievements of the Western intellect. The memorable variations on
the theme of the new social order (which, as we have seen, he designates as
Geneva thought in acknowledgement of its source in Rousseau) had come to
constitute in the course of the nineteenth century the fundamental vision
"underlying today's civilization."[11]

This intellectual unity held out the possibility of a more concrete Western
unity in the future. Dostoyevsky thus looks to the West in an attempt to
discern the practical outcome of the promise of a new universal order inherent
in the intellectual hegemony of Geneva thought. Before turning to his scrutiny
of Geneva practice in the West, it must be noted that this scrutiny is conducted
in terms of the particular peoples of the West. Although he regards the divisive nationalism of the nineteenth century as a "new form of democracy," he
recognizes the existence of actual particularities in the West that precede
modern nationalism. Indeed, he was captivated by the "perfect organisms" of
Europe, "the work of centuries."[12] This is evident in his repeated avowals of
reverence for the "sacred wonders" of Europe, and in the obvious delight
with which he discusses the characteristics peculiar to the various Western

9 *DW*, p. 457 (Sept. 1876); *UD*, I, p. 54.
10 *NRY*, p. 380.
11 *The Adolescent*, p. 212 (II,1,iv).
12 *PS*, p. 36; *WNSI*, p. 109.

peoples, while always relating these characteristics to the larger question of social order.[13] Dostoyevsky appears to think that a tendency towards national particularity existed even during the full flowering of Latin Christian civilization. The Reformation was thus concerned with the emancipation of peoples, as well as individuals, from the Roman Catholic order. With the final breakdown of the traditional Western unity, the assertion of particularity became increasingly relentless, so much so that in the modern West "even the most general philosophical and social teachings" acquire a "national shading": "over there, everything rests upon a firm national foundation. Each nation believes in itself, to the point where it almost assumes that it is destined to conquer the whole world for its particular nationality."[14] Dostoyevsky's account of the historical fate of the Geneva idea in the West is thus inseparable from his scrutiny of the particular peoples of the West.

The New Order and the Western Peoples

France

It is natural that in his consideration of the West Dostoyevsky would turn first to France. Since the eighteenth century, Russian Westernism had looked to France as the supreme model of civilization. Those Russians who strove to become Europeans strove above all to become Frenchmen. This worship of French civilization persisted into the nineteenth century, undiminished even by the war with Napoleon. Dostoyevsky suggests that the Russian attraction to France can be attributed to an inherent "taste for beauty." In *The Gambler* a Russian expounds this theme in a discussion with an Englishman concerning the love of a young Russian woman (perhaps symbolic of Russian Westernism) for a "disenchanted" French liberal:

A Frenchman, Mr. Astley, is a finished and beautiful type. You, as a Briton, may not agree; I, as a Russian, don't agree either—perhaps, if you like, from sheer

---

13 Dostoyevsky does, of course, make observations about various Western peoples that bear no apparent relation to the concern with social order which chiefly determines his scrutiny of the West. These observations, largely negative in character, are to be found mostly in his private correspondence (though in rare instances they do find their way into some of the minor characterizations of the novels—the Marmeladovs's landlady in *Crime and Punishment*, for instance). The fact that comments concerning, for example, the personal integrity and intelligence of the German lower class or the drinking habits of the Swiss are restricted almost entirely to his correspondence indicates that he himself certainly did not regard them as part of his important thought about the West. These comments may illustrate Dostoyevsky's capacity for extreme irritability when abroad, or even for prejudging the personal characteristics of foreigners, but they contribute nothing to the understanding of his critique of the West, and certainly cannot be taken as evidence of a chauvinistic hatred of everything Western. We shall thus disregard them as being of interest only in relation to his personal biography. This applies equally to those comments in his correspondence concerning, for instance, the Italian peasants, which are adulatory but which do not bear on the question of the Western crisis of order.

14 *UD*, II, p. 4; *NP*, p. 215.

envy; but our young ladies may be of a different opinion.... The French national type, I mean the Parisian, had begun to be cast in an elegant mould while we were still bears. The Revolution was the heir of the nobility. Now the vulgarest Frenchman may have manners, modes of behaviour, ways of speech, and even ideas, of a thoroughly elegant form, without his own initiative, soul, or heart playing any part in it; he has inherited it all. In themselves they may be the shallowest of the shallow, the lowest of the low. Well, Mr. Astley, I must tell you now that there is no creature on earth more frank and trustful than a good, intelligent, not too affected Russian young lady. A de Grieux, appearing in some character, wearing a disguise, may conquer her heart with extraordinary ease; he appears in an elegant shape, Mr. Astley, and the young lady takes that shape for his own soul, the natural form of his soul and heart, and not for a garment he has inherited . . . and Russians are very sensitive to beauty and have a taste for it.[15]

When the Russians were converted to Christianity under Vladimir in 988, the decision for Byzantine Christianity was supposed to have been determined by the superior beauty of the liturgy which the Russian envoys witnessed in the Cathedral of Saint Sophia.[16] France, like Byzantium, satisfied a Russian love of beauty, and something more besides: France was to uprooted Russians the true home of that idea that promised to satisfy their thirst for order. Although the Russians imbibed the Geneva idea in the cloistered tranquillity of German universities, they assumed that this idea had its genuine life in the streets of Paris. Turgenev's depiction of the death of Rudin (in the novel of the same name) on a Paris barricade of 1848 captures perfectly the ethos of the Russian liberal idealists of the 1840s.

It is to a Russian need for beauty and for order, then, that Dostoyevsky ascribes the fact that France, more than any other country in the West, is the "second fatherland" of Westernized Russians. Thus, in the revolutionary year of 1848, the Russians followed events in Paris as closely as if the fate of their own deepest aspirations were in the balance.[17] In 1870 they lamented France's ignominious defeat by the Germans in the Franco-German war as though it were their own. Like Versilov, they regarded the defeat of France and the subsequent burning of the Tuileries during the Commune as equivalent to the sounding of the "death knell" over all Europe.[18]

Napoleon III's defeat at Sedan in 1870 appeared to signify the final eclipse of France as a great power. Surely the nation which had experienced the catastrophes of Waterloo and Sedan within a half-century must renounce any claim to European hegemony. France, however, still refused to give up its desire to play a leading role in the West. Dostoyevsky observed that, remarkably enough, most of the West was not averse to supporting France in its refusal: "To this day [1876], the most insignificant happening in France

---

15 *The Gambler*, p. 159.

16 Mouravieff, *A History of the Church of Russia* (New York, 1971), p. 12.

17 This is according to Dostoyevsky's own testimony before the tribunal investigating the Petrashevsky circle. See J. Drouilly, *La pensée politique et religieuse de Dostoïevski* (Paris, 1971).

18 *The Adolescent*, p. 467 (III,7,ii).

arouses in Europe more sympathy and attention than any important Berlin event."[19] He maintains that the persistence of France's claim to the leadership of the West is not without foundation, for the ultimate justification of its pre-eminence has always really been, not the *gloire militaire* won by its armies, but its moral stature. France is "the nation of genius, *par excellence*," one of those nations which rules over humanity by virtue of the exercise of an influence which can best be compared to that of Athens over ancient civilization. France has long been the "land of the first step, the first test, the first ideational initiative." The magnificence of its attempt to embody the Roman Catholic idea had accorded it the spiritual leadership of the medieval West.[20] The history of the modern West, moreover, actually dates from Louis XIV's apotheosis of the State:

It is a remarkable fact that in France everything dates from Louis XIV.... But most remarkable of all is the fact that everything in all Europe dates from Louis XIV.... Perhaps it is because he was the first to say, "*L'état c'est moi*." This thrilled everybody; it took all Europe by storm.[21]

According to Dostoyevsky, France's "incontestable and predominant influence on all the European peoples" has been due for centuries to the brilliant determination with which it has striven to be the embodiment of a principle of social order that could constitute an inspiration to other peoples.[22] Since 1789 France had devoted itself to the fulfillment of a new idea of order. The final outcome of this effort would determine whether or not it could continue, even after Waterloo and Sedan, to claim the leadership of the West.

From the Revolution to the inauguration of the Third Republic in 1870, the rule of France had been shared almost entirely between the Monarchists (whether Bourbon or Orléanist) and the Bonapartists. Those of the nobility and clergy who would not reconcile themselves to the destruction of the traditional order refused to recognize any regime in France as legitimate, except that of the Bourbon monarchy. Throughout the Revolutionary and Napoleonic eras they aided the enemies of France. In the immediate aftermath of the Bourbon Restoration (1815-1830), they revenged themselves upon Revolutionary France in the "white terror"; and under Charles X (1825-1830) it appeared that they might actually succeed in a genuine revival of the old order, without any of the concessions to the principles of 1789 which Louis XVIII (1815-1825) had granted in his Constitutional Charter. The overthrow of their hopes in the revolution of 1830 which brought the more liberal Duke of Orléans, Louis Philippe (1830-1848), to the throne made them no less intractable. The power which they continued to enjoy in rural France, where much of the peasantry still accepted the guidance of the local *seigneur* and the

19 *DW*, p. 250 (March 1876).
20 *DE*, pp. 46, 148-49; *DW*, pp. 250-51, 575 (March 1876; Jan. 1877); *The Devils*, p. 258 (II,1,vii).
21 *WNSI*, p. 126 (7).
22 *DE*, p. 148.

priest, and even in Paris, where the ancient family names were still held in awe by those with high social aspirations, encouraged them to adhere relentlessly to their hopes. Their determination was, for Dostoyevsky, the refusal of a "corpse" to acknowledge its own death.[23]

The Bonapartist imperialism which arose in the wake of the Revolution was, in Dostoyevsky's view, the most successful political movement in France during the nineteenth century. But it was devoid of any idea of social order, living or dead. The Empire, whether that of the uncle or the nephew, was predicated on military glory abroad and order at home. Neither bore a genuine relation to the liberal principles which the Bonapartes tended to invoke. Later avowals of the goal of a European union of liberal states notwithstanding, Napoleon I's imperialism had shown itself to have no ultimate end other than conquest for conquest's sake.[24] While Napoleon III did further the cause of Italian liberation from Austria, his defence of Pope Pius IX against the Italian liberals, his hopes for the annexation of Belgium, and his attempt to transform the Mexican republic into a Roman Catholic empire ruled by the Archduke Maximilian of Austria, all bore a highly dubious relation to the universal furthering of "the rights of man."[25] The incongruity, apparent in the Bonapartes' foreign policy, of the association of imperialism with liberal principles was less pronounced in their domestic rule. This bore unashamedly the stamp of military dictatorship, with a minimum of lip-service to the principles of 1789.[26] Nonetheless, Dostoyevsky thought that, despite its lack of an idea, Bonapartism, or "Caesarism," had proven to be the most effective regime France had known since the Revolution. He points to France's peculiar susceptibility to the temptation of "Caesarism," a susceptibility which continually threatened the life of the Third Republic after 1870.[27]

Social order in France since the Revolution had thus been most directly determined by those who were without an idea of social order, or by those whose idea was dead. What had become of the Geneva vision of order which was so intimately associated with the Revolution?

The original bearers of the Geneva idea during the Revolution had been the republicans. Prior to the founding of the Third Republic in the aftermath of Sedan, they had exercised political power for only two very brief periods:

23 *UD*, III, p. 82.
24 So far as Russians were concerned, Napoleon's attack on Russia in 1812 demonstrated the boundlessness of his military ambitions. For Dostoyevsky's discussion of the Russian victory over Napoleon see *DW*, p. 1045 (Jan. 1881).
25 Ibid., p. 457 (Sept. 1876).
26 See *WNSI*, chaps. 2, 7.
27 *DW*, p. 817 (Sept. 1877). Dostoyevsky points, for instance, to the crisis of May 16, 1876. President MacMahon's dissolution of the legislative assembly in an attempt to redefine the uncertain distribution of powers within the constitution precipitated the sort of crisis which Dostoyevsky thought could easily topple the Republic. In his view, the inability of the various parties to present a united front against MacMahon's unilateral extension of his powers, and MacMahon's popularity with the army and the common people, brought a military dictatorship within easy reach of France. See ibid., pp. 740-42, 816-21 (May-June, Sept. 1877).

1789 to 1795 and 1848 to 1851. And it was quite possible, in Dostoyevsky's estimation, that the Third Republic would be of short duration. Contemplation of the meagre successes of French republicanism since its birth leads him to remark:

It is difficult to conceive unluckier men than the French republicans with their French republic. Soon one hundred years will have elapsed since, for the first time, this institution came into existence. Since then every time (now it is the third time) adroit usurpers have confiscated the republic for their benefit, no one has risen in its serious defense, save some negligible group. Not even once has there been strong popular support. Besides, during periods when the republic chanced to exist, only a few people regarded it as a final, and not a transitory thing. Nevertheless, no men are more convinced of the country's support than the French republicans.[28]

Dostoyevsky points out that the transitoriness of republican regimes has much to do with the unfavourable circumstances which have attended their establishment. The opportunity to realize the Geneva idea always came in the wake of a traumatic upheaval which left most Frenchmen too anxious and insecure to give thought to anything beyond their immediate interests. The circumstances in which the Third Republic was born were especially unfavourable: it had to accept most of the disgrace of defeat in a war which it had not started, and yet refusal to continue Napoleon III's war with the Germans would have entailed the greater disgrace of conceding defeat too easily. Although "disgrace was ahead of them, disgrace was behind them," the republicans enthroned themselves with "a light heart, despite everything." For Dostoyevsky it is this complacency which makes their situation not only "tragic," but "comical." The "comical" aura that he attributes to the French republicans is similar to that "ridiculousness" characteristic of the Russian liberals of the 1840s. Their failure since 1789 to give practical effect to their ideas made them appear to be entirely "abstract men" in whose parlance the word "republic" was something "comically idealistic." These bearers of Geneva thought had proven to be "quite impotent." By the latter part of the nineteenth century, France could no longer take seriously the "liberal, gray-haired old men making themselves look younger and imagining themselves still young."[29]

Dostoyevsky thought that the fundamental factor in the practical impotence of the republicans was their failure to gain the support of the bourgeoisie. The ascendancy of the middle class in France had been a concomitant of the French Revolution; indeed, the French bourgeoisie was "a child of the republic." The republicans had contributed directly to the rise of the middle class by confiscating and selling, at deflated prices, the enormous land-holdings of the nobility and clergy. Measures such as this so enriched the middle class that it was able, eighty years later, to finance payment of the

28 Ibid., p. 813 (Sept. 1877).
29 Ibid., pp. 814-17, 736-37 (Sept., May-June 1877).

huge indemnity to the Germans with remarkable ease. In general, these measures surrendered France to "the boundless sovereign power of the bourgeoisie," a sovereignty which Dostoyevsky considers to be the single most important factor determining the question of social order in modern France. Since 1795, however, the newly ascendant bourgeoisie had evinced a pronounced aversion for the republic. This was not fully explained by reference to the natural mistrust, and even contempt, of the industrious and acquisitive for "abstract men" and "idealists." The bourgeoisie had come to consider the republicans to be "unreliable," not so much because of their comical aspect, but because of the close neighbourship of the republic with "communism." Having successfully ousted the nobility and the clergy from the foremost position in France, according to the saying—"*Ôte-toi de là que je m'y mette!*"—the middle class did not intend to be ousted in turn by the "fourth estate" which their own industrial enterprise had brought into being.[30] The formula of "freedom, equality, and brotherhood" had come to inspire the workers also, and the particular emphasis which they placed upon equality posed a distinct threat to the recently acquired power of the bourgeoisie. The spectre of communism had come to haunt the middle class even during the Revolution. Although the "Conspiracy of the Equals" (1796) led by Babeuf was easily crushed, the bourgeoisie had come to fear some of the possible implications of "freedom, equality, and brotherhood." When the opportunity came, in the person of Napoleon, the republic was sacrificed to imperial "order."[31] Although, later, the bourgeoisie was not particularly pleased with the restored Bourbon monarchy, its ingratitude to the republicans became obvious in its undisguised pleasure at the Orléanist regime ushered in by the revolution of 1830. And it was even more pleased when the revolution of 1848 finally resolved itself into Bonapartist rule rather than that of the Second Republic.

Though comical and pathetic "little old men," were not the republicans still the bearers of the only living idea of social order present in modern France? Was it utterly inconceivable that this idea could eventually bear fruit? Indeed, was not their very rejection by the middle class indicative of the steadfastness with which they guarded the purity of the Geneva vision of order? Dostoyevsky's response to such questions is to attribute the impotence of French republicanism to a misunderstanding on the part of the bourgeoisie. The middle class had been incorrect in its assessment of the "unreliability" of republicanism, for the republic is "the most natural expression and form of the bourgeois idea," and republicans are "an incarnation of the bourgeoisie in the strictest meaning of the term."[32]

30 Ibid., pp. 254, 251, 737, 253, 618 (March 1876; May-June, Feb. 1877).
31 Dostoyevsky refers to Napoleon I as the "executor of the first historical phase of the event which began in 1789," that is, the phase of bourgeois domination of the Revolution. Ibid., pp. 834, 724 (Sept., May-June 1877).
32 Ibid., pp. 737-38, 254 (May-June 1877; March 1876).

The intimacy between the republicans and the "third estate" during the Revolution had given birth to an idea of social order which Dostoyevsky designates as "bourgeois liberalism."[33] Bourgeois liberalism is for him, most simply, that interpretation of Geneva thought which is wholly in accord with the needs and aspirations of the bourgeoisie. Freedom, for the French republican or bourgeois liberal, signifies the liberation of economic activity from the inhibitions imposed upon it by the Roman Catholic church, by outmoded feudal organizations such as the guild, and by the absence of an efficient system of coinage, transport, and communication. Freedom is thus linked more with comfortable self-preservation than with the moral striving so central to Geneva thinking.

What is *liberté*? Freedom. What freedom? Equal freedom for each and all to do as they please within the limits of the law. When may a man do all he pleases? When he has a million. Does freedom give each man a million? No. What is the man without a million? The man without a million is not one who does all that he pleases, but rather one with whom one does all that one pleases.

Equality is understood as "equality before the law" rather than the equality of capacity for moral goodness which is implied in Geneva thought.[34]

The interpretation which the French liberals give to freedom and equality makes it difficult to perceive in their talk of brotherhood anything more than a pious platitude. Brotherhood is invoked only in a negative manner, as a restraint upon the individual's pursuit of comfortable self-preservation. Even then the need for limit is preached, not in accordance with a vision of social harmony, but in reference to the right of other individuals to make their lives comfortable. According to Dostoyevsky, the reconciliation of individual freedom with social unity envisaged in Geneva thought is nullified in bourgeois

---

33 For instance, in *UD*, III, p. 147.

34 *WNSI*, pp. 109-10 (6). Dostoyevsky was doubtless acquainted with the economic liberalism propounded by Adam Smith, Malthus, and Ricardo. See, for instance, *UD*, I, p. 50. He presents the gist of the teaching of these British liberals in the words of the aspiring businessman, Luzhin, in *Crime and Punishment:* "If, say, I've been told in the past, 'Love thy neighbour as thyself,' and I did, what was the result of it?... The result of it was that I tore my coat in half to share it with my neighbour, and both of us were left half naked... But science tells us, 'Love yourself before everyone else, for everything in the world is based on self-interest. If you love only yourself, you'll transact your business as it ought to be transacted, and your coat will remain whole.' And economic truth adds that the more successfully private business is run, the more solid are the foundations of our social life and the greater is the general well-being of the people. Which means that by acquiring wealth exclusively and only for myself, I'm by that very fact acquiring it, as it were, for everybody..." (p. 167 [II,5]). Although clearly aware of the teaching embodied in English-speaking economic liberalism, Dostoyevsky's concern is with the teaching itself, not with questions of intellectual history associated with it. Thus, his account of French bourgeois liberalism ignores the question of any intellectual debt which it might owe to the English-speaking liberal tradition. Moreover, his account makes no direct reference to any particular exponent of bourgeois liberalism in France itself.

liberalism. The vision of social harmony is sacrificed to "a principle of individualism, a principle of isolation, of intense self-preservation." In a social order in which each personality "fights for what it wants, . . . demands its rights," and "desires to separate," social cohesion, insofar as it exists, is dependent on contracts between calculating individuals rather than on mutual love.[35]

Since 1789 French liberalism had given ample proof of its loyalty to the bourgeois economic order. It was the liberals who ruthlessly defended the sanctity of private property against the Babouvists in 1796, and against the socialists and workers of Paris during the "June Days" of 1848 and the Commune of 1870. Dostoyevsky thought it abundantly clear that "no one on earth" was more hostile to the aspirations of the "fourth estate" than the "strict" republicans. In deference to the bourgeoisie, French liberalism had established as its highest goal the mere political form of the republic: "The form is the whole hope of the republic . . . salvation is sought in the form. . . . Most positively there dwells in every French republican the fatal conviction, dooming him, that the word "republican" suffices; that to call the country "a republic" suffices to make it happy—at once and forever."[36]

The vision of social order entertained by the French liberals was, in fact, identical in substance to that most bourgeois of all regimes, the "July monarchy" of Louis Philippe (1830-1848), with the sole difference that it was called a "republic" and there was "no king (i.e. of course, a 'tyrant')."[37] Symptomatic of this exclusive emphasis on the formal realization of the Geneva idea was the inordinate love of eloquence characteristic of French liberals. All those orations in the National Assembly, the Convention, and the clubhouses during the Revolution may have been utterly sincere, but by the middle of the nineteenth century French liberalism had degenerated into a love of eloquence for eloquence's sake. The tendency of the liberals to become comic figures was nowhere more pronounced than in their love of eloquence. This was particularly so when they were out of power:

the legislative body maintains six liberal deputies, six permanent, irremovable, genuine liberal deputies. . . . There shall be no more of them, you can rest assured; nor shall there be fewer. . . . Naturally, all necessary measures are taken to prevent them from talking too much. But they are allowed to chatter a little. Annually, at a set time, they discuss urgent questions facing the government, and the Parisian fairly melts with rapture. He knows that there will be eloquence and he is happy. Of course he knows very well that it will be eloquence and nothing more, that there will be words, words, and more words, and that nothing whatever will come of these words. But even so he is highly pleased. . . .[38]

---

35 WNSI, pp. 110-11 (6).
36 DW, pp. 737, 254, 815 (May-June 1877; March 1876; Sept. 1877).
37 Ibid., p. 737 (May-June 1877).
38 WNSI, pp. 135, 126-29 (7). The most outstanding embodiment of French liberal eloquence was apparently Lamartine: "Ce n'est pas l'homme, c'est une lyre." UD, II, p. 119.

Dostoyevsky predicted that the bourgeoisie would eventually recognize that they had nothing to fear from the republic. The situation of the Third Republic was precarious indeed; but it would probably survive because the bourgeoisie had finally acknowledged French liberalism as a natural ally. The liberals clearly craved such an acknowledgment. The Third Republic, after all, had been erected on the corpses of the Paris communards.[39]

To Dostoyevsky it was clear by the latter part of the nineteenth century that the "nation of genius" had failed to realize its own new word to humanity. France's attempt to embody a new social order based on the Geneva idea had proven "groundless," had "burst like a soap bubble." The only promise uttered during the Revolution which had been fulfilled was that of the Abbott Sieyès: "What is the third estate? Nothing. What ought it to be? Everything."[40] The impressive outward show of order which France presented to the world was the expression, not of a unanimous adherence to an idea of social order, but of the successful domination of one social class.[41] With the complete triumph of the bourgeoisie over the Geneva idea, France had apparently said all it had to say to the West. Of all the hope, devotion, and energy inspired by the Geneva vision in France, apparently the only thing left was "the bourgeois liberal with his immortal principles of '89. Meagre sustenance."[42] As an idea of social order, bourgeois liberalism was perhaps "meagre" indeed: its emphasis on individual rights seemed to preclude a truly cohesive society, and it was, moreover, inseparably associated with the triumph of one part of the French people over the rest. Dostoyevsky, however, does not exclude the possibility that French liberalism might prove adequate to save France from the perpetual state of disunity threatening it. Also, he does not exclude the possibility that bourgeois liberalism could serve to unite the West as a whole, for his scrutiny of the other major peoples of the West was to leave him convinced that the Geneva idea had nowhere been perfectly realized, and that nowhere had an alternative idea of order been effectively spoken.

Dostoyevsky thought that the most serious rivals to France's claim to the leadership of the modern West were the English-speaking nations and Germany.

39 *UD*, II, p. 90.
40 *WNSI*, p. 109 (6); *UD*, III, p. 82.
41 Despite the epoch of revolution, imperial wars, and final defeat through which France had lived, it maintained throughout the nineteenth century an appearance of self-confident unity which Dostoyevsky found impressive, and sometimes oppressive. Corresponding to the external regimentation imposed by the state, Dostoyevsky perceived what seemed to be a tremendous inner conformity emanating "from the very soul" of the French people. Paris in particular exuded an impressive sense of unanimity and stability: "What orderliness! What prudence; what well-defined and solidly established relationships; how secure and perfectly delimited everything is; how content everyone is..." *WNSI*, pp. 126, 88, 87 (7,5).
42 *UD*, III, p. 147.

The English-Speaking World:
England and the United States

The Russian capacity for entering into the spirit of alien peoples, on which Russian Westernism prided itself, was faced with a formidable challenge in the English. Versilov is able to be a Frenchman in France, a German in Germany, and even a Hellene in ancient Greece, but he makes no claim to be an Englishman in England.[43] Despite its eminent role in the development of the modern West, England's influence on Russian Westernism was slight compared with that of France or Germany. In *The Gambler* Dostoyevsky has a Russian offer an Englishman a partial explanation of this relative lack of influence: "Much to your displeasure I must own that Englishmen for the most part are angular and inelegant, and Russians are very sensitive to beauty and have a taste for it." The Russian, however, does observe that the Englishman's inelegance may very well conceal "originality of character," and even "beauty of soul."[44] Dostoyevsky was, indeed, impressed by the obstinate "originality" of the English character. He thought that it is precisely this originality or eccentricity which makes the English so inaccessible to Russians and to other Western peoples.

Dostoyevsky, however, is not content to subscribe entirely to the common Russian opinion, learned from French vaudevilles, that an Englishman must simply be regarded as a "queer fellow" and an "eccentric":

But what is a queer fellow?—He is not always a fool or so naive that he cannot guess that not everywhere in the world are things run in the same way as somewhere at home, in his own corner. On the contrary, Englishmen are a level-headed nation with broad views. As navigators—and besides, enlightened ones—they have seen a great many people and customs in all countries of the world. They are extraordinary and gifted observers.[45]

Dostoyevsky maintains that the eccentricity for which the English are notorious is not entirely due to an unconscious self-absorption which renders them blithely indifferent to the ways of other peoples. It is also a type of arrogance. English "queerness" stems from a "haughtiness" which refuses to consider the ways of any other people to be on the same level as those of a "son of old England." The chilly, dignified haughtiness of the Englishman has its source in an imperturbable national self-confidence which, for Dostoyevsky, is the most striking feature of the English character: "Thus, in England all Englishmen equally respect themselves, perhaps solely because they are Englishmen. This alone, it would seem, should prove sufficient for a close bond and the people's communion in that country."[46]

Dostoyevsky considered England the most "solid" political entity in Europe; but political stability alone did not account for England's importance

---

43 *The Adolescent*, p. 470 (III,7,iii).
44 *The Gambler*, p. 159 (17).
45 *DW*, p. 889 (Nov. 1877).
46 Ibid., pp. 890, 263-64, 283 (Nov. 1877; March, April 1876); *UD*, II, pp. 143, 160.

in the West. The pre-eminent position occupied by England was due chiefly to the prodigious growth of English commerce and industry in the nineteenth century. In a vivid passage in *Winter Notes on Summer Impressions* Dostoyevsky gives voice to a feeling of awe before the apparently boundless material power which confronted him in the London of 1862:

A city as unfathomable as the ocean, bustling day and night; the screech and roar of machines; railroads passing over the houses (and soon under them too); that boldness of enterprise; that apparent disorder which is actually bourgeois orderliness in the highest degree; that polluted Thames; that air saturated with coal dust; those splendid commons and parks; those terrible sections of the city like Whitechapel with its half-naked, savage, and hungry population. A city with its millions and its world-wide commerce, the Crystal Palace, the International Exposition.... Ah, yes, the Exposition is astonishing. You sense the terrible force which has drawn these people without number from all over the world into a single herd; you become aware of a colossal idea; you sense that here something has been achieved, that here there is victory and triumph. You sense that it would require great and everlasting spiritual denial and fortitude in order not to submit, not to capitulate before the impression, not to bow to what is, and not to deify Baal, that is, not to accept the material world as your ideal....[47]

A confident England spoke, in every corner of the world, with a voice too powerful to be ignored. But could England's social order serve as the basis of a renewed Western civilization? For Dostoyevsky, this is to ask whether English imperialism speaks to humanity by virtue of sheer material power, that is as "Baal," or by virtue of an idea capable of binding people together in a shared vision of their final destiny.

Dostoyevsky regards the "English Parliament" and "Anglo-Saxon law" as the constitutive elements of the English social order.[48] But in neither does he discern an idea of universal scope. What there is of fundamental thought about social order is, for him, to be found in the contending parliamentary factions of Whig and Tory. These parties had been united in rejecting French liberalism, and yet they seemed to offer no alternative for the West as a whole. The traditional order which the Tories wished to preserve was specifically English; while the liberty for which the Whigs struggled seemed to be a liberty appropriate only for Englishmen.[49] Dostoyevsky claims, furthermore, that the "liberties of Englishmen" do not even apply to all Englishmen, for

47 *WNSI*, pp. 90-91 (5). During his first trip to Europe in 1862, Dostoyevsky spent a week in London. Here, at the World Exhibition of 1862, he saw the Crystal Palace (built for the Exhibition of 1851), which was to become such an important symbol in *Notes from Underground*. He also visited Herzen several times, and apparently met with Bakunin. See L. Grossman, *Dostoevsky* (London, 1974), pp. 265-69.
48 England is almost always associated in Dostoyevsky's writing with the parliamentary tradition. See, for instance, *The Idiot*, p. 410 (III,4); *BK*, p. 854 (XII,9); *DW*, pp. 889-90 (Nov. 1877). For a reference to "Anglo-Saxon law" as the basis of English social order, as "Democracy or... formal equality" is of the "French (Romance) world," see *NP*, p. 225.
49 See, for instance, *DW*, p. 576 (Jan. 1877).

the conflict between Whigs and Tories is conducted on the basis of a fundamental consensus which actually excludes a large part of the English people
from genuine membership in English society.[50] According to Dostoyevsky,
the solid English unity is, in fact, a unity of the upper-class minority inspired
by a fear of the new social phenomenon which English industry had
engendered—the proletariat. The "parliamentary procedure of a free
people"—England's pride and the envy of other peoples[51]—does not represent the whole truth about English order. Dostoyevsky bears witness to the
less edifying underside of modern England's political and economic success:

In London you behold throngs of such dimensions and in such surroundings as you
will see nowhere else in the world. . . . [O]n Saturday night a half-million workers,
male and female, together with their children, flood the city like a sea, flocking
especially in certain sections, and celebrate the Sabbath all night until five in the
morning; that is, they stuff themselves and drink like animals, enough to last the
week. This disposes of the week's savings, of all that was earned with sweat and
malediction. . . . They all race against time to drink themselves insensate. The
wives do not lag behind their husbands but get drunk with them; the children run
and crawl about among them. . . . The people are everywhere the people, but here
everything was so colossal, so dazzling, that you seemed to be actually touching
what you had previously been able only to imagine. Here, in fact, you do not see a
people, but rather, a systematic, submissive, fostered loss of consciousness. And
you sense, as you behold these pariahs of society, that for a long time to come the
prophecy will not come to pass for them, that for a long time to come they will be
given neither palm branches nor white robes, and that for a long time yet they will
appeal to the throne of the Most High, "How long, oh Lord!". . . These millions
of beings, abandoned, expelled from the human feast, shoving and crushing each
other in the subterranean darkness into which their elder brothers have pushed
them, grope for any gate at all to knock at, and seek an exit in order not to be
smothered in the dark underground.[52]

In Dostoyevsky's view, England was actually made up of two different
peoples. The parliamentary and legal institutions had become the instruments
by which the lower class was prevented from discovering an exit out of the
"subterranean darkness." He did acknowledge the efforts of the best
Englishmen to alleviate the gulf between the two peoples. Yet England had
produced a Malthus, as well as a Dickens.[53]

50 See, for instance, Governor von Lembke's proposition to Peter Verkhovensky in *The De-*
    vils, p. 319 (II,4,iii).
51 For instance, the "pugilist," Keller, in *The Idiot*: "You know, I love reading in the pa-
    pers about the English Parliament. I—I don't mean what they're discussing there (I'm af-
    raid I'm no politician), but the way they talk to each other, the way they behave like
    politicians: 'the noble viscount sitting opposite,' 'the noble earl who shares my opinion,'
    'my honourable opponent who has astonished Europe by his proposal'—I mean, all those
    flowery expressions, all this parliamentary procedure of a free people; that's what's so
    fascinating to a chap like me!" (p. 410 [III,4]).
52 *WNSI*, pp. 92-94 (6).
53 See Dostoyevsky's letter of 1 Jan. 1868; *DW*, pp. 75, 82, 350 (1873; June 1876); *The
    Adolescent*, p. 439 (III, 5, iii); *NRY*, p. 295; *UD*, I, p. 50, II, p. 84, III, p. 60.

The question of social order in England, as in France, was for Dostoyevsky tied to the emergence of the bourgeoisie as the dominant class. English order was, above all, bourgeois order. The solid unity of "old England" was a unity having its source in the dominance of one part of the English people over their countrymen, a dominance which was only reinforced by the prevailing form of English Christianity. The "state Anglican religion" appeared to Dostoyevsky to provide no alternative to the bourgeois order: "It is the religion of the wealthy, and openly so."[54] England thus lacked an idea which could guarantee the ultimate solidarity of its own people, let alone the West as a whole.

Dostoyevsky does not explicitly concur with Herzen's characterization of the United States as a cruder version of English civilization. The existence of an Anglo-American civilization was, however, assumed among Russians, and Dostoyevsky's assessment of the American role in the future of the West tends to reflect his view of England's possibilities.

The United States was, according to him, the only nation in the West other than England which had achieved a solid and durable political organization, if at the price of a civil war.[55] Although he said very little about American civilization, he seemed to think that "Americanism" would be a predominant force in the West, eclipsing even the material power embodied in London.[56] He alludes often in his writings to the attraction which the bare thought of America held for uprooted Russians. For those cut off from the living life of an integrated social order, America signified a fresh, vigorous, renewed life.[57]

Yet Dostoyevsky thought that Americanism, despite its impending success, would not breathe new life into Western civilization. With reference to the United States he reiterates his teaching that "the development of a people and its future life is determined only by what this people believes in, what it considers an ideal of good and truth." Such an idea may have been present at the origin of the "Northamerican States"; but the original "spirit" had rapidly disappeared.[58] According to Dostoyevsky, the American liberal idea had early lent itself to the justification of the exploitation of one group by another. For instance, during the American civil war "many most advanced liberals declared themselves to be on the side of the plantation owners on the ground that Negroes were Negroes and inferior to the white race, and therefore that the right of might was the prerogative of white men."[59] The victory of the North

---

54 *DW*, p. 264 (March 1876); *WNSI*, pp. 98-99 (5).
55 *DW*, p. 283 (April 1876). For a reference to the American Civil War, see *NU*, p. 108 (I,7).
56 *UD*, II, p. 71: "Americanism will set in for a short while."
57 *CP*, p. 511 (VI,6); *The Adolescent*, pp. 46, 213 (I,3,iii; II,1,iv); *BK*, pp. 650, 699 (X,6; XI,4).
58 *UD*, II, p. 91.
59 *The Idiot*, p. 329 (II,10). It can be assumed that Radomsky speaks here for Dostoyevsky. See also *WNSI*, p. 63 (3); *CP*, p. 61.

in the war, moreover, had merely established a new form of slavery, that of the worker in the northern factories. By the latter part of the nineteenth century, American liberalism had clearly become the instrument of the commercial and industrial elite. Americanism was thus equivalent to the triumph of the bourgeoisie. The American bourgeoisie, furthermore, enjoyed their dominance without hindrance from the restraints still imposed on their French and English counterparts by the abiding presence of traditions from before the age of modern industry.[60] Dostoyevsky's understanding of Americanism as a massive attempt to organize human beings primarily for material ends,[61] combined with a boundless political self-confidence, is expressed by Captain Lebyadkin (in *The Devils*) in a memorable image: "I read in the papers the biography of an American. He left his huge fortune to factories and to the applied sciences, his skeleton to the students of the academy there, and his skin to be made into a drum with the proviso that the American national anthem might be beaten on it day and night."[62]

Germany

Although the Russians hesitated in the face of English queerness, they manifested no such reluctance to enter into the life of that other "great, proud, and peculiar people"—the Germans.[63] The attitude of Russian Westernism towards the German people was that attitude of reverence which the pupil feels for the teacher, for, as Stepan Verkhovensky observed, the Germans had been the teachers of the Russians for two hundred years. Indeed, in the middle of the nineteenth century Russian Westernism was still "at school, at some German *Peterschule*, sitting over a German book and repeating its everlasting German lesson." Dostoyevsky makes it clear that Stepan Verkhovensky and Versilov imbibed much of their liberal idealism in Germany.[64] The close association of education with the Germans in his writing reflects the common Russian perception of Germany as a land inhabited largely by professors. His own respect for the intellect of the people which produced Kant, Schiller, and Hegel was immense.

The respect of the student for the teacher was not, according to Dostoyevsky, incompatible with a pronounced inclination among Russians to be critical of, and even "heartily dislike," the Germans. In a letter to his niece from Germany, he himself expresses the suspicion that there may be something "limited" about the Germans, even though they are doubtless the most

---

60 See *The Devils*, p. 148 (I,4,iv); *BK*, p. 899 (XIII,2).
61 In Dostoyevsky's writing "America" possesses the same symbolic value as "railroads" or "bread." See, for instance, *NP*, p. 387.
62 *The Devils*, p. 270 (II,2,ii).
63 *DW*, p. 729 (May-June 1877).
64 *The Devils*, pp. 23-25, 303 (I,1,i; II,4,i); *The Adolescent*, p. 475 (III,8,i); *BK*, p. 652 (X,6); *DW*, pp. 221, 394 (Feb., July-Aug. 1876); *UD*, II, pp. 73, 84, III, p. 160.

"scholarly" of peoples.[65] In *The Diary of a Writer*, however, he suggests that this suspicion, shared by other peoples, may be mistaken:

As regards German wit and German apprehension... there exist several opinions. The French, who... never liked the Germans, always have considered, and now regard, the German mind as being a bit tight but, of course, by no means blunt. They perceive in the German intellect, as it were, some inclination to avoid always the straight issue in everything, and, on the contrary,... to make out of a single proposition something bisyllabic, biarticulate. Among us, Russians, there has always circulated a great number of anecdotes about the tightness and dullness of the Germans, notwithstanding all our sincere admiration of their learnedness. But it seems to me that the Germans merely possess too strong a distinctiveness, too obstinate a national peculiarity, to the degree of haughtiness, which, at times, makes one indignant, and which, for this reason, leads to erroneous conclusions regarding them. However, at first, on a foreigner—especially if he is a newcomer to Germany—the German, in truth, sometimes produces a strange impression in social intercourse.[66]

Dostoyevsky delights in relating anecdotes which illustrate the obstinate "national peculiarity" of the Germans. However, the distinctiveness of the German people, whatever its effect on other peoples, is in his view expressive of a genuine national character which has "grown organically."[67] The German people thus possess that profound sense of nation so conspicuously absent among uprooted Russians. Because of their deeply rooted national self-confidence, the Germans, like the English, do not exude a very great modesty; they too are not averse to contemplating their own image in a mirror. What expresses itself as haughtiness in the English tends in the Germans to take the more vulgar form of boastfulness, an "unbecoming" and "surprising" trait of the German people.[68]

Although he refers to an inherent tendency towards self-complacency and "petty bragging" in the German character, Dostoyevsky considered German arrogance too important a phenomenon to be reduced to a mere question of character traits. His fascinated observation of the German people yielded a more significant explanation of their aggressive self-confidence. This explanation is concerned most immediately with the implications of the Franco-German war. While in Dresden in 1870, he witnessed the mobilization and departure of the Saxon troops for the front and was impressed by what he saw:

what vigour in those faces, what a serene, cheerful and, at the same time, grave expression in their eyes! They were all young men and, when looking at some company marching, it was impossible not to admire their wonderful military drill, their orderly step, their rigidly punctilious alignment, and, at the same time, the remarkable freedom which I had never before observed in a soldier... these Ger-

---

65 *DW*, p. 221 (Feb. 1876); letter of 30 Dec. 1870.
66 *DW*, p. 394 (July-Aug. 1876).
67 "with them, things have grown organically from their national character." *NP*,
      pp. 212, 214.
68 *UD*, III, pp. 69, 74; *DW*, pp. 457, 375, 732 (Sept., July-Aug. 1876; May-June 1877).

mans marched without being driven with a rod—as one man, with perfect resoluteness and full certitude in victory.

Dostoyevsky confesses to having felt afraid for the French, though he was then certain that they would defeat the Germans. Upon the return of the victorious German troops shortly thereafter, the inhabitants of Dresden became "drunk" with their success.[69] Dostoyevsky was apparently most shocked by the manner in which scholarly Germany was taken up into the "raging chorus" of German nationalism. In a letter written to his niece from Dresden during the siege of Paris he reports:

By far the greatest excitement and pride exists among the professors, doctors, and students... the professors are extraordinarily arrogant. I encounter them every evening in the public library. A very influential scholar with silver-white hair loudly exclaimed, the day before yesterday, "Paris must be bombarded!" So that's the outcome of all their learning.[70]

The frenzy of self-congratulation which erupted in Germany in the aftermath of the war with France was not simply the natural after-flush of a stunning military triumph.[71] The war was also a prodigious political event for the German people. Through it the political unification of Germany was achieved. At Versailles a humiliated France bowed, not only to Prussia, but to the newly emergent German Empire. The Germans had long possessed "economic prosperity, civilization, science"; but until 1870 they had lacked political unity. The relative lateness of Germany's organization into a political unit thus rendered German nationalism more aggressive than that of Western peoples who had long taken their political self-articulation for granted.[72]

The stridency of German nationalism also owed much to the manner in which Germany achieved political unification. In 1864, two years before the battle of Sadowa and six before Sedan, Dostoyevsky predicted that Prussia would "assemble Germany by force."[73] He continued, after the fulfillment of this prediction, to regard the German state as something "unnatural" and "forced," despite its apparent inevitability. Although Bismarck's reliance on "blood and iron" was doubtless effective, the political unity thus achieved was a "mechanical" and merely external unity. Dostoyevsky doubted the durability of a state which owed so much to military triumphs:

That which today may seem durable is, maybe, nothing but a fantasy... the present generation of the Germans has been bribed with successes; it is intoxicated

69 DW, pp. 374-75 (July-Aug. 1876).
70 Letter of 30 Dec. 1870; DW, p. 667 (April 1877).
71 Dostoyevsky, however, takes this factor into consideration: "A people who have rarely been vanquishers but who have been so strangely often vanquished,—that people unexpectedly... conquered an enemy who nearly always conquered everybody!... the Germans could not help but grow proud to the point of intoxication." DW, p. 732 (May-June 1877).
72 DE, p. 166; DW, p. 283 (April 1876); UD, II, p. 74.
73 UD, I, p. 127.

with pride, and is restrained by the iron hand of its leaders. Still, perhaps in the not distant future, when these leaders pass into another world, ceding their place to other men, the questions and instincts which have temporarily been suppressed will be brought to the foreground. It is also quite probable that the energy of the initial impulse of the consolidation will be exhausted, and, instead, the oppositional energy will again be restored, and that it will undermine that which has been accomplished.[74]

The fear, only half-acknowledged and yet hauntingly persistent, of political dissolution enhanced immeasurably the vehemence of German nationalism.

While pointing to the unnatural character of the modern German state, Dostoyevsky nonetheless affirms the complete naturalness of the yearning which brought it into being. He maintains that the ostentatious nationalism of modern Germany is the most recent manifestation of a conviction deeply rooted in the history of the German people. Germans have for centuries believed that they are destined to speak the final word of social order to the West:

Throughout his whole history [the German] has been dreaming of, and thirsting for, his unification, for the proclamation of his proud idea. . . . The German is already fully convinced of his triumph and that no one can assume his place at the head of the world and of its renaissance. He believes in this haughtily and undeviatingly; he believes that there is nothing on earth higher than his spirit and his word, and that only Germany can utter it.[75]

The Germans had persistently sought the political unification which their mission seemed to presuppose. Well before 1870 they would gladly have agreed to exchange "half of their scientific fame" for that political unity long ago achieved by England and Russia.[76] The instinctive groping for a political foundation from which to speak the German word to humanity finally eventuated in the German Empire of Bismarck. The lateness and unnaturalness of Bismarck's state did not alter the fact that the German people had long felt summoned to unify the West according to a new idea of order. Indeed, the Germans felt the obligation of this summons as intensely as the French, and perhaps more intensely than the English-speaking peoples.[77] For Dostoyevsky, however, the content of Germany's vision of order was less definite than its desire to transmit this vision to the West.

There would be ample reason to conjecture that the German conception of order is closely related to the Geneva idea. Modern German nationalism first emerged decisively in opposition to French imperialism, but it derived much of its theoretical justification and practical efficacy from the "new form

---

74 *NRY*, p. 230; *DW*, pp. 731-33 (May-June 1877). Dostoyevsky also refers to the "illusory solidity" of Germany in *UD*, II, p. 71; and he observes that the image of the "colossus with feet of clay" may be applicable to the new German colossus, in *DE*, p. 129.

75 *DW*, p. 564 (Jan. 1877).

76 Ibid., pp. 283, 731 (April 1876; May-June 1877).

77 Dostoyevsky thought that the English, more than the other great peoples of the West, tend to live within themselves. *UD*, III, p. 47.

of democracy" which France fostered throughout the West. The intellectuals and politicians who attempted to rally the German people against Napoleon found inspiration in the notion of "the self-determination of a free people." Moreover, the Prussian state which defeated Napoleon at Leipzig had modelled itself after the rationalized French liberal state; and, in general, Napoleon's reorganization of the chaotic patch-work of German kingdoms, duchies, and principalities was indispensable to the political realization of German nationalism. The consolidation of German political unity in 1870 thus owed much to French liberalism.

Liberal idealism enjoyed a practical success in France only insofar as it became bourgeois liberalism, and was thereby able to enlist the support of the dominant social class. Napoleon's policies had greatly furthered the ascent of the German middle class to economic dominance. Throughout the nineteenth century it gradually achieved a social recognition consonant with its economic mastery, and within the new German nation-state it was granted a glimpse of the political influence it was to wield with more confidence after the turn of the century. Dostoyevsky considered the middle class so important in modern Germany that he tended to cast the German people as a whole in its image. There is a certain ambivalence in his depiction of the German bourgeois. By way of contrast with the incapacity of uprooted Russians for sustained work, he praises the capacity of the German bourgeois for sustained, methodical effort towards the achievement of a definite goal.[78] Yet at the same time he professes amusement and consternation at this capacity (in the words of Alexey in *The Gambler*):

everywhere among these people every house has its *Vater*, dreadfully virtuous and exceedingly honest. So honest, in fact, that it's terrible to go near him. Every one of these *Vaters* has a family, and in the evening they all read improving books aloud to one another. The elms and chestnut trees rustle above the little cottage. There is the sunset, and a stork on the roof, and everything is extremely touching and poetic.

Suppose the *Vater* has already got together a few gulden, and is counting on handing over his trade or his bit of land to the eldest son; to this end the daughter is not given a dowry and remains an old maid. To this end also the younger son is sold into bondage or the army, and the money is added to the capital of the household. . . . It is all done out of nothing but honesty . . . things are no easier even for the elder son; he has his Amalchen, with whom his heart is united—but they can't get married because not enough money has been scraped together yet. They wait virtuously, and, smiling in all sincerity, they too go like lambs to the slaughter. Amalchen's cheeks are sunken, she is growing withered. At last, after about twenty years, the fortune has increased; the gulden have been honestly and virtuously amassed. The *Vater* gives his blessing to the forty-year-old son and the thirty-five-year-old Amalchen, with her withered breasts and her red nose. . . . Thereupon he weeps, moralizes, and dies. The elder son is now transformed into a *Vater* and the whole story begins all over again . . . and after some five or six more generations

---

78 Dostoyevsky illustrates the German capacity for work with lengthy anecdotes drawn from his own experiences in Germany. See, for instance, *DW*, pp. 391-95 (July-Aug. 1876).

there emerges Baron Rothschild himself, or Hoppe and Co., or the devil knows who. Well, sir, what a majestic spectacle! a century or two's continuous labour, patience, intelligence, honesty, strength of character, steadfastness, foresight, and storks on the roof! What more can you want?[79]

Germany's evolution into a bourgeois liberal state seemed probable in light of the strong presence of the bourgeoisie, and of a liberal thought eager for practical effect and at least partially willing to accommodate itself to bourgeois aspirations.

Dostoyevsky, however, discerned something in the German middle class which distinguished it from that of France, England, or the United States. This difference was for him extremely significant, though its nature was obscure. It was expressed most clearly in the unusual docility of the German middle class.[80] Unlike its French or Anglo-American equivalents, the German bourgeoisie appeared willing to limit its dominance for the sake of an obedience not always in accord with its most obvious aspirations. Rather than adopt liberalism for its own ends, the German bourgeoisie had maintained a definite distance from it, in deference to a different vision of order. German intellectuals may have been enthralled by "freedom, equality, and brotherhood," but the German middle class tended to pay homage elsewhere.

The object of this homage eluded Dostoyevsky's precise definition. However, the task of understanding the content of Germany's vision was, for him, obviously imperative. The emergence of Germany as the most powerful state on the European continent, consequent upon its victory over France, had made it a likely arbiter of Western civilization.[81] In a letter written to his niece from Germany, just prior to the final capitulation of France, Dostoyevsky declares that now "the Germans will at last show us their real faces."[82] If this face was not to be that of the bourgeois liberal, to whom would it belong? He did not find an adequate answer to this question in the still commanding presence of the Prussian *Junker*, nor did he think it was contained in Lutheranism. Other than a terse, inconclusive reference to "paganism" in modern Germany,[83] he offers no positive indication of the uniquely German idea of order. Indeed, he indicates that the idea animating the German people may be, in essence, a negation. In *The Devils* he translates the Franco-German rivalry in modern Europe into a musical analogy in which the initially self-assured melody of the *Marseillaise* is gradually overcome by the increasingly authoritative strains of *Mein lieber Augustin*:

> It began with the menacing strains of the *Marseillaise*:
> Qu'un sang impur abreuve nos sillons!

---

79 *The Gambler*, pp. 41-42 (4).
80 *BK*, pp. 651-52 (X,6); *OW*, p. 34.
81 Dostoyevsky seems to have thought it possible that the entire European continent would eventually come under German hegemony. *UD*, III, p. 80; *DW*, p. 912 (Nov. 1877).
82 Letter of 17 Aug. 1870.
83 *UD*, III, p. 12.

A flamboyant challenge was heard, the flush of future victories. But suddenly, mingling with the masterly variations on the national anthem—somewhere on one side, from below, from some corner, but very close, came the trivial strains of *Mein lieber Augustin*. The *Marseillaise* ignored them; the *Marseillaise* reached the climax of intoxication with its own grandeur; but *Augustin* was gaining strength, it was getting more and more insolent, and suddenly the strains of *Augustin* began to blend with the strains of the *Marseillaise*. The latter was apparently getting angry; unable to ignore *Augustin* any longer, it tried to shake it off, to brush it off, like some obtrusive, insignificant fly, but *Mein lieber Augustin* was hanging on firmly; he was gay and self-confident, he was full of joy and arrogance, and the *Marseillaise* suddenly somehow became terribly stupid: it could no longer conceal its resentment and exasperation; it was a wail of indignation, tears, and oaths with arms outstretched to Providence:

> *Pas un pouce de notre terrain, pas une de nos fortresses.*

But already it was forced to sing in time with *Mein lieber Augustin*. Its melody passed in a most stupid way into that of *Augustin*, it drooped and died. Only from time to time could a snatch of the original tune be heard: *qu'un sang impur . . .* but immediately they passed most mortifyingly into the horrible waltz. Finally, it was utterly subdued: it was Jules Favre sobbing on Bismarck's bosom and giving away everything, everything. . . . But now it was *Augustin's* turn to assert himself: hoarse sounds were heard, one had a feeling of countless barrels of beer, the frenzy of self-glorification, demands for milliards, expensive cigars, champagne and hostages; *Augustin* passed into a wild roar.

Dostoyevsky intimates that the "wild roar" in which *Mein lieber Augustin* culminates may express no idea other than "long live German pride."[84]

Dostoyevsky thought it no accident that the national day of the new German state commemorated the victory over France at Sedan. For modern Germany seemed to be animated chiefly by a "terrible animosity" towards France. Bismarck would have reduced France to a "nonentity" if it had been within his power to destroy Paris and transfer the ownership of French land to Germans. As it is, he was prepared to attack France again at a moment's notice.[85] For Dostoyevsky this animosity is not only "terrible" but also "significant." It is so significant that it cannot be restricted to Bismarck and the nineteenth century, but must be perceived as a fundamental constituent of the German spirit throughout its history. The German animosity towards France is, moreover, too significant to be reduced to talk of a racial enmity between German and Gaul. Dostoyevsky maintains, rather, that Germany has tended to reject, not France itself, but those ideas of social order—first Roman Catholic and then Genevan—which France has striven to embody. Thus Bismarck's attack on Roman Catholicism within Germany (the *Kulturkampf*),

---

84 *The Devils*, pp. 326-27 (II,5,i); *UD*, II, p. 71.
85 *UD*, III, pp. 114, 170; II, p. 41. Dostoyevsky thought that France's rapid material recovery after the Franco-German war was a source of great anxiety for Bismarck. He considered it very possible that Bismarck would, on the slightest pretext, scotch the French desire for a war of *revanche* before France became strong enough to wage it. See *DW*, pp. 565, 732-34 (Jan., May-June 1877).

otherwise inexplicable, could be understood as the latest manifestation of Germany's traditional denial of French visions of order. In Dostoyevsky's view, the modern Franco-German rivalry is "a battle of two civilizations very different from each other," a battle which the war of 1870 had failed to resolve decisively.[86] The word which Germany was preparing to speak to the West from its new position of power would clearly constitute a radical rejection of the liberal idea. But the positive content, if any, of its own vision of universal union remained shrouded in darkness.

Towards a New World Order

Bourgeois Liberal Democracy

From his scrutiny of the Western peoples Dostoyevsky concluded that, despite its apparent fragmentation, the West is indeed moving towards a new unity, towards an embodiment of a new "formula of the union of men upon the earth."[87] The possibility of this union resides in the two crucial circumstances of the modern West: the emergence of the bourgeoisie everywhere as the dominant social class, and the intellectual hegemony of the liberal idea of order. The amalgam of these two sovereign facts of modern Western life gives rise to the social formula of "bourgeois liberal democracy." In this formula the West seeks the restoration of its lost unity, and ultimately the unity of all humanity. The "bourgeois social form" embodied so eloquently in France is now beginning to reign "throughout the world in eternal imitation of the great nation."[88]

Whatever the particular form of the various Western regimes, the trend towards democracy, or universal suffrage, is unmistakable. And whatever the particular version of bourgeois liberalism which animates these democracies, the modification of the Geneva idea is fundamentally the same.[89] Freedom is indissolubly associated, not with moral striving, but with the satisfaction of needs. The right of individual freedom is the right to "the multiplication and the rapid satisfaction of needs"; and people are encouraged in their natural tendency to interpret need in material terms. Capitalist liberalism seeks social cohesion on the basis of the universal extension of the right to material satisfaction: "Selfishness displaces the old unifying principle, and the whole

86 *DE*, pp. 167-68.
87 *PS*, p. 88.
88 *WNSI*, p. 141 (8).
89 For Dostoyevsky, as we have seen, Germany does not quite come within the rubric of bourgeois liberal democracy; and insofar as it rejects this new formula of social order, its place in the West poses a grave problem. Dostoyevsky does not doubt that Germany is a Western nation which, moreover, aspires to hegemony over the entire West. Nevertheless, its reluctance to accept the new social formula being realized in France, Britain, and the United States leads him to make an important distinction within the West. He distinguishes between the "outermost Western world" of the great liberal democracies, and the Germanic world. (See, for instance, *DW*, p. 730 [May-June 1877]).

system breaks up into a multitude of individuals, each with a full set of civil rights.'' This all-encompassing extension of individual rights is the pre-requisite of a social order in which "everything is settled by agreement," that is, a contractual social order.[90] The durability of the fundamental social contract, according to an apologist in *The Idiot*, is guaranteed by "the universal necessity of living, eating, and drinking," which can never be adequately satisfied without some degree of "association" and "solidarity of interests."[91] This appeal to material self-interest may be an appeal to sheer "piggishness"; yet bourgeois liberal democracy, founded on a "realistic" appraisal of human beings, claims to be the only hope for a workable social order in a world ruled by the "individualist instinct."[92]

Dostoyevsky could discern in the coming order of "the rights of man" nothing more elevated than the "bourgeois solution to the problem of comfort."[93] He maintained that capitalist liberalism will go to some lengths, however, to conceal the aridity of its contractualism with an attractive décor. While it assumes a relatively honest appearance in Americanism, in French liberalism it adopts a façade of elegance, and even nobility. The French bourgeoisie proclaim openly that "money is the highest virtue and human obligation," and yet they love "to toy with nobility of character." The longing of the French bourgeoisie for an aura of "ineffable nobility," which would not impede them from amassing capital, inspired melodrama, that incomparable contribution of France to the bourgeois world order:

vaudeville, though it attracts the bourgeois, does not satisfy him fully.... He needs something lofty, he needs ineffable nobility, he needs emotion, and melodrama contains all of these.... Melodrama will not die as long as the bourgeois lives.... The bourgeois takes great pleasure in lecturing himself and his [wife] at every opportunity, and even considers this a most sacred and pressing duty....

The melodrama contains lofty characters and lofty sermons. Here there is no humour; it is rather the pathetic triumph of all that [the bourgeois] admires. What he likes most is political tranquillity and the right to amass money for the building of a more placid home. And this is the spirit in which melodramas are written nowadays.[94]

90 *UD*, III, p. 160; *BK*, p. 369 (VI,3); *The Adolescent*, p. 217 (II,2,ii); *The Idiot*, p. 232 (II,2). See also *DW*: "Oh , it goes without saying that man always, at all times... has been inclined to perceive and understand liberty only in the sense of making his life secure through money hoarded by the exertion of every effort and accumulated by all possible means. However, at no time in the past have these tendencies been raised so cynically and so obviously to the level of a sublime principle as in our Nineteenth Century. 'Everybody for himself, and only for himself, and every intercourse with man solely for one's self'—such is the ethical tenet of the majority of present-day people, even not bad people, but, on the contrary, labouring people who neither murder nor steal" (p. 649 [March 1877]). Dostoyevsky refers to two other popular liberal social formulae: "*Chacun pour soi et Dieu pour les tous*" and "*Après moi, le déluge*," in *PS*, p. 67.
91 *The Idiot*, pp. 411-12 (III,4).
92 *UD*, II, pp. 5, 7; *WNSI*, p. 114: "the individualist, isolationist instinct which stands aloof and demands its rights with sword in hand."
93 Dostoyevsky uses this phrase in a letter of 18 Feb. 1868 to Apollon Maykov.
94 *WNSI*, pp. 146-47 (6). Dostoyevsky focuses particularly on the role of melodrama in endowing marriage with a sacrosanct and "ineffably noble" character, for he thought that

Dostoyevsky thought that the wedding of the awesome material power called forth by capitalism with the doctrine of the "rights of man" would elicit the allegiance, or at least the acquiescence, of an ever greater portion of humanity. The adornment of Anglo-American "knowhow" with French "moral order," and even "ineffable nobility," must surely prove irresistible. More than a century of the dynamic economic activity of the middle class had laid the material foundations of a new universal civilization. The railway and the telegraph—"the reduction of distances and the transmission of ideas through the air," in Father Zosima's words—and, above all, the stock exchange are for Dostoyevsky "artistic expressions" of the movement towards a universal bourgeois civilization.[95] Bourgeois liberal democracy may succeed where the Roman Catholic order finally failed, for as never before the world appears to be "getting more and more united and growing into a brotherly community" through "commerce, maritime navigation, markets, factories," and the principle of the "rights of man." Material necessity and individual egoism may thus eventually prove to be the solid, if unedifying, cornerstones of a new, unified Western civilization. The bourgeoisie, no longer compelled to persuade the West that they are the incarnation of human perfection, are now able to "pose tranquilly and majestically before the entire world."[96]

Yet although bourgeois liberal democracy is "terrifically cocksure," it is at the same time permeated with fear and self-doubt. Dostoyevsky thought that there was ample reason for capitalist liberalism to be perennially ill at ease and "afraid of something," for while on the verge of its conclusive triumph, the bourgeois world order was becoming increasingly overcast with "dark clouds."[97] He attributed responsibility for the darkness hovering over Western civilization to two fundamental shortcomings within liberal democracy itself.

First, liberal democracy had failed to tame the divisive nationalism to which it made such an important contribution in the nineteenth century. The notion of the universal realization of the "rights of man" was proving less potent in the modern West than the kindred notion of the collective right of peoples to determine their own destiny. And these two notions showed themselves to be far less compatible than liberal theory had assumed. The increasing fragmentation being brought about by liberal nationalism in practice was

in actuality marriage in France had become little more than a "wedding of assets" (ibid., p. 139 [8]). For his corrosively satirical and highly amusing account of marriage in bourgeois France, and indeed of the entire attempt of the French bourgeoisie to conceal its "craving for personal material welfare" (DW, p. 650 [March, 1877]) with a noble façade, see the chapters entitled "Bribri and Ma Biche" and "Essay on the Bourgeoisie" in WNSI. These chapters establish Dostoyevsky as perhaps the foremost pre-1917 Russian critic of Western middle-class mores.

95 The Idiot, p. 413 (III,4); DW, pp. 664, 670 (April 1877); BK, p. 369 (VI,3).
96 BK, p. 369 (VI,3); DW, p. 601 (Feb. 1877); The Idiot, p. 411 (III,4); WNSI, p. 117 (6).
97 WNSI, pp. 87, 90, 100, 102, 116-17, 124 (5,6,7); DW, p. 782 (July-Aug. 1877); UD, II, p. 160.

exacerbated by the apparent emptiness of the promise of world-wide community contained in the dynamic economic activity of the bourgeoisie. To Dostoyevsky it was increasingly apparent, by the latter part of the nineteenth
century, that the West's commercial and industrial activity entailed, instead, a
divisive economic imperialism which could very easily plunge the world into
conflicts of immense magnitude "for the sake of some trivial stock-exchange
interests. . . ."[98] The agents of future world union, the railway and the stock
exchange, had become the instruments of an intense rivalry among the
capitalists of the Western nation-states. Having manifested itself already in the
scramble for markets and raw materials in the non-Western world, this rivalry
must inevitably erupt with violence in Europe itself. The Franco-German war,
moreover, had disrupted the tenuous concord which, with minor exceptions,
had been maintained among the European powers since the Vienna Settlement
of 1815. The bewildering array of alliances forged in Europe after 1870 had
failed to restore the balance of power, and had actually heightened the international tension. Writing in *The Diary of a Writer* in 1881, Dostoyevsky maintains that the "unnatural" political situation prevailing in the West will culminate in war:

huge, final, disintegrating political war, in which all powers will have a share, and
which will break out in our century, perhaps even in the coming decade. . . . Do
you rely upon the wisdom of statesmen and upon their refusal to undertake a war?
When was it possible to place any reliance upon that wisdom? Do you put your
trust in Parliaments, and believe that they will foresee the results and refuse the
money for the war? But when have Parliaments foreseen results and refused money
to the slightest insistence of a man in power?[99]

The colossal destruction of war which awaited the West did not bode well for
the "bourgeois solution of the problem of comfort."

    The other great failure of capitalist liberalism is, if possible, even more
significant. It was clear to Dostoyevsky that the offer of equal rights to all
individuals was failing to secure the unanimous acquiescence in the fundamental social contract which liberal democracy presupposes. In *The Idiot* he
has Lebedev observe that railways which bring material goods to satisfy the
needs of humanity, "without a moral basis for that action," may quite deliberately "exclude a considerable part of humanity from the enjoyment of what
they bring."[100] The lower classes were encouraged to multiply and satisfy
their needs; but they were not granted the means of satisfaction. The universal
extension of equal rights was thus arousing the envy and resentment of the
poor rather than securing their acquiescence in the capitalist order. The possession of equal rights in a contractual order is meaningless without the power
to participate effectively in defining and enforcing the terms of the contract.
Those who do have this power, in effect, possess the rest "as a slave."[101] By

98 *DW*, p. 670 (April 1877).
99 *PS*, p. 87.
100 *The Idiot*, p. 413 (III,4).
101 *BK*, p. 369 (VI,3); *PS*, p. 85.

the latter part of the nineteenth century the Western bourgeoisie, fearful of the possibly disastrous consequences of the slaves' resentment, had begun tentatively to move towards the "welfare state," to purchase the tranquillity of the lower orders. But Dostoyevsky doubted that the Western workers would be ultimately appeased by "little concessions." For the moment they seemed content to drown their resentment in drink, but would they not, sooner or later, drown it in blood instead of drink?[102]

Socialism

The resentment of the "fourth estate" in Western industrial society had come to be justified and directed by socialism. Writing in 1881, Dostoyevsky maintained that the potent alliance of the workers' unsatisfied needs with socialism constituted a dire threat to the emerging bourgeois liberal order:

the proletarian is in the street. Do you think he will wait and starve in patience as he used to? After he has tasted political socialism, after the International, after the Socialist Congresses and the Paris Commune? No, it will not now be as it used to be. They will hurl themselves upon Europe. . . .[103]

It is to the nation of "the first step," France, that Dostoyevsky looks for the genesis of "political socialism" or "communism." The birth of French liberalism was accompanied, almost simultaneously, by the birth of French socialism. As early as 1796 Babeuf and Buonarroti had spurned those "positive acquisitions" which the liberals deemed sufficient to consider the French Revolution completed. They would not accept bourgeois liberalism as the fulfillment of the Geneva vision:

These proclaimed a new word of their own, namely, the necessity of universal fellowship not for the equal distribution of rights allotted to a quarter, or so, of the human race, leaving the rest to serve as raw material and a means of exploitation for the happiness of that quarter of mankind, but, on the contrary—for universal equality, with each and every one sharing the blessings of this world. . . .

Progressive minds had only too well grasped the fact that despotism had merely assumed a new guise . . . that the new world-conquerors (the bourgeois) proved, perhaps, even worse than the former despots (the nobility); that "Liberté, Egalité, Fraternité" is but a high-sounding phrase, and nothing but a phrase.[104]

These progressive minds declared that the natural course of the Revolution had been prematurely interrupted, that the realization of the "rights of man" required a radical social, as well as political, transformation.

As in his analysis of socialism in Russia, Dostoyevsky identifies three successive yet intimately related varieties of European socialism: utopian or idealistic, scientific, and political or revolutionary. The utopian socialism of the French—Saint-Simon, Fourier, and George Sand—made its appearance

102 *DW*, p. 664 (April 1877); *PS*, p. 86; *BK*, p. 368 (VI,3).
103 *PS*, p. 87.
104 *DW*, pp. 729, 346-47 (May-June 1877; June 1876).

first. Rather than adjust their vision of freedom, equality, and brotherhood to accommodate the middle class which had risen to dominance in the wake of the Revolution, the utopian socialists advocated the substantial equality of goods as a prerequisite of genuine freedom and brotherhood. Their explicit attack on private property deprived them at the outset of the support of the powerful. Instead of calculating ways and means of seizing power themselves, they expected the persuasive effect of their teachings alone to usher in the "new Christianity" or the "phalanstery." This adamant refusal to compromise with actuality seemed tantamount to a preference for "dreams" and "fantasy" over "realism."[105] While for Dostoyevsky there was certainly something naive and fantastic in the penchant of utopian socialism for drawing up remarkably detailed blueprints of heaven on earth, he nevertheless regarded it as a movement of paramount significance for the West, for utopian socialism contained, in embryonic form, the fundamental components of the later, more effective forms of socialism. First, it was infused with a high moral earnestness which seemed very attractive beside the realism of bourgeois liberalism. Utopian socialism's obviously genuine thirst for justice leads Dostoyevsky to assert that, on moral grounds, the leadership of Europe belongs to these socialists, "notwithstanding their apparent weakness and fantasticality."[106] Secondly, the utopian socialists assumed that their thirst for justice could be slaked by the actualization of formulations of reason. They were utterly confident that the problem of social order was soluble by human reason alone:

The frantic [idealistic] socialist sets desperately to work on the future fraternity, defining it, calculating its size and weight, enticing you with its advantages, explaining, teaching, telling of the profit each stands to gain from the fraternity and just how much each will win; he determines in advance what each personality will look like and what burden each will carry, and determines in advance the division of earthly wealth; what part each one will merit and how much each in return must pay to the community at the expense of his individuality....[107]

This tendency to apotheosize human reason culminated in the development of scientific socialism. The fervid moral earnestness of utopian socialism tended to become, in scientific socialism, an imperturbable assurance of the inevitability of its triumph. This assurance was derived in part from a rational or scientific doctrine of historical progress (as formulated, for instance, by Marx) which purportedly rendered socialism less naive and more certain of realization: "there is no *right* here whatsoever—there is only *history*, a historical course of events."[108] The doctrine of historical necessity, combined with a continuing sense of moral superiority, made scientific

105 Ibid., p. 252 (March 1876).
106 Ibid., p. 252 (March 1876).
107 *WNSI*, pp. 114-15 (6).
108 *DW*, p. 619 (Feb. 1877). In this passage Dostoyevsky observes that the notion of historical progress first became effective in bourgeois liberalism.

socialism a theory which promised to bear potent fruit in the realm of practice. This promise was truly realized only when scientific socialism allied itself with the resentment of the poor, and became political socialism. Whereas utopian socialism had been wary of such an alliance, the scientific socialists eventually came to the conclusion that the bourgeoisie, as the product of a particular historical and social necessity, would never be educated to cede its place to another stage in the "historical course of events." The middle class would have to be forcibly ousted from its dominant position, just as it had previously ousted the nobility.[109]

The Crisis of Order and the Future of the West

To Dostoyevsky it was increasingly apparent that the failures of liberal democracy were grave enough to call radically into question its aspiration—just on the verge of fulfillment—to a new universal order. The crisis of liberal democracy, in his view, entailed grave consequences for the West: the West faces an upheaval "such as there has never been before"; Europe is a powder-keg "just waiting for the first spark"; the time has come for something "sempiternal, millenarian," something "colossal, elemental, and dreadful"; "immense cataclysms" await the West.[110] Although he did not pretend to be a soothsayer, Dostoyevsky did attempt to illumine the thick darkness which he perceived descending upon the "land of holy miracles." In this attempt he was led to make particular predictions concerning the future of the West—some of them prophetic, and others less accurate. It must be emphasized, however, that the import of his account of the modern Western quest for order does not depend on the accuracy of the scenario which can be constructed from his various predictions. What is important is the accuracy, or lack thereof, with which he discerned the lineaments of the crisis of order faced by the West.

At the centre of Dostoyevsky's thought about the future of the West are the two fundamental conflicts which, in his view, have their source in the nature of liberal democracy itself. As we have noted, he thought that the intense rivalry of the bourgeois nation-states would erupt into wars of thitherto inconceivable magnitude. He envisaged also an extension and intensification of the struggle between bourgeois liberalism and political socialism which would eventually see the entire bourgeois West threatened with an immense revolution. He did not explicate the relationship between these enormous conflicts, but he clearly associated them very closely, speaking of them almost in the same breath.[111]

He seems to have anticipated the outbreak first of a great war involving all the Western powers. The heart of the "inevitable and not far distant" war

109 Ibid., pp. 618-20 (Feb. 1877).
110 UD, III, p. 148; DW, pp. 258, 562, 724, 908 (March 1876; Jan., May-June, Nov. 1877).
111 PS, pp. 86-87.

would be the struggle between France and Germany. The enmity between these nations had not abated in the aftermath of the Franco-German war of 1870, and the desire of France for a war of *revanche* was surpassed only by the desire of Germany for undisputed hegemony over Europe. The war between these great nations would draw in England, Austria, Italy, and perhaps Russia on one side or the other. Dostoyevsky thought that a war that would cost so much blood must unquestionably end quickly; but if the outcome of the war were not definitive, then the West would in the future face "ten times greater" effusions of blood. He appears to have thought that the national struggles would likely eventuate in the emergence of Germany as the ruler of continental Europe, with a powerful English-speaking order on one side and Russia on the other.[112]

Yet the elemental national struggles, whatever their outcome, are overshadowed in significance for him by the possibility of a "colossal revolution" posed by the diffusion of political socialism throughout the West. He did not explore the question of the workers' participation in the internecine bourgeois wars, but his anticipation of an "all-European battle" indicates that he thought the Western workers might be persuaded initially to put national honour ahead of international proletarian solidarity. He apparently also thought, however, that the bourgeois states would be terribly weakened by their wars, and that the workers would finally refuse to shed their blood in an alien cause. For he was convinced that revolution would come, and not long after the era of great wars.[113]

Dostoyevsky predicted that "communism will surely come and triumph." Liberal democracy will perhaps prove so tenacious that the victory of communism will require "centuries of terrible discord," and cost "one hundred million heads" and "floods of blood." But political socialism, initially weaker than its adversary, will finally prove itself stronger. The bourgeoisie must at last yield to the inevitable: "The fourth estate is coming; it knocks and batters at the door, and if the door be not opened, it will be broken down."[114] Those who are bound by liberal democracy will doubtless be resolute in the defence of their material interests. Yet when defeat looms large before them they will "scatter like lightning"; for liberal democracy is fundamentally a union of individuals for the purpose of "saving their bellies," and this is one of the most impotent of all the ideas which can bind people together.[115] Bourgeois liberalism lacks an idea with moral appeal, and the conservative idea is little more than a "corpse." For Dostoyevsky, socialism thus embodies the only significant moral idea present in the political life of the modern West, and for this reason it is likely in the future to prevail

112 *DW*, pp. 829-34 (Sept. 1877); *UD*, III, p. 80.
113 *PS*, p. 87; *UD*, II, p. 150; *DW*, p. 833 (Sept. 1877).
114 *UD*, II, pp. 101, 150; *DW*, pp. 253, 621 (March 1876; Feb. 1877); "And finally the triumph of eight million proletarians and arsonists," *UD*, II, p. 70; *PS*, p. 86.
115 *PS*, pp. 83, 85.

over its rivals.[116] This vision endows socialism with an unconquerable resolve which enables it to survive, and even transform into moral victories, defeats which would have utterly crushed its opponents.

Yet at the same time as he affirms the future triumph of communism, Dostoyevsky declares that "after a bit it will fall."[117] Political socialism may derive much strength from the relative attractiveness of its aspiration to justice; but its potency in practice depends on its close alliance with the far less attractive envy and resentment of the dispossessed. In Dostoyevsky's view, this alliance detracts seriously from the moral appeal of the socialist idea. To the mass of the exploited workers socialism has come to signify simply the plunder of property owners. The triumph of political socialism may thus ultimately entail no more than a transfer of economic power from one social class to another. To quote Versilov:

Un beau matin, despite all their "balanced budgets" and "absence of deficits", all the governments will get so hopelessly bogged down in their debts that they'll decide to suspend payment and declare themselves bankrupt . . . those who never held any shares, indeed, never possessed anything, that is, all the penniless beggars, will refuse to accept a liquidation based on former holdings, and the struggle will begin. . . . Well, then, after seventy-seven defeats, the beggars will wipe out the shareholders, take their shares away from them, and, of course, become shareholders themselves. Perhaps they'll introduce some innovations, and perhaps they won't. Most likely they'll go bankrupt too.[118]

The triumphant paupers may blithely ignore or even suppress socialist doctrine so that they can concentrate on the enjoyment of their newly won power, just as the bourgeoisie had ignored liberal ideas after successfully confronting the feudal order with its "*Ôte-toi de là que je m'y mette.*" A future union of workers for the sake of "filling their bellies" is, for Dostoyevsky, a distinct possibility. Such an eventuality would signify the indirect victory of the bourgeois ethos and the moral fall of socialism.

Socialism is deprived of its universal moral appeal insofar as it becomes historically effective in political socialism or communism. In Dostoyevsky's view, communism is finally an expression of the envy and resentment of those who do not possess the means to realize their right to the "multiplication and the rapid satisfaction of needs." The future triumph of communism, then, cannot be permanent, for it will be the triumph, not of humanity, but of one part (albeit the vast majority) of humanity. In the absence of a genuine reconciliation between the former "shareholders" and the new "shareholders," the perpetual struggle between rich and poor will continue. As the expression and self-justification of a particular class, communist "brotherhood" will inevitably be confronted by what Dostoyevsky calls the "protest of individuality."[119] This protest is already raised against communism by

116 *UD*, II, pp. 170, 109.
117 Ibid., p. 101.
118 *The Adolescent*, pp. 210-11 (II,1,iv); *NRY*, p. 370.
119 *UD*, II, p. 9.

capitalist liberalism, which has never hesitated to invoke the sacred right of individual freedom to protect bourgeois privileges.[120] Yet the "protest of individuality" has a dimension beyond that of bourgeois defensiveness. As in Russia (with Nechayev-Peter Verkhovensky), so in the West a more fundamental questioning of socialism was taking shape, a questioning heralded, for instance, by Max Stirner's rejection of the idea of "humanity" in the name of the "unique individual." Bourgeois liberalism and radical individualism (or "existentialism," to use a later term) would be united in raising this fundamental question: what real inducement is there for the stronger, wealthier, or more intelligent individual to "make a sacrifice" for a common good or "brotherhood" which represents merely the aspirations of the weak and dispossessed among humanity? Though probably the most effective historical force in the future, communism is still in need of a "moral enticement" sufficiently strong to quell the "protest of individuality" which it will evoke.[121] Without such a moral enticement it will have to resort to violence, which will engender further violence in response, and the West will be denied the unity of order for which it yearns.

Dostoyevsky's inquiry into the problem of social order in the West leads him to conclude that the modern West is in the midst of a crisis for which it may be impossible to propose any solution.[122] Yet in the absence of a new order the West is faced with two equally desolate possibilities. It may undergo a lingering dissolution, continuing indefinitely to perform the outward bodily functions of a civilization, but dead at the heart. In this case it will continue to exist only as a magnificent museum in which, as Ivan Karamazov professes:

Every stone... speaks of such ardent life in the past, of such a passionate faith in their achievements, their truth, their struggles, and their science, that I know beforehand that I shall fall on the ground and kiss those stones and weep over them and—and at the same time be deeply convinced that it's long been a graveyard and nothing more.[123]

Alternatively, the West may suffer "perturbations which the human mind refuses to believe, considering their realization as something fantastic."[124] And perhaps both possibilities will come to pass.

This, however, is not Dostoyevsky's final word concerning the future of Western civilization. He distinguished on the horizon of the West the presence

---

120 *WNSI*, p. 108 (6).
121 *UD*, I, p. 99. It should be noted that this protest will include that of national "individualities." See *The Adolescent*, pp. 468, 470 (III,7,ii,iii); *NRY*, p. 370; *NP*, p. 357; *DW*, pp. 250, 667 (March 1876; April 1877); *UD*, II, p. 4. Although Dostoyevsky was acutely aware of the still significant presence of national particularity in the West, and regarded socialism itself as a "French doctrine," he nevertheless considered it to be, like bourgeois liberalism, an essentially universal, cosmopolitan, and even anti-national doctrine.
122 *UD*, II, p. 144.
123 *BK*, p. 269 (V,3).
124 *DW*, p. 908 (Nov. 1877). Dostoyevsky envisaged the possibility even of humanity's annihilation of itself. See *BK*, p. 374 (VI,3).

of a "social formula" which might serve as the final Western solution to the crisis of order. The most concise expression of this barely glimpsed solution is found in his rough notes, immediately following a reference to future inter-necine conflicts in the West: "The Pope—leader of communism."[125] Dos-toyevsky thought that this social formula constitutes a possible culmination of Western thought and practice.

"The Pope—leader of communism" as the final Western social formula represents an alliance of what Dostoyevsky considered to be the two most significant historical forces in the modern West. As we have seen, he thought that the eventual triumph of socialism could be consolidated only if it were able to provide a moral enticement of sufficient strength to appease the protest of individuality which may not want to sacrifice itself for the common good. In Dostoyevsky's view, the chief source in the West of such a moral entice-ment remains the Church. Roman Catholicism has traditionally been the most effective bearer of the morality of individual self-renunciation—precisely the sort of morality which a future socialist order will need. Dostoyevsky's pre-diction that communism must turn to religion for the moral enticement needed to consolidate itself is not implausible (especially in the light of what has transpired in Russia itself since 1917). But the notion that communism will find in the Roman Catholic Church the necessary moral enticement depends on two far more questionable assumptions.

The social formula assumes, first, that Roman Catholicism will remain sufficiently strong in the West to be considered seriously as the moral prop of the socialist state. Dostoyevsky certainly conceded that the humiliation of Pope Pius IX at the hands of the new Italian state (particularly in 1870) was symbolic of the position into which the church was being forced in the modern West. Pius' resolute defiance of modern Italy, and of modernity in general, had inspired merely the indifference, or laughter, of the liberal and socialist West:

at the fatal moment when he had been deprived of both Rome and the last parcel of land, and when only the Vatican had been left in his possession,—at that same moment, as if on purpose, he proclaimed his infallibility, and at the same time the thesis: Without mundane possessions Christianity cannot survive on earth. . . .

Oh, isn't it true that this would sound funny and insignificant to politicans and diplomats of Europe! The downtrodden Pope, imprisoned in the Vatican, appeared to them during the last years as such a nullity that it would have been a shame to pay any attention to him. Thus many progressives of Europe have been reasoning, especially the witty and liberal ones. The Pope delivering allocutions and issuing syllabuses, receiving the devout, damning while dying—in their view resembled a buffoon performing for their entertainment.[126]

---

125 *UD*, II, p. 133. The same idea is expressed in published form in 1871 in *The Devils*, p. 419 (II,8).
126 *DW*, pp. 735-36 (May-June 1877). Note also the consensus of Stepan Verkhovensky's liberal circle in *The Devils*: "We had long ago prophesied that the Pope would assume the role of a simple archbishop in a united Italy, and had no doubt whatever that this

By the 1870s the Roman Catholic Church had apparently become too insignificant even to inspire the anti-clericalism long fashionable among modern Europeans.

Dostoyevsky, however, argues that the dismissal of Roman Catholicism as a "trifling matter" in our age of "humanitarian ideas, industry, and railways" betrays a shallow understanding of religion, and an incomplete grasp of the most recent historical trends. A religion which has been "organically living in the world one thousand years" does not die "in an instant"; and events in later nineteenth-century Europe demonstrated that Roman Catholicism was still very far from its death-bed. Although France had long before renounced Roman Catholic order in favour of the Geneva idea of order, it is to this nation that Dostoyevsky turns for indications of the enduring strength of Roman Catholicism. One of these indications was the fact that, "despite 1789," the Pope had been able to depend throughout the nineteenth century on French support of his temporal power.[127] France finally abandoned Rome to the Italian liberals only when forced to do so by the war with Germany in 1870.

For Dostoyevsky the most significant indication of the abiding strength of Roman Catholicism was the influence of ultramontanism in France, and throughout Europe. He focuses particularly on the crisis of Seize Mai (1876) in France, precipitated by President MacMahon's dissolution of the Republican assembly. According to his interpretation of the crisis, MacMahon's attempt to assume greater powers—a situation amounting almost to a monarchist coup d'état—was engineered by the clerical party in France, which aimed at attaining political power through MacMahon in order to scotch Bismarck's Kulturkampf against the Roman Catholic Church with French arms. Dostoyevsky's long and intricate discussion of this crisis in The Diary of a Writer (May-June 1877) is concerned with making the point that the Roman Catholic Church remains a sufficiently powerful presence in the West to influence decisions concerning war and peace in the country which is the very womb of modernity, and to inspire the implacable hostility of Bismarck, the shrewdest and most powerful statesman in the West. He maintains that the evident strength of ultramontanism in modern Europe should give pause to those who merely laughed at Pius IX's proclamation of the dogma of infallibility at the Vatican Council of 1870. The weakness of the throne in the West did not necessarily imply the weakness of the altar. The refusal of Roman Catholicism to die makes it a potential source of that moral enticement, or "consolidating force," which will be required by the modern West. And this consolidating moral force, thanks to Pius IX's proclamation, will tend increasingly to be centred in the person of the Pope. Although the Pope cannot claim the command of many regiments, he can continue to claim, by virtue of his moral authority, the command of many hearts and minds.

thousand-year-old problem was a trifling matter in our age of humanitarian ideas..."
(p. 48 [I,1,ix]).
127 The Devils, p. 48; DW, p. 736 (May-June 1877); DE, p. 46.

The second questionable assumption underlying "the Pope—leader of communism" is that Roman Catholicism would ever consent to an alliance with communism. The Roman Catholic Church had long associated itself with the monarchs of Europe, and continued to do so after 1789. For instance, in the crisis of *Seize Mai* the clericals had placed their hopes in the monarchist cause, embodied in the Comte de Chambord. Dostoyevsky argues, however, that it was the clericals who were using the monarchists rather than the contrary. And he points to signs in nineteenth-century France—for instance, the "social Catholicism" of Lamennais and Lacordaire[128]—that once the clericals became convinced of the impotence of the European "right" they might be open to an alliance with the "left." He points in particular to the largest and most influential Roman Catholic order, the Jesuits, who have always shown a proclivity towards accommodation with popular political and social trends.[129] Dostoyevsky adduces other evidence of the possibility of a future understanding between the Roman Catholic Church and the Western left, an understanding which he characterizes most explicitly in a passage in *The Diary of a Writer:*

Catholicism . . . will manage to seduce the leaders of the underground war. It will say to them: "You have no centre, no order in the conduct of the work: you are a force scattered all over the world. . . . I shall be your rallying centre, and I shall attract to you all those who still believe in me."
One way or another the alliance will be formed. Catholicism does not wish to die, whereas social revolution and the new social period in Europe are indubitable: the two forces, unquestionably, will have to come to an understanding, to unite.[130]

"The Pope—leader of communism" emerges as a final possibility from Dostoyevsky's empirical observation of the modern Western attempt to construct a new order "deduced solely from rational principles." Doubtless certain fundamental questions continue to obtrude themselves: has the possible development of liberalism and socialism into "the Pope—leader of communism" been sufficiently substantiated? or the possibility that the Roman Catholic Church would ever participate in such an order? Yet Dostoyevsky's expression of the final Western social formula (which he does not put forward as a certainty) was never intended to stand or fall according to the amount of empirical evidence which could be marshalled to support it. His approach to the fundamental problems, as he himself once asserted, is that of a "realist *in the higher sense.*"[131] The ultimate concern of his critique of the West is with

128 For his reference to these "greatest representatives of Catholicism" in the nineteenth century, see *UD*, I, p. 93.
129 *DW*, pp. 728, 735-36, 911 (May-June, Oct. 1877).
130 Ibid., p. 912 (Nov. 1877). See also ibid., pp. 256-58 (March 1876).
131 This remark was reported by N. Strakhov, and is quoted in E. Sandoz, *Political Apocalypse, a Study of Dostoevsky's Grand Inquisitor* (Baton Rouge, 1971), p. 53. (The italics are mine.) See also *DW*: "The aim of art is not to portray these or those incidents in the ways of life but their general idea, sharp-sightedly divined and correctly removed from the whole multiplicity of analogous living phenomena" (p. 90 [1873]).

those ideas of life which constitute the essence underlying the historical phenomena of Western civilization. The social formula—"The Pope—leader of communism"—represents the modern, outward appearance of an idea of order living within the inner heart of the West. Dostoyevsky's empirical observation of the modern Western crisis leads him to this formula; but for its fuller elucidation and justification we must turn from his explicitly political writings to the higher expression of his "realism" in his art.

FOUR

THE FINAL WESTERN SOCIAL FORMULA

"The Grand Inquisitor"

Dostoyevsky presents his definitive elucidation of the final Western social formula in "The Grand Inquisitor." This short writing, considered by him to be the "culminating point" of *The Brothers Karamazov*, can be regarded as the culmination also of his religious and political thought—his "final statement" concerning the question of human order.[1] The importance which he attached to his critique of the West is perhaps most conclusively established by the fact that his final statement about human order is also his final statement about the West. The thought about human order contained in "The Grand Inquisitor" is of universal import. But clearly, for Dostoyevsky, this thought is at least initially inseparable from the consideration of the meaning of Western civilization. It can hardly be an accident that the universal themes of this writing, which represent the distillation of years of Dostoyevsky's thought about the "mystery of man," are expressed by a Western character. The Grand Inquisitor is, with minor exceptions, the only attempt at a portrayal of a non-Russian figure in Dostoyevsky's art. Dostoyevsky's willingness thus to risk the aesthetic effect of his "final statement" bears eloquent testimony to the significance which the question of the West held for him. Our concern with finding in "The Grand Inquisitor" an elucidation of the social formula—"The Pope—leader of communism"—will bring us inevitably into the presence of Dostoyevsky's timeless thought. The same concern, however, will determine the limits of our consideration of this thought, for this chapter does not pretend to plumb all the "fathomless depth" of "The Grand In-

---

1 See Dostoyevsky's letter of 10 May 1879 to N. A. Liubimov.

quisitor'' which, as Nicholas Berdyaev maintains, has ''never yet been properly explored.''[2]

The exposition of the final Western social formula is the primary concern
of the Grand Inquisitor's monologue. Apart from this monologue, the only
constituents of the writing itself are Ivan Karamazov's brief ''literary introduction,'' and the silent figure of Christ. Ivan's authorship of ''The Grand
Inquisitor,'' and the presence within it of Christ, both serve to integrate it
within *The Brothers Karamazov* as a whole. Yet although it thus points, on
the one hand, to Ivan's ''rebellion'' against God and, on the other, to the
Christian teachings of Father Zosima, ''The Grand Inquisitor'' can be approached, at least initially, as an independent writing. Ivan himself maintains
that, with regard to the Inquisitor's monologue, ''the only thing that matters is
that the old man should speak out, that at last he does speak out and says aloud
what he has been thinking in silence for ninety years.''[3] This assertion is made
in response to Alyosha's question concerning the meaning of that silent presence to which the ''old man'' addresses himself, and it could serve equally as
a response to the question of Ivan's own relation to ''The Grand Inquisitor.''
It is my intention to heed Ivan's assertion by examining the Inquisitor's
monologue first in isolation from the thought either of Ivan or of Father
Zosima.

Before consideration of what is said in the monologue, note should be
made of who, precisely, is speaking. The Grand Inquisitor, as Ivan points out
in his ''literary introduction,'' is a cardinal of the Roman Catholic Church in
sixteenth-century Spain ''during the most terrible time of the Inquisition,
when fires were lighted every day throughout the land to the glory of
God...'' (291; V,5). He therefore embodies Roman Catholicism, not at the
time of its apogee in the twelfth century, but at the time of its desperately
militant attempt during the Counter-Reformation to preserve itself by means
of the Spanish sword. The Inquisitor, close to death at ninety years of age,
stands near the end of Roman Catholic civilization in the West, and at the
beginning of the modern quest for a new order. Though rooted in a particular
time and place, the old man's vision extends in both directions to encompass
the entire history of Western civilization, from the ancient Roman Empire to
the new Rome which he anticipates after the fall of modern liberalism and

2 N. Berdyaev, *Dostoevsky* (New York, 1957), p. 210. It is hoped that a consideration of
   ''The Grand Inquisitor'' within the context of Dostoevsky's critique of the West will
   shed further light on its meaning. For a thoughtful, comprehensive introduction to the
   structure and themes of this extraordinarily complex writing, see E. Sandoz, *Political
   Apocalypse* (Baton Rouge, 1971). See also V. Solovyov, *Lectures on Godmanhood* (London, 1948), XI-XII for a philosophical exposition of some of the writing's chief themes. It
   is probable that Solovyov's account of the temptations was based in part on discussions
   with Dostoyevsky himself. For a brief summary of the range of critical opinion concerning
   ''The Grand Inquisitor'' see R. L. Cox, ''Dostoevsky's Grand Inquisitor,'' *Cross Currents* (Fall 1967), pp. 427-28.
3 *BK*, p. 293 (V,5). Further references in this chapter to *The Brothers Karamazov*—by page
   numbers, part, and chapter—will be given in parentheses after each text.

socialism. "The Grand Inquisitor" is meant to be a teaching about Western civilization as a whole. And beyond this, it is meant to be a teaching about humanity as a whole, for the Inquisitor's fundamental concern is to articulate the social order which most closely corresponds to human nature.[4] In this endeavour he looks to the history of the West for evidence of the truth of his teaching, and for an answer to the question of its realizability.

The Inquisitor sets his account of the best social order within the framework provided by the biblical account of Christ's temptation in the wilderness (Matthew 4:1-10). He claims that the "prodigious miracle" of the story of the three temptations lies in the fact that the questions posed in them should have appeared among men at all, particularly at such an early date in human history, for the posing of these questions evinces an insight into everything which is most fundamentally at issue in the problem of human order, an insight arrived at prior to the centuries of historical experience which have since borne it out:

> If it were possible to imagine, for the sake of argument, that those three questions of the terrible spirit had been lost without leaving a trace in the books and that we had to rediscover, restore, and invent them afresh and that to do so we had to gather together all the wise men of the earth—rulers, high priests, scholars, philosophers, poets—and set them the task of devising and inventing three questions which would not only correspond to the magnitude of the occasion, but, in addition, express in three words, in three short human sentences, the whole future history of the world and of mankind, do you think that the entire wisdom of the earth, gathered together, could have invented anything equal in depth and force to the three questions which were actually put to you at the time by the wise and mighty spirit in the wilderness? From these questions alone, from the miracle of their appearance, one can see that what one is dealing with here is not the human, transient mind, but an absolute and everlasting one. For in those three questions the whole future history of mankind is, as it were, anticipated and combined in one whole and three images are presented in which all the insoluble historical . . . contradictions of human nature all over the world will meet. (295-96; V,5)

The Inquisitor's social formula is founded on his own interpretation of, and response to, the three "everlasting" questions posed to Christ in the wilderness. To him, each question reveals a fundamental truth about human nature—or, more precisely—a fundamental human need which is actually present in people and verifiable in their historical experience. The only order which can be considered final is that order which satisfies the three basic human needs articulated in the temptations.

The Inquisitor's elaboration of his social formula proceeds in terms of the three human needs revealed in the temptations. This elaboration, however, assumes his recognition of one primal human need, which determines his interpretation of the others. Note must be taken of this chief need, or "torment," of humanity which constitutes the unifying theme of the Inquisitor's discourse. This need, of "every man individually and of mankind as a whole

4 Cf. Aristotle, *Politics*, 1253a 1-18, 1281a 2-4.

from the beginning of time,'' is the need for order itself. We have seen that in Dostoyevsky's thought the need for order is tantamount to the need for a religion, in the broadest and yet most literal meaning of a ''binding together.'' This teaching is reflected in the Inquisitor's assertion that ''man's universal and everlasting craving . . . can be summed up in the words 'whom shall I worship?'.'' The need for religion inevitably becomes, according to the Inquisitor, the yearning for a common religion, for the existence of differing reverences casts doubt upon all of them:

It is this need for *universal* worship that is the chief torment of every man individually and of mankind as a whole from the beginning of time. For the sake of that universal worship they have put each other to the sword. They have set up gods and called upon each other, 'Give up your gods and come and worship ours, or else death to you and to your gods!' And so it will be to the end of the world, even when the gods have vanished from the earth: they will prostrate themselves before idols just the same. (298; V,5)

According to the Inquisitor, the primal human yearning for order has never enjoyed complete and permanent satisfaction because the great movers of humankind have not been unanimous in according it the recognition it deserves. Throughout history the Caesars have been opposed by the Christs, who have placed freedom higher than the need for order. In their sanctioning of the free individual in separation from the mass, the preachers of freedom (encompassed symbolically for the Inquisitor in the figure of Christ) have repeatedly encouraged disorder. The Inquisitor accuses these preachers of behaving as though they hated human beings and wished to mock them, or, at best, as though they were blithely indifferent to the most elementary facts of human life. Surely those who truly love human beings would recognize and make provision for the fact that they suffer from disorder as from a disease—a disease which they are too weak to endure for the sake of freedom (300; V,5).

The Inquisitor interprets the entire history of the West in terms of the struggle between the advocates of order and the advocates of freedom, between those who take human beings as they actually are and those who estimate them too highly. According to his interpretation, the ancient world was just within sight of success in its Herculean attempt at a permanent solution to the problem of order when it was undermined by Christ's affirmation of personal freedom. It had been the enormous accomplishment of Roman Catholicism to salvage what remained of the ancient order, and on this basis to re-integrate the isolated individual within a ''Christian civilization'':

''Was it not you who said so often in those days, 'I shall make you free?' But now you have seen those 'free' men,'' the old man adds suddenly with a pensive smile. ''Yes, this business has cost us a great deal,'' he goes on, looking sternly at him, ''but we've completed it at last in your name. For fifteen centuries we've been troubled by this freedom, but now it's over and done with for good.'' (294; V,5)

For fifteen centuries the West had been in fragments, but it had finally become whole again thanks to the Roman Catholic reconciliation of Rome with Christ.

This wholeness, however, was to be of short duration. Turning towards the future, the Inquisitor anticipates with foreboding the dissolution of Roman Catholic order in the series of events being initiated in his own time by the "dreadful new heresy" which had arisen in the "north of Germany" (290; V,5). He does envisage, beyond this period of chaos, a renewed attempt at order; but he prophesies that this attempt will be futile unless and until the variants of liberal-socialist thought which will inform it give way before his social formula. Although he considers his formula to be the best for all human beings at all times, he clearly thinks that its actualization is most likely in the modern West, in the aftermath of the internecine struggle between bourgeois liberalism and political socialism. Addressing in the figure of Christ all the teachers of freedom, he nevertheless proposes his formula particularly in opposition to the Christ who is the "great idealist" of Geneva thought (306-307; V,5).

It is evident that the Inquisitor's social formula is founded, not only on the conviction of the primacy of the human need for order, but also on the conviction that the satisfaction of this need is incompatible with the affirmation of freedom. The dissonance of freedom and order is sounded throughout his discourse. However, it is important to recognize (as Alyosha does) that the Inquisitor's opposition of freedom to order stems from a particular understanding of freedom. For the Inquisitor, as for Geneva thought, the affirmation of freedom is synonymous with the affirmation of the individual as a separate "conscious will," as an isolated being endowed with reason and will.[5] Yet the Inquisitor does not share the Geneva hope that the separate individual can be re-integrated within the social union through the mediatory power of love. Because freedom and social cohesion are ultimately antithetical, freedom is an intolerable burden for humanity: "nothing has ever been more unendurable to man and to human society than freedom! . . . I tell you man has no more agonizing anxiety than to find someone to whom he can hand over with all speed the gift of freedom with which the unhappy creature is born" (296, 298; V,5). The Inquisitor maintains that freedom, though intolerable, is a fact of life which cannot simply be abolished. It can, however, be transferred into the hands of a few rulers who will exact from the majority of humanity absolute obedience in all things large and small, thereby granting them the order for which they yearn. A final solution to the problem of order is possible for the Inquisitor only on the basis of the positing of a radical inequality among human beings. Dostoyevsky has him state this inequality most explicitly in the rough notes for the novel: "But the strengths of mankind are various. There are the strong and there are the weak."[6]

The Inquisitor's attribution to human beings of a fundamental need for order is therefore subject to a decisive qualification: there are those, inevitably a minority, who are strong enough to renounce the satisfaction of this need.

5 Cf. Raskolnikov's dream in *CP*, p. 555 (VII,2).
6 *NBK*, p. 82.

The existence of two sorts of human beings can militate against order when the strong demand comparable strength from the weak, as did the "great idealist," Jesus. But when the strong are also compassionate, then the most complete order becomes possible. The "millions and scores of thousands of millions" of the weak, anxious to surrender the conscious will which alienates them from the spontaneous life of complete social integration, will be able to place their freedom in the hands of the "great and strong" who consent to "endure freedom and rule over them . . ." (297; V,5). The appeal to an evident inequality among human beings by way of justifying the absolute rule of a minority of free individuals over the mass of humanity, who are equal only in their slavery and free only because they gratefully accept the assurance of their rulers that they are free, recalls Shigalyov's scientific reinterpretation of the Geneva idea. Unlike the taciturn Russian, however, the Spanish cardinal is more than willing to elaborate his formula for the only earthly paradise possible for human beings.

The First Temptation

The first temptation to which Christ was subjected is interpreted by the Inquisitor as follows:

And do you see the stones in this parched and barren desert? Turn them into loaves, and mankind will run after you like a flock of sheep, grateful and obedient, though forever trembling with fear that you might withdraw your hand and they would no longer have your loaves.' But you did not want to deprive man of freedom and rejected the offer, for, you thought, what sort of freedom is it if obedience is bought with loaves of bread? (296; V,5)

The rejection of the loaves constitutes a rejection of the first, and most self-evident, of the three principal means whereby individuals can be relieved of their burdensome freedom—for in this first temptation is revealed the truth that the weak will give up the prerogative of individual freedom to those who assure them that this prerogative is merely a chimera, that the real concern of human life is the multiplication and satisfaction of natural needs. According to the Inquisitor, "heavenly bread"—synonymous with such notions as the right to "freedom," or "moral responsibility," or the "spiritual dimension" of human life—cannot compare in the eyes of the weak with "earthly bread." This preference has its source in the fundamental need of human beings for at least the minimum satisfaction of their natural inclinations, for the minimum protection from hunger, cold, and the numbing hopelessness of material poverty. Despite the obviousness of this need, its strength has repeatedly been underestimated by the preachers of heavenly bread. Yet can the offer of heavenly bread have any impact upon people who are subject to the tyranny of unsatisfied natural desires? This is the question posed in the first temptation.

Those strong enough for the most inflexible disciplining of their inclinations by the conscious will may perhaps be able to contemplate virtue while suffering the pangs of hunger; but there still remain the weak, "numerous as the sand of the sea," who cannot ignore their pain. According to the Inquisitor, it is terribly unjust to add to the suffering of the majority of humanity the additional burden of moral guilt because of their preference for earthly bread. The "great idealists" are all too quick to condemn precisely where they should show compassion. Those who love human beings with a genuine love will not condemn them for a yearning too strong to struggle against, but will attempt to alleviate their suffering by satisfying this yearning. The Inquisitor thus stands with those who declare: "Feed them first and then demand virtue of them!" (296; V,5). The meaning of this declaration is elaborated by Dostoyevsky himself in a letter in which he discusses explicitly the first temptation:

Rather than go to the ruined poor, who from hunger and oppression look more like beasts than like men, rather than go and start preaching to the hungry abstention from sins, humility, sexual chastity, wouldn't it be better to *feed* them first? . . . give them *food* to save them; give them a social structure so that they always have bread and order—and then speak to them of sin—Command then that henceforth the earth should bring forth without toil, instruct people in such science or instruct them in such an order, that their lives should henceforth be provided for. Is it possible not to believe that the greatest vices and misfortunes of man have resulted from hunger, cold, poverty, and the impossible struggle for existence?[7]

Those self-styled teachers of humanity who have evinced an apparent indifference to the enormous suffering which material poverty has inflicted and continues to inflict upon the vast majority of their fellow beings are accused by the Inquisitor of exhibiting a dire lack of commonsense, or worse, a reprehensible severity.

Although the first temptation discloses a truth which is "absolute and everlasting," it anticipates also the "future history of mankind," for the issue which it raises was to be especially predominant in a certain epoch of history. The Inquisitor, present at the barely discernible incipience of this epoch, foresees the full course of its development:

You replied that man does not live by bread alone, but do you know that for the sake of that earthly bread the spirit of the earth will rise up against you and will join battle with you and conquer you, and all will follow him, crying 'Who is like this beast? He have given us fire from heaven!' Do you know that ages will pass and mankind will proclaim in its wisdom and science that there is no crime and, therefore, no sin, but that there are only hungry people. 'Feed them first and then demand virtue of them!'—that is what they will inscribe on their banner which they will raise against you and which will destroy your temple. (296; V,5)

The historical epoch anticipated here is that of the modern West. The allusion to Prometheus (whom Marx regarded as "the foremost saint and martyr in the philosophical calendar")[8] indicates perfectly the Inquisitor's understanding of

---

7 Letter of 7 June 1876 to V. A. Alexeyev.
8 See E. Voegelin, "The Formation of the Marxian Revolutionary Idea," *Review of Politics,*" XII (1950), pp. 275-302.

the spirit of Western modernity as a rebellion against the insubstantial, other-
worldly notion of heavenly bread on behalf of the tangible, earthly need of
those who suffer here and now. The traditional Christianity which the Inquisitor himself represents must face the consequences of its failure to accord
sufficient recognition to actual human suffering: "we shall again be persecuted and tortured. . . ." After tearing down the Roman Catholic "temple,"
the modern rebels will embark upon the construction of an alternative order:
"A new building will rise where your temple stood, the dreadful Tower of
Babel will rise up again . . ." (296-97; V,5).

The builders of the new Tower of Babel are not named, but in the letter
previously quoted Dostoyevsky specifies the historical movement alluded to
by the Inquisitor:

Here is the first idea which was posed by the evil spirit to Christ. Contemporary
socialism in Europe . . . sets Christ aside and is first of all concerned with bread. It
appeals to science and maintains that the cause of all human misfortune is poverty,
the struggle for existence and an oppressive environment.[9]

Socialism is thus specified as the most effective historical embodiment of the
Promethean attempt to alleviate the suffering of the "millions, numerous as
the sand of the sea" who hunger for the earthly bread which has been denied
them. According to Dostoyevsky, the compassion of socialism for human
suffering is combined with an understanding of suffering as ultimately material in origin, as the consequence of "poverty, the struggle for existence and
an oppressive environment." Despite the apparent nobility of its intentions,
then, socialism inevitably develops into a form of political materialism. The
modern Western rebellion against Roman Catholic order in the name of
earthly suffering culminates in the materialism of communism and its rival,
bourgeois liberalism. The Inquisitor thus anticipates, not only the destruction
of Roman Catholic order, but also the overcoming of the Geneva idea by the
appeal to earthly bread.

The ultimate insufficiency of any order which fails to protect the mass of
humanity from "hunger, cold, poverty, and the impossible struggle for existence" is painfully demonstrated for the Inquisitor in the imminent breakdown of Roman Catholic civilization. The future practical success of modern
political materialism will constitute an indisputable lesson concerning the
crucial place which material need occupies in human existence. The final
triumph of socialism over its liberal rival will indicate that it has learned this
lesson more thoroughly and has demonstrated a superior capacity for distribut-
ing bread equitably and efficiently. Nevertheless, in the face of the lesson
concerning humanity's need for earthly bread, the Inquisitor reaffirms the
primacy of the need for order and, evaluating socialism in terms of this need,
he finds it deficient. He certainly does not deny that materialism is capable of
functioning as a religion; indeed, he acknowledges that earthly bread may

9 Letter of 7 June 1876.

well be the most incontestable object of worship which can be offered to humanity. What could be more evident to the perception, and the inclination, of the masses than natural satisfactions? The meaning of earthly bread is obvious, and it enjoins no troublesome chastisement of natural inclination for the sake of some obscure "spiritual destiny." Rather than setting the conscious will against natural impulses, the religion of earthly bread encourages human beings to exercise the will only insofar as it serves these impulses. The consequent atrophying of the conscious will can only facilitate the overcoming of isolation and the individual's re-integration within the social unit.

Yet despite his acknowledgment of the primal appeal of earthly bread, the Inquisitor judges it to constitute an inferior idea of life, ultimately incapable of satisfying the human need for order. The futility of the modern attempt to found a new order on the universal satisfaction of material needs will finally become inescapably clear: "No science will give them bread so long as they remain free. . . . They will, at last, realize themselves that there cannot be enough freedom and bread for everybody, for they will never, never be able to let everyone have his fair share" (297; V,5). Those who would give humanity "fire from heaven" will be compelled to recognize that the universal and fair distribution of bread will never be realized in a society which has not completely overcome individual freedom. For inevitably there will be those who, unwilling to attune their desires to the collective, will demand more than their "fair share" of life's goods. What could induce these more strongly desiring individuals to "make a sacrifice" for the whole? The inadequacy of political materialism is manifest for the Inquisitor in its inability to furnish a conclusive answer to this question.[10] The socialist argument that competitive individualism is itself a product of the socio-economic environment is ultimately no more than wishful thinking. For the available evidence concerning the "always vicious and always ignoble race of man" does not encourage hope for a flowering of human goodness within a more "rational" environment (297; V,5).

The inability of socialism to secure the compliance of every conscious will in the social union necessarily implies the failure, not only to distribute bread effectively among human beings, but also to give them the order which they desire above all. The Inquisitor thus adds a significant qualification to his initial declaration that human obedience can be bought with bread. In summoning up the spectre of the rebellious individual against the new Tower of Babel, he asserts that any renunciation of individual freedom called forth by

10 UD, II, p. 156. As Dostoyevsky has Father Zosima declare in his rough notes: "And don't dream, materialists, that mutual advantage will force you to construct an order like that of a regular society. This cannot be, for your society will require sacrifice from everyone, but a corrupt desire will not want to sacrifice. A strong desire and great talent will not want to be compared with mediocrity, and since there will be no moral tie . . . except for the mutual advantage of bread, then the great and powerful will arise with his savagery and confederates, and you will begin to destroy each other in eternal enmity and you will devour each other, and that's the way it will finish" (NBK, p. 107).

the need for material satisfaction can only be temporary. To assume that the alienated individual will be reconciled to the collective through a certain transformation of external material structures is to fail to penetrate to the roots of humanity's attachment to the conscious will. The builders of the modern Tower of Babel do not grasp the significance of human freedom, and will thus never be able to possess it. They will break their hearts "for a thousand years" with their tower, without being able to complete it.

For the Inquisitor, the truth of modern political materialism lies in its profound appreciation of the need for earthly bread. Its fatal error lies in its disregard of the continuing need for heavenly bread. Communism is correct in inscribing on its banner—"Feed them first and then demand virtue of them!"—but its tendency to concentrate on the first part of this slogan to the exclusion of the second betrays an incomplete understanding of human nature. Thus, while castigating the "great idealists" for their failure to heed the teaching about human order expressed in the first temptation, the Inquisitor nevertheless acknowledges the ultimate validity of their refusal to uphold earthly bread as humanity's highest end:

> With the bread you were given an incontestable banner: give him bread and man will worship you, for there is nothing more incontestable than bread; but if at the same time someone besides yourself should gain possession of his conscience—oh, then he will even throw away your bread and follow him who has ensnared his conscience. You were right about that. For the mystery of human life is not only in living, but in knowing why one lives. Without a clear idea of what to live for man will not consent to live and will rather destroy himself than remain on the earth, though he were surrounded by loaves of bread. (298; V,5)

Earthly bread is necessary, but it is not sufficient, for the final solution to the problem of order. Human beings can be finally relieved of the burden of their freedom only if the distributors of the loaves satisfy another human need—the need for a "moral enticement."[11] This need and the means by which it can be met are explicated in the course of the Inquisitor's interpretation of the second temptation.

The Second Temptation

"Man is born a rebel" (295; V,5). According to the Inquisitor, the primary source of this "rebelliousness" is the insistence of human beings on regarding themselves as something more than the product of nature. The striving to transcend the limitations of natural necessity expresses itself particularly in the tendency to measure human existence against an ultimate good. In spinning its fine web of necessity around human beings, socialism forgets their insistent need to know that what is necessary can also be called "good." And if they cannot affirm the goodness of the order which provides them with bread, then they will finally reject this order and its bread, whatever the

11 *UD*, I, p. 99.

consequences for their natural wants. Against the modern Tower of Babel, then, the Inquisitor asserts the human propensity for making moral distinctions. Whether or not human beings are in truth entirely a product of chance and necessity, they are in fact beings who insist on perceiving themselves as something more. This tendency seems so deeply rooted as to be impervious to any amount of re-education according to the laws of "utility" and "necessity." Insofar as people tend, not only to make moral distinctions, but to insist on making these distinctions for themselves, their propensity for moral judgment is intimately associated with the assertion of the individual conscious will. The "conscious will" can thus be more precisely designated the "*conscience*."[12] For the Inquisitor the personal conscience is the mainspring of human freedom. Those who understand human freedom as directed primarily towards natural, rather than moral, ends will never be able to possess it.

According to the Inquisitor, the personal conscience has been no less important than the desire for earthly bread in inspiring that rebelliousness which has undermined human order throughout history. The nearly complete order of antiquity was doomed when the individual began to reject the "strict ancient law" in order to "decide for himself with a free heart what is good and what is evil" (a movement associated above all with the names of Socrates and Jesus) (299; V,5). The ensuing moral chaos had been alleviated by Roman Catholicism's massive effort to establish a solid morality which defined good and evil clearly for all. But the Inquisitor perceives, in the "dreadful new heresy" of Luther appearing in his own time, a renewed assertion of the personal conscience which can only issue in another epoch of moral chaos. He knows that the personal conscience will resist the threat of fire with which the Roman Catholic order vainly defends itself, and he knows that it will finally resist also the offer of earthly bread with which the builders of the modern Tower of Babel will attempt to tame it. These builders ignore at their peril the depth of the human attachment to the conscience. Like the yearning for material goods, this attachment is an "eternal problem"[13] which centuries of historical experience have made impossible to ignore, at least for those who are genuinely and intelligently concerned with human happiness.

This "eternal problem" does admit of a solution, according to the Inquisitor. Despite his appreciation of the obduracy of the personal conscience, he insists still on the primacy of the human desire for order. His conviction that human beings ultimately wish to be induced to give up their freedom remains unshaken. For him, the proper estimation of the personal conscience is merely the prerequisite for capturing it: "whoever knows this mystery of mankind's existence knows how to go about subduing him, and who can, subdues him."[14] The "mystery" of the conscience is that "there is nothing more alluring to man than . . . freedom of conscience"; at the same time,

12 *NBK*, p. 80.
13 Ibid., p. 80.
14 Ibid., p. 80.

"there is nothing more tormenting, either" (298-99; V,5). In this paradox resides the possibility of relieving human beings of their freedom.

According to the Inquisitor, human beings strive for an ultimate good only in order finally to attain to a condition of happy repose. When the longed-for tranquillity eludes them and the moral quest becomes a perpetual striving, then the personal conscience becomes a torment—particularly for the "thousands of millions" of the weak who lack the spiritual capacity to sustain the arduous struggle for final peace of mind. If there is indeed an ultimate end to the moral quest, surely knowledge of it will be vouchsafed only to the few thousand of the strong, who are more like gods than human beings. For the weak, the freedom of conscience which they find so alluring issues only in "unrest, confusion, and unhappiness . . ." (301; V,5). To the Inquisitor this is demonstrable from the historical experience of the West just as surely as is the tenacity with which humanity upholds the prerogative of the personal conscience. Gazing into a distant future in which the Protestant conscience has been translated through Geneva thought into the right of each individual to decide independently "with a free heart" what is good, the Inquisitor predicts that the mass of humanity will come to rue the day that simple acquiescence in the given morality of the Roman Catholic order was rejected:

They will pay dearly for it. They will tear down the temples and drench the earth with blood. But they will realize at last, the foolish children, that although they are rebels, they are impotent rebels who are unable to keep up with their rebellion. Dissolving into foolish tears, they will admit at last that he who created them rebels must undoubtedly have meant to laugh at them. (300-301; V,5)

The Inquisitor does not claim that individuals will cease to be moral beings, for the need to make moral judgments is too deeply rooted. He thinks, however, that in the aftermath of the trials in store for them, human beings could be persuaded to relinquish the right to make such judgments *for themselves*, "with a free heart." Yet the sacrifice of personal conscience, which the modern individual will be only too willing to make, will be merely temporary unless it is accepted by those with the knowledge to hold it "captive for ever" (299; V,5).

According to the Inquisitor, this knowledge is disclosed in the second temptation. The temptation, properly interpreted, not only reveals that human beings will surrender their freedom only to those who can fully appease their conscience, but reveals also the most effective means of appeasement:

There are three forces, the only three forces that are able to conquer and hold captive for ever the conscience of those weak rebels for their own happiness—these forces are: miracle, mystery, and authority. You rejected all three and yourself set the example for doing so. When the wise and terrible spirit set you on a pinnacle of the temple and said to you: 'If thou be the son of God, cast thyself down: for it is written, He shall give his angels charge concerning thee: and in their hands they shall bear thee up. . . .' (299; V,5)

The "rebels" have to be taught that the question of good is a "mystery" which must be believed rather than known, that it is not the "free verdict of their hearts nor love that matters, but the mystery which they must obey blindly, even against their conscience." Remembering the "horrors of slavery and confusion" to which a "free mind" brought them, they will gratefully accept the assurance that the ultimate good is inaccessible to human knowledge (301, 303; V,5). The "authority" of those who preach the "mystery" will be confirmed, above all, by "miracles," or the appearance of miracles, for when freedom of conscience becomes too agonizing "what man seeks is not so much God as miracles." Human beings are ultimately unable to carry on without a miracle, so much so that even in the modern age which has banished miracles they will find new miracles for themselves and will worship the pseudo-miracles of the modern "witch-doctor" (300; V,5).[15]

The Inquisitor maintains that in Western history the preaching of "miracle, mystery, and authority" has come within the special province of the Roman Catholic Church. And he foresees no serious rival arising to contend with the traditional supremacy of Roman Catholicism in this matter. It would thus appear that when modern people begin to yearn for "miracle, mystery, and authority," they will have no choice but to return to that morality which they have spurned with such cavalier disregard for their own happiness. The Roman Catholic Church may again be compelled to hide itself in the catacombs; but the Inquisitor thinks it possible that the day will come when it will be sought out in its hiding place and asked to renew its possession of the human conscience. This time will come when humanity's striving after knowledge of good and evil becomes completely transformed into the directionless striving after knowledge for its own sake which is characteristic of modern science:

Freedom, a free mind and science will lead them into such a jungle and bring them face to face with such marvels and insoluble mysteries that some of them, the recalcitrant and the fierce, will destroy themselves, others, recalcitrant but weak, will destroy one another, and the rest, weak and unhappy, will come crawling to our feet and cry aloud: 'Yes, you were right, you alone possessed his mystery, and we come back to you—save us from ourselves!' (303; V,5)

The Inquisitor's social formula is based on his interpretation of the first two temptations. It can therefore now be stated in the following way: those who would rule over humanity for its happiness must be both distributors of "loaves" and preachers of "miracle, mystery, and authority." Properly interpreted, and regarded in the light of historical experience, the first two temptations reveal that people will ultimately consent only to an order which provides them with both earthly and heavenly bread. Only to rulers who simultaneously satisfy their physical and moral appetites will people relin-

15 For an interesting discussion of the manner in which the Inquisitor's understanding of "miracle, mystery, authority" differs from that of the New Testament, see R. L. Cox, "Dostoevsky's Grand Inquisitor," *Cross Currents* (Fall 1967), pp. 427-44.

quish forever their freedom for the sake of that social re-integration which is their most fundamental desire. Because it is based on two "eternal" or "everlasting" truths about human nature, the Inquisitor's social formula applies to human beings everywhere and always.

The very timelessness of the Inquisitor's formula, however, must inevitably render it more or less "abstract," despite his citing of concrete historical evidence for its validity. Yet "abstractness" implies a certain dissociation of theory and practice which the Inquisitor, of all people, must not admit. For he is concerned with the *actual* happiness of human beings, a concern which leads him to refuse to ask too much of them and to found his social formula on human beings as they actually *are* rather than as they *ought* to be. The Inquisitor cannot remain content with a teaching which is the best in theory, though it may never be realized in practice. For him, this would be equivalent to siding with the "great idealists," who do not love humanity sufficiently. His entire enterprise requires that his social formula be realizable. The confident assurance with which he does anticipate the realization of his formula has its source in his interpretation of the third temptation.

The Third Temptation

The third and last "torment" of humanity is the need for "universal unity," for the union of all in a "common, harmonious, and incontestable anthill . . ." (302; V,5). The Inquisitor avers that the human yearning for order will not be satisfied by the idea alone of an ultimate good, even when this idea is provided in conjunction with earthly bread, for human beings need also to give a practical living expression to the object of their belief, and they need to do so in unity with others. The unity sought is ultimately universal, for the co-existence of differing ideas of life tends to undermine the certainty of those who live by them. For the Inquisitor the human need for a universal order is not to be satisfied by the appeal (which Christianity, for instance, has made) to a universality which is "spiritual" in nature. The universality for which humanity has always yearned is a visible universality; therefore, in the Inquisitor's thinking, "universal" is synonymous with "world-wide" (or "ecumenic," as first defined by the Roman historian, Polybius).[16] According to the Inquisitor, then, human beings require an actual world-wide social order corresponding to the "miracle, mystery, and authority" which they obey—an order, moreover, which grants them at least the minimal satisfaction of their material wants. This is to say that human beings will ultimately settle for nothing less than the realization, not merely in a dream but in actuality, of the Inquisitor's social formula.

The Inquisitor interprets the offer of the "kingdoms of the world" in the third temptation as the offer of the most powerful instrument for satisfying the human need for universal unity—the universal state. The universal state is the

16 See E. Voegelin, *Order and History* (Baton Rouge, 1974), vol. IV, pp. 114-34.

prime vehicle for the actualization of the social order ruled by keepers of humanity's conscience who are also distributors of its bread. History for the Inquisitor is important chiefly as the realm of the appearance and progressive development of this vehicle. (Indeed, his ecstatic certainty concerning the future realization of his final solution to the problem of order makes his view of history reminiscent of that modern Western "philosophy of history" developed from Vico to Marx.)[17]

According to the Inquisitor, the dawn of history coincides with the first tentative efforts towards the construction of a universal order. The persistence with which human beings have moved towards the universal state, even in its most rudimentary form, reflects at least a half-conscious awareness of its importance for their happiness:

Mankind as a whole has always striven to organize itself into a world state. There have been many great nations with great histories, but the more highly developed they were, the more unhappy they were, for they were more acutely conscious of the need for the world-wide union of men. The great conquerors, the Timurs and Genghis Khans, swept like a whirl-wind over the earth, striving to conquer the world, but, though unconsciously, they expressed the same great need of mankind for a universal and world-wide union. (302; V,5)

The work of the Timurs and the Genghis Khans is a striking manifestation of the human impulse towards the universal state; but, in them, this impulse remained merely unconscious, and hence failed to bear fruit. The conscious aspiration towards the construction of the universal state first appeared in the ecumenic empires of Persia, Macedon, and Rome. The Inquisitor focuses upon the last as the culmination of ancient humanity's striving for universal unity.

Humanity had possessed, in the Roman Empire, a splendid and apparently "eternal" instrument for its happiness. Yet just when it seemed that the human struggle towards order had achieved final success, Rome was undermined by the rebellion of the personal conscience, which found its most effective vehicle in Christianity. Despite its aura of finality, the Roman state had failed to understand properly the moral dimension of human life. This failure condemned humanity to a thousand years of the disease of disorder. The external political and legal structures of Rome proved extraordinarily durable, however, even after the life had gone out of them; the "sword of Caesar" remained at hand for the use of new architects of world-wide order (302; V,5). In its attempt to have Christianity serve order rather than disorder, the Western church did not spurn this sword, and the accommodation which it reached with the remnants of the Roman state gave birth to that Roman Catholic order which was to define Western civilization for centuries. Although it evinced a more profound appreciation of the need for heavenly bread, Roman Catholic order was also to be finally undermined by the asser-

17 See K. Löwith, *Meaning in History* (Chicago, 1949), pp. 1-19.

tiveness of the personal conscience, and also by the attempt to alleviate the sufferings of material deprivation. But in its rejection of Roman Catholic civilization, the modern West has not repudiated the "sword of Caesar"; indeed, it apotheosizes the state—still fundamentally the universal state of Rome—and opposes it to any other instrument of human order (69; II,5). Because of its wholehearted adoption of the state, the modern West tends to overcome the divergence of loyalties once rendered inevitable by the uneasy compromise achieved in the Middle Ages between the Roman church and the Roman state. The modern state, moreover, in consciously founding itself solely on reason, is bound up with a science which holds out possibilities for the control of human and non-human nature beyond anything dreamt of in the past. For these reasons, the modern Western state must be regarded as the most effective instrument of social order that the world has yet seen. The "sword of Caesar" could prove, in its modern embodiment, to be more powerful than it ever was in ancient Rome or in medieval Europe. But who will wield this formidable instrument?

As we have already noted, the Inquisitor predicts that it is socialism which will finally inherit Caesar's sword. We have also noted, however, his expectation that the triumph of socialism will be short-lived unless it can offer humanity something more than earthly bread. Among the socialists there will be those sufficiently "scientific" to realize that the full compliance of the individual in the socialist order will require a "moral enticement." In order to preserve itself, socialism will at last be compelled to seek out preachers of "miracle, mystery, and authority." The Inquisitor thus foresees that the socialist state, following those driven to despair by the "jungle" into which freedom of conscience has led them, will turn to the Roman Catholic Church as the most practised adept in the realm of "miracle, mystery, and authority." This time, however, the alliance between church and state will be more complete than the compromise of the past allowed. The two will enter into the indivisible union expressed in the formula—"The Pope—leader of communism"—which is the outward historical expression of the Inquisitor's social theory. When socialism surrenders its highly organized system for the satisfaction of material needs into the hands of Roman Catholicism, then the keepers of humanity's conscience will also be the distributors of its bread. The problem of social order will be at last solved in actuality. Human beings will finally come into possession of that yearned-for earthly paradise which has always eluded them:

And then we shall finish building their tower ... and we alone shall feed them in your name ... the flock will be gathered together again and will submit once more, and this time it will be for good. Then we shall give them quiet, humble happiness, the happiness of weak creatures, such as they were created. ... They will grow timid and begin looking up to us and cling to us in fear as chicks to the hen. They will marvel at us and be terrified of us and be proud that we are so mighty and so wise as to be able to tame such a turbulent flock of thousands of millions. They will be helpless and in constant fear of our wrath, their minds will grow timid, their eyes will always be shedding tears like women and children, but at the slightest sign from us they will be just as ready to pass to mirth and laughter, to bright-eyed gladness and happy childish song. . . . And they will have no secrets from us. . . . The most tormenting secrets of their conscience—everything, everything they will bring to us, and we shall give them our decision for it all. . . . And they will all be happy, all the millions of creatures, except the hundred thousand who rule over them. (297, 303-304; V,5)

The Goal of the Final Western Social Formula

Reason and Love of Humanity

The modern Western quest for an "order deduced solely from rational principles" speaks its final word in the Grand Inquisitor's description of the future earthly paradise. The Inquisitor's conception of the universal state is presented in opposition to the universal state of "freedom, equality, and brotherhood" which was the original object of the modern Western project; but Dostoyevsky clearly regards the Inquisitor's tyranny as more a reformulation than a negation of the Geneva idea. In the most important respects the Inquisitor is in accord with the Geneva vision: out of love of humanity he aspires to an earthly paradise which has its foundation in reason. This dependence on reason, not explicit in his own words, may seem incongruous with the crucial role which "miracle, mystery, and authority" play in his social formula. "Miracle, mystery, and authority," however, are for him merely instruments of order required by his "realistic" appraisal of humanity as it actually is. This "realistic" assessment of human nature is wholly free of any traditional religious or philosophical preconceptions.[18] The Inquisitor's social formula is a logical inference, derived solely from the historical and natural evidence available to him. It is in this sense that his idea of order can be considered as "rational" as that of Geneva thought, despite his position as a representative of Roman Catholicism at its most militant. The Inquisitor's formula for tyranny, moreover, is not only in concordance with the original intent of the modern quest for a new order, but affirms it more fully. His deeper love of humanity inspires a more uncompromising, even ruthless, rationality than that evinced by the proponents of the Geneva idea. For him, where humanity's happiness is at stake, hesitation before the consequences of reason is equivalent to a lack of charity, for the rational approach to human existence, if combined with courage and lucidity, does yield the solution to the problem of order. The Inquisitor's reinterpretation of the idea of "freedom, equality, and

---

18 This would include, of course, the preconceptions of Roman Catholicism. The very difficult issue of the Inquisitor's precise relation to Roman Catholicism will be taken up in the final chapter, when we concern ourselves with Dostoyevsky's judgment of Western Christianity.

brotherhood," so that it corresponds to what humanity *actually* is, is thus presented as having its source in the most consistent possible affirmation of the foundational principles of the Geneva vision.

In its salient features the Inquisitor's social formula corresponds to Shigalyov's reinterpretation of the Geneva idea. As we have seen, Shigalyov also is a "fanatic lover of mankind," who therefore yearns for the earthly paradise in actuality rather than merely in a dream. This yearning for certainty leads him also to the most uncompromising application of reason to the problem of social order. The rigorous observation of humanity as it actually is yields to both Shigalyov and the Inquisitor the fundamental insight into human inequality. This inequality pertains, not simply to obvious differences in natural endowment, but to something fraught with far graver consequences for Geneva thought: human beings are unequal in their capacity to endure freedom. This truth, vouchsafed by the truly rational assessment of humanity, requires that transposition of terms which turns the universal order of "freedom, equality, and brotherhood" into a tyranny. Freedom is only for the few who are able to endure it, and they in turn rule absolutely over the many, who are equal brothers in their utter subjugation.

In the thought of the Inquisitor and Shigalyov, then, Dostoyevsky's critiques of Russian Westernism and of the West converge. The "great idea" which originally commanded the allegiance of the best Russian Westernists is the same idea which stands at the centre of the modern Western project. In each case, the progressive self-revelation of this idea culminates in the word of tyranny. The question raised at the end of my exposition of Dostoyevsky's critique of Russian Westernism is decisively answered by him in "The Grand Inquisitor." Due to the relative absence of solid foundations of life in Russia, Russian Westernism did indeed take Western ideas to extremes which tended to make them unrecognizable to the West itself. But this tendency immediately to regard as an axiom what is merely an hypothesis in the West discloses, rather than falsifies, what lies concealed in the hypothesis. For Dostoyevsky, then, Russia may be likened to a hot-house in which Western ideas bear fruit more quickly than within the more mature, and hence delimited, cultures of the West. The Geneva idea of order ultimately expresses itself as a tyranny, not because it has been sown in improper soil, but because of what is most fundamentally inherent in the idea itself.

Yet the inner necessity of the relation between Versilov's earthly paradise and that of the Inquisitor, between the liberal idea of "freedom, equality, and brotherhood" and tyranny remains to be disclosed. It is primarily through what is revealed about the Inquisitor's ultimate motivation that Dostoyevsky attempts to show this inner necessity. This attempt centres on the problematic relation between reason and love of humanity, both of which are essential to the Geneva idea and to the Inquisitor's tyranny.

The Inquisitor has much to say about the means of ensuring the consent of the weak to the future universal state; but he is singularly reticent concerning those who are to rule. His own aspiration to absolute rule is apparently motivated by an "incurable" love of humanity (307; V,5). His humanitarianism is expressed in the avowal that only consequent upon the actualization of his social formula will it be possible "for the first time to think of the happiness of men" (295; V,5). Indeed, he asserts that all previous social orders have been founded on an insufficient love of humanity. In the rough notes Dostoyevsky has him declare explicitly that his idea of order is rooted in a love of humanity greater than that of Christianity, the so-called "religion of love": "Inquisitor: God as a merchant. I love humanity more than you do."[19] The Inquisitor's love of humanity, moreover, is attested to by Ivan in response to Alyosha's accusation that the Spanish cardinal is nothing more than a tyrant in the usual sense:

What I'd like to ask you is why your Jesuits and Inquisitors have united only for some vile material gains? Why shouldn't there be among them a sufferer tormented by great sorrow and loving humanity? You see, let us suppose that among all those who are only out for filthy material gains there's one, just one, who is like my old Inquisitor, who had himself fed on roots in the wilderness, a man possessed, who was eager to mortify his flesh so as to become free and perfect; and yet one who had loved humanity all his life and whose eyes were suddenly opened and who saw that it was no great moral felicity to attain complete control over his will and at the same time realize that millions of other of God's creatures had been created as a mockery, that they would never be able to cope with their freedom, that no giants would ever arise from the pitiful rebels to complete the tower, that the great idealist had not in mind such boobies when he dreamt of his harmony. Realizing that, he returned and joined—the clever fellows. That could have happened, couldn't it? (306-307; V,5)

Ivan is responsible for the Inquisitor and his words, and therefore should be expected to know him intimately. His depiction of the suffering servant of humanity sounds the major chord in the self-justification of the rulers of the future universal state. The profound love of humanity animating the Inquisitor entails a voluntary assumption of suffering which imbues his figure with a certain "lofty sadness" (306; V,5). There is something undeniably attractive in the image of the exceptional person who, unable to cure himself of his compassion for lesser people, renounces his own solitary happiness in order to serve their happiness by bringing "some sort of supportable order" into their lives. Although Alyosha is the "hero" of *The Brothers Karamazov*,[20] Dostoyevsky seems to be serving notice of the inadequacy of understanding the rulers of the universal state in terms of the picture which is usually conjured up by the word "tyrant." The rulers of the universal state will portray themselves as people who have been compelled to acknowledge, finally and to their great sorrow, that tyranny is the price of human happiness, a price which will be paid by the tyrants themselves: "And they will all be happy, all the millions of creatures, except the hundred thousand who rule over them. For

19 *NBK*, p. 75.
20 See Dostoyevsky's foreword to *The Brothers Karamazov*.

we alone, we who guard the mystery, we alone shall be unhappy'' (304; V,5). This image of the hundred thousand sufferers maintaining a lonely and loving vigil over their weaker fellow humans imbues the Inquisitor's social formula with a potent moral aura. This formula is thus able to evince the most sober realism without being in the least prosaic.

The Inquisitor associates his suffering with the guarding of a ''mystery'' or a ''secret.'' Closer examination of this ''secret'' reveals that his love of humanity is rendered ambiguous by the very suffering which lends it such a heroic aspect. The Inquisitor's ''sorrow'' and Shigalyov's ''despair'' are only partially attributable to their realization that tyranny is the only possible solution to the problem of human order. This realization points to the more fundamental insight into human life which is ultimately responsible for their suffering. The Inquisitor himself comes close to revealing this insight, which the rulers keep from the weak ''for their own happiness,'' when he states that ''beyond the grave they will find nothing but death.'' However, he then hastens to qualify this assertion by adding that ''if there were anything at all in the next world'' it would not be for such as they. It is Alyosha, with Ivan's concurrence, who gives explicit expression to the Inquisitor's secret: ''godlessness, that's all their secret. Your Inquisitor doesn't believe in God—that's all his secret!'' (304-305, 307; V,5). The Inquisitor's consideration of humanity as it actually is is indissolubly associated with the insight, implicit throughout his monologue, that human life is a finiteness unencompassed by any over-arching meaning. It is the vision of human life as meaningless, perpetual becoming which is at the root of the suffering of the future tyrants. There is nothing spurious in their suffering, then, and in this regard the image of the sorrowing lover of humanity cannot be considered a deception. However, the insight into human life responsible for this suffering casts a profound shadow over the other component of Ivan's image. Is the knowledge that there is no answer to the why of human existence, other than the indifferent silence of death, compatible with a love of humanity? Can the Inquisitor love those whom he knows to be nothing more than ''unfinished experimental creatures created as a mockery'' (307; V,5)? This question is rendered acute by the suspicion inevitably fostered in any attentive hearer of his monologue concerning his attitude towards his ''flock.'' His refusal to demand too much, to estimate the ''weak and base'' creatures too highly, treads too fine a line between loving solicitude and contempt. He thus invites the question which Dostoyevsky poses to the builders of the universal state: ''Do you love or despise mankind, you, its coming saviours?''[21]

The issue of the compatibility of love of humanity with the insight into the ''finality of becoming'' (to adopt Nietzsche's phrase) remains largely implicit in the Inquisitor. To attribute such an insight too explicitly to a sixteenth-century Roman Catholic cardinal would perhaps run the risk of

21 See Dostoyevsky's letter of 10 May 1879 to N. A. Liubimov.

making him anachronistic, thereby detracting from the artistic power of the "poem"—(which is what "The Grand Inquisitor" ultimately is, for Dostoyevsky as much as for Ivan [288; V,5]).[22] It is possibly for this reason that Dostoyevsky's further analysis of the suffering "saviours" of humanity is embodied in Ivan, the modern Russian author of the poem. We have noted that Dostoyevsky's critiques of Russian Westernism and the West itself merge into one because of his conviction that modern Russia functions as a "laboratory" in which the final results of Western "hypotheses" become observable more rapidly than in the West itself. The conjunction of the two critiques is epitomized in Ivan. On the one hand, he represents the furthest development of Russian Westernism, in its Shigalyov phase. In a letter to his publisher Dostoyevsky refers to Ivan as the "synthesis of contemporary Russian anarchism," and in another letter, to K. P. Pobedonostsev, he characterizes him as a socialist of today."[23] On the other hand, Ivan, who intends to leave Russia for the "precious graveyard" of Europe, is the poet of the final Western solution to the problem of order (269; V,3). Dostoyevsky does place some distance between the young Russian socialist and the Grand Inquisitor; for instance, in reply to Alyosha's urgent question as to whether he is "with" the old man, Ivan laughingly refers to "The Grand Inquisitor" as "only a stupid poem of a stupid student, who has never written two lines of poetry in his life" (308; V,5). But there is no such hesitation concerning Ivan's relation to the Inquisitor in the rough notes for the novel. Here, the two characters are tersely but decisively united: "Ivan—Inquisitor! Inquisitor!"[24] Therefore, although the most subtle aspects of Dostoyevsky's further analysis of the motivation underlying the future universal state may be embodied of necessity in Ivan and other Russian characters, it should be clear that this analysis is meant to pertain equally to the West.

In his rough notes for *The Brothers Karamazov*, Dostoyevsky has Ivan state the chief point of his accord with the Inquisitor: "I am with the old man's idea, because he loves humanity more."[25] Ivan affirms the Inquisitor's universal state because it is the social order which corresponds most faithfully to a genuine love of humanity. In the two chapters leading up to "The Grand Inquisitor" ("The Brothers Get Acquainted" and "Rebellion"), he makes it clear that for him the requirements of love constitute the criterion against which all human thought and practice must be measured; and in these same chapters he stipulates what love requires. The first requirement is an infinite compassion for human suffering. For Ivan, the measure of love is the degree of agony which a person is capable of experiencing at the knowledge of the "human tears with which the earth is saturated from its crust to its

22 Dostoyevsky's concern with presenting his thought while conforming to the requirements of art is evident, for instance, in his discussion of the character of Father Zosima. See his letter of 7 Aug. 1879 to N. A. Liubimov.
23 Letters of 10 May 1879 and 19 May 1879.
24 *NBK*, p. 75.
25 Ibid., p. 79.

centre. . . ." So that his "case" is clearer he speaks particularly of the suffering of the innocent, and his cruel cataloguing of the tortures undergone by
little children evokes in Alyosha that very agony which is the mark of love.
This agony is not, however, the highest expression of love for Ivan; rather, he
yearns for its overcoming in the actualization of justice (285-88; V,4). The
person who loves is the thirster after justice.

Ivan does not understand justice legalistically, as retribution for the
suffering inflicted by some human beings upon others. He seeks, not vengeance, but the end of all suffering, including that of the torturers who deserve
to suffer. He yearns for an all-encompassing reconciliation, in which "the
mother will embrace the torturer who had her child torn to pieces by his dogs,
and all three will cry aloud: 'Thou art just O Lord!'" (286; V,4). Ivan's thirst
for justice thus reveals itself as a thirst for perfection itself, for the "harmony" in which "all the offensive and comical spectacle of human
contradictions"—of which human suffering is one principal manifestation—
"will vanish like a pitiful mirage . . ." (275; V,3). Ivan's thirst for justice,
however, can find no satisfaction in the thought of a harmony which transcends the earth, nor in the anticipation of a harmony to be attained in the
indefinite future. He demands justice here on earth, and immediately. For if
justice is actual only beyond the earth, or on the earth in some distant future,
then the "spectacle" of human imperfection will persist as a source of pain to
those who love humanity. Their pain will remain unassuaged, just as the
suffering of the innocent will, in actuality, remain without consolation. Out of
the love he bears for humanity, then, Ivan rejects any notion of justice which
postulates a gulf between the idea and its imminent actualization on earth. His
return of the "entrance ticket" to any harmony which cannot be present for
him here and now constitutes perhaps the most forceful expression of the
modern repudiation of the traditional concept of a transcendent justice. But no
less does it represent a forceful attack on the modern immanentization of this
transcendent justice in the doctrine of historical progress. Ivan's rejection of
progressivism is reminiscent particularly of Belinsky's well-known condemnation of Hegel:

Surely the reason for my suffering was not that I as well as my evil deeds and sufferings may serve as manure for some future harmony for someone else. I want to
see with my own eyes the lion lie down with the lamb and the murdered man rise
up and embrace his murderer. I want to be there when everyone suddenly finds out
what it has all been for. All religions on earth are based on this desire, and I am a
believer. . . . Listen: if all have to suffer so as to buy eternal harmony by their suffering, what have the children to do with it—tell me, please? It is entirely incom-
prehensible why they, too, should have to suffer and why they should have to buy
harmony by their sufferings. Why should they, too, be used as dung for someone's
future harmony? . . . I renounce higher harmony altogether . . . if the sufferings of
children go to make up the sum of sufferings which is necessary for the purchase of
truth, then I say beforehand that the entire truth is not worth such a price . . . I
don't want harmony. I don't want it, out of the love I bear to mankind. . . . I'd
rather remain with my suffering unavenged and my indignation unappeased, *even if*

I were wrong. Besides, too high a price has been placed on harmony. We cannot afford to pay so much for admission. (285-87; V,5)[26]

Love of humanity requires, above all, the immediate realization of justice. For the sake of certainty concerning this realization, Ivan is willing to lower his sights when it comes to justice itself. "The Grand Inquisitor" reflects this readjustment. Renouncing the perfect, but distant and perhaps unattainable, harmony, Ivan opts instead for the immediate alleviation of human suffering promised in the Inquisitor's social formula. The universal state is a "paradise" which can at least be actual, rather than merely a dream. There seems to be no indication in Ivan's argument of how the immediate achievement of human happiness would atone for past suffering; but the abolition at least of the present and future suffering of the majority of human beings is promised in the universal state. It should be emphasized that, although Ivan's thirst for immediate justice entails the rejection not only of Greek philosophy and biblical revelation but also of progressivist liberalism and socialism, his social formula is not so much a negation of the Geneva idea as a logical extension of the principles inherent in it. For Ivan, too, renounces love of God and immortality in favour of a love of humanity which expresses itself in the yearning for an actual earthly paradise. Dostoyevsky intends Ivan's argument for justice on earth to constitute the very heart of the self-justification of the modern Western project, both in its origin in Geneva thought and in its furthest development in political socialism. In Ivan, Dostoyevsky discloses that the question of the West is for him essentially a question about the possibility of achieving justice on earth. The builders of the new Tower of Babel are building "for the sake of bringing heaven down to earth" (26-27; I,5).

Despite the emphasis on practice implied in Ivan's thirst for justice on earth, he shares in the fundamental characteristic which Dostoyevsky attributed to Russian Westernism—the willingness to "sacrifice one's self, to sacrifice everything for truth." Although Ivan gently mocks the Russian "boys" who "do nothing nowadays but talk of eternal questions," even while snatching a free moment in a pub, he himself is pre-eminently one of these Russian boys (273, 268; V,3). He cannot resist subjecting his own thirst for justice to a theoretical examination. The ambiguity which Dostoyevsky discerned at the heart of the universal state, implicitly present in the ambivalence of the Inquisitor's attitude towards his "sheep," is made the explicit subject of theoretical analysis by Ivan himself.

The nature and possibility of "love of humanity" is a question which preoccupies Ivan throughout the novel. If love of humanity is the major

---

26 Cf. Kant's reluctance to formulate a philosophy of history, in the third thesis of his "Idea for a Universal History from a Cosmopolitan Point of View," in I. Kant, *On History* (New York, 1963); and see Hegel's words concerning the fate of many "an innocent flower" in the introduction to his philosophy of history, in G. W. F. Hegel, *The Philosophy of History* (New York, 1956), pp. 32-33.

premise of his argument for the Inquisitor's social formula, it is a premise which is far from self-evident for him. Significantly, his most sustained argument for immediate earthly justice (in the chapter entitled "Rebellion," immediately preceding "The Grand Inquisitor") commences with a confession of his inability to comprehend the very "love of humanity" which inspires his rebellion against other conceptions of a more distant justice:

> I never could understand how one can love one's neighbours. In my view, it is one's neighbours that one can't possible love, but perhaps only those who live far away. . . . To love a man, it's necessary that he should be hidden, for as soon as he shows his face, love is gone. . . . Theoretically it is still possible to love one's neighbours, but at close quarters almost never. (276-77; V,4)

Ivan's compassion impels him to repudiate any notion of justice which tends to disregard actual human suffering. Yet his experience of the insuperable difficulty of loving actual people calls that compassion into question.

Ivan's passion for truth compels him to seek out the principle which might serve as the basis of a love for humanity. He is able to discern no such principle in nature, according to the testimony of another character in the novel, Miusov, a liberal of the 1840s:

> I will tell you . . . a very interesting and most characteristic anecdote about Mr. Ivan Karamazov himself. Only five days ago, at a certain social gathering, consisting mostly of ladies, he solemnly declared during an argument that there was absolutely nothing in the whole world to make men love their fellow-men, that there was no law in nature that man should love mankind, and that if love did exist on earth, it was not because of any natural law. . . . (77; II,6)

Understood according to the modern science of nature, "humanity" is the chance product of an indifferent material necessity. Insomuch as the science of nature is able to provide any criterion at all for the behaviour of these "accidental" beings, it can only point to the satisfaction of natural needs as the chief concern of each. According to Ivan's scientific understanding of nature, then, self-preservation, and even comfortable self-preservation, would have priority over "love of mankind." Ivan's difficulty in loving actual people is not counteracted by any natural principle which might ultimately encourage such love.

He is thus forced to acknowledge that his compassion for human suffering must be based on the love of a "hidden" humanity. Without the conviction of a "higher" humanity somehow present in actual people, love of humanity simply would not exist. Love of humanity is necessarily the love of an idea of humanity; it is a "duty" undertaken for the sake of this idea, rather than a natural impulse. We have seen that an important theme of Dostoyevsky's elucidation of the Geneva idea, particularly in its original liberal expression, is the ambiguity of its professed love of humanity. In his presentation of Ivan's idea of order this theme becomes crucial. Ivan, while affirming "love of humanity" as the very corner-stone of the universal state, vehemently

rejects the Geneva distinction between humanity as it actually is, and humanity as it could be and will be in the future. But the abolition of what little
distinction Geneva thought retains between humanity as it *is* and as it *could*
be deprives Ivan of the theoretical basis of that love which supposedly inspires
his argument for justice on earth. He therefore faces an impasse. Unless he is
willing to renounce his love of humanity, he must reconsider the possibility of
an orientation towards a humanity not rooted in the here and now. Ivan's
acknowledgment of the necessity of the idea of "immortality" would seem to
indicate his movement towards such an orientation. For him, the idea of an
"eternal" humanity provides the most profound and comprehensive guarantee possible for the love of actual human beings. To quote Miusov again:

he solemnly declared . . . that if love did exist on earth, it was not because of any
natural law but solely because men believed in immortality . . . and that if you were
to destroy the belief in immortality in mankind, not only love but every living force
on which the continuation of all life in the world depended, would dry up at once.
Moreover, there would be nothing immoral then, everything would be permitted,
even cannibalism. (77; II,6)

Ivan, however, rejects the concept of immortality, despite his recognition of its necessity. For Ivan, immortality is a "lie," and his love of truth
compels him to reject it. He will not participate in the self-deception of a
"John the Merciful":

I read somewhere about "John the Merciful" (some saint) who, when a hungry and
frozen stranger came to him and begged him to warm him, lay down with him in
his bed and, putting his arms around him, began breathing into his mouth, which
was festering and fetid from some awful disease. I'm convinced that he did so from
heart-ache, from heart-ache that originated in a lie, for the sake of love arising
from a sense of duty, for the sake of a penance he had imposed upon himself.
(276; V,4)

Ivan's turning away from eternity is expressed most explicitly in the novel in
his response, "over the brandy," to his father's anxious queries:

But tell me all the same: is there a God or not? Only seriously, mind! I want it
seriously now.
    No, there's no God . . .
    Ivan, is there immortality, I mean just of some sort, just a tiny little one?
    No, there's no immortality, either.
    None at all?
    None at all. (155-56; III,8)

This repudiation of the "lie" of God and immortality would seem simply to
be in accord with Ivan's status as a representative of atheist socialism. With
his recognition of the final consequences of his insight into the finality of
becoming, however, he moves beyond socialism to "nihilism."
    The term "nihilist" was first introduced into Russian intellectual life by
Turgenev. In *Fathers and Sons* he applied it to those Westernists of the 1860s
who sought the destruction of all the traditional objects of reverence for the

sake of a new, socialist order. According to this popular usage of the word in latter nineteenth-century Russia, "nihilism" and "revolutionary" socialism were indistinguishable. Dostoyevsky, however, perceived in nihilism an independent theoretical stance which ultimately excludes socialism. Ivan is a nihilist, not only because he seeks the destruction of the old gods, but, more importantly, because he knows that all gods are human inventions, that the moral ends to which human beings have submitted themselves are not sustained in the nature of things. The source of this insight is his "Euclidean" mind (274; V,3), that is, his reason—reason, however, which is more consistently and courageously applied than in liberalism or even "scientific" socialism. Ivan's recognition of the necessity of the idea of an eternal good, or God—both as a component of the Inquisitor's social formula and as the basis of that love of humanity which supposedly inspires the formula—does not alter his fundamental insight. At the outset of his argument for justice on earth, he quotes approvingly Voltaire's dictum: "*S'il n'existait pas Dieu il faudrait l'inventer*. And, to be sure, man has invented God" (274; V,3).

Ivan immediately qualifies the preceding observation by maintaining that he decided long before not to speculate as to whether "man has created God or God has created man." Yet, as I have noted, for Ivan the propensity of human beings to measure their existence against an ultimate moral good, expressing itself in notions such as "God" and "immortality," is manifestly a propensity for self-deception. The fact that he is careful to temper this insight in his discussion with Alyosha indicates that he too must be engaged in deception, if not of himself, then of those he is trying to convert to the universal state. For the unqualified avowal of the nihilist insight would negate his argument for justice on earth. This nihilist insight consigns humanity entirely to the realm of chance and necessity, and, as we have seen, for Ivan there is no basis for the love of humanity in this realm. The fact that the accidental creature insists on deluding itself that its existence has some overarching meaning can elicit only the contemptuous laughter, or in some exceptional cases the grudging respect, but never the love, of the nihilist. Shigalyov perceives the incompatibility of science and socialism, but he is oblivious to the more fundamental incompatibility of science with the love of humanity which still underlies his system. In Ivan, however, the tension between reason and love asserts itself as a problem which must be resolved.

The contradiction between Ivan's love of humanity and his nihilism manifests itself in him throughout the novel. The rebel out of love of humanity is also the teacher of the formula *par excellence* of nihilism—"everything is permitted." Smerdyakov, his most proficient pupil, explains the formula most precisely: "This you did teach me, sir; . . . if there's no everlasting God, there's no such thing as virtue, and there's no need of it at all" (743; XI,8). The direct practical consequence of this teaching is parricide, one of the most ignominious of crimes for those who live within the horizon of good and evil. Despite Ivan's horror when confronted with this consequence of nihilism, he never repudiates his "everything is permitted." Indeed he signifies his theoretical acceptance of parricide when, speaking of his father and his brother, he is able to declare contemptuously: "One reptile will devour another reptile, and serve them both right!" (164; III,9). That a professed lover of humanity could speak thus of his own family is, to say the least, paradoxical. Another and perhaps more striking instance of Ivan's "contradictoriness" is revealed by Lise Khokhlakov: the man who maintains that a single tear of an innocent child cannot be compensated by any yet-to-be attained harmony is apparently able to affirm the "goodness" of feeling enjoyment at the sight of the crucifixion of a four-year old child (685; XI,3). Ivan's thought and practice thus reflects an irresolvable contradiction. The contradiction is stated most concisely by another of Dostoyevsky's nihilist characters, Kirilov (in *The Devils*): "God is necessary and so must exist. . . . But I know that He doesn't exist and can't exist."[27]

It would seem that the very nature of Ivan's dilemma points towards his resolving it through the complete affirmation of the nihilist insight and its consequences, for he is, above all, a theoretical man, willing to sacrifice everything for truth. Moreover, the knowledge, once attained, that God is an "invention"—no matter how necessary an invention—must surely preclude any genuine return to life within the horizon of good and evil. Ivan's profession of love for humanity must thus be regarded as more or less spurious to the extent that his movement into nihilism is more or less complete.

The implications of Ivan's nihilism for his vision of social order must now be considered. The question of the Grand Inquisitor's attitude towards those he would rule can be given a clear answer. He cannot possibly love humanity; and, in the absence of love, his solicitude for human weakness must be regarded as an expression of contempt. His contempt may be mitigated by love to the extent that his nihilism is incomplete. But allowance for such a possibility does not alter Dostoyevsky's fundamental observation that the universal state will be ruled by tyrants who, despite their protestations, do not love humanity. What, then, will be the source of their aspiration to rule?

Alyosha's initial, instinctive imputation to the Inquisitor of a lust for "filthy earthly gains" takes on a new force in the light of the preceding discussion. Dostoyevsky's entertainment of the possibility that the rulers of the future universal state will be driven by the sheer desire for power is reflected particularly in Peter Verkhovensky's adoption of Shigalyov's "system." Verkhovensky himself admits to Stavrogin that his enthusiasm for Shigalyov's social formula is the enthusiasm of a "rogue," that he is "not a socialist at all . . . but some sort of ambitious politician. . . ."[28] This ambition has theoretical significance, however, for his disavowal of socialism ultimately stems, not from his "roguishness," but from his nihilism. Modern science has taught him to acknowledge the sovereignty of chance and neces-

27 *The Devils*, p. 611 (III,6,ii).
28 Ibid., p. 422 (II,8).

sity. Yet this issues in an active, unappeasable *libido dominandi* rather than in paralysis. In his case, then, nihilism and political order are compatible. He willingly consents to undertake the role of tyrant, as the only political activity appropriate to those strong enough to be nihilists.[29] It may thus be a matter of indifference whether or not the rulers of the universal state love those whom they rule. The desire for power, if not love, will spur them to adopt the Inquisitor's social formula, thereby at once satisfying their power-lust and the yearning of the weak for order.

Nevertheless, Dostoyevsky implies that the relation between nihilism and the future universal state is highly uncertain. Verkhovensky adopts Shigalyov's system because he happens to be driven by the *libido dominandi*. Yet even if the desire for power over others were the chief passion of all nihilists, the result could be a perpetual struggle within the ranks of the strong rather than the formation of a stable social order. It is as easy to envisage titanic wars among various tyrannies in which the weak would be sacrificed to the power-lust of their nihilist rulers as it is to envisage the attainment of the final earthly paradise. It is by no means clear, moreover, that there is any necessary relation at all between nihilism and the aspiration to power over others. There seems to be no reason why the formula "everything is permitted" should entail political activity more than the private seeking of pleasure or—if the vision of life's meaninglessness becomes unendurable—self-annihilation. This uncertainty is reflected particularly in Ivan. Immediately subsequent to his justification and presentation of the Inquisitor's social formula, he seems to disavow any personal inclination to join the ranks of those who are constructing the universal state: "Good Lord, what do I care? I told you all I want is to live to thirty and then—dash the cup to the floor!" (308; V,5). The "dashing of the cup to the floor" as a likely consequence of his nihilism is elaborated by Ivan in Dostoyevsky's rough notes for the novel:

I have reflected, perhaps one could steep oneself in gambling, in chess, become a banker and play the stock-market, become a courtier. But . . . I came to the conclusion that I . . . could not do these things. You can't get rid of the idea. It will continue to live like a worm. Only one thing remains: Beastly voluptuousness, with all its consequences, voluptuousness to the point of cruelty, crime, even to the point of the Marquis de Sade. That would carry you for a while . . . I have come to the conclusion that up to 30 you can get by with the power of life . . . with the fascination of the cup, that is, with deceptions, and then one has to destroy oneself.[30]

Becoming a banker is as likely a "deception" for the nihilist as becoming a tyrant, and both possibilities are overshadowed by a yearning for release from the absurdity of existence. To quote Nietzsche, Europe's "first perfect nihilist," the insight into the finality of becoming can be "deadly."[31] The threat which this insight poses to the possibility of sustained political activity

29 See ibid., pp. 418-22 (II,8).
30 *NBK*, pp. 72-73.
31 F. Nietzsche, *The Use and Abuse of History* (London, 1909), p. 84.

is but one aspect of the threat which it poses to life itself. Dostoyevsky's analysis of the motivation of those who would rule the universal state thus seems to indicate the impossibility of its actualization. The modern Western quest for order, in its reliance on reason alone, carries within itself the seeds of a nihilism ultimately inimical to any order.

The Man-God

Ivan, however, is the author of "The Geological Upheaval" as well as "The Grand Inquisitor." If these two writings are looked at in conjunction, an extraordinary resolution of the problem which has been raised becomes dimly perceptible. Our knowledge of what is said in "The Geological Upheaval" depends on the following summary, offered by the "Devil" in conversation with Ivan:

> there's no need to destroy anything. All that must be destroyed is the idea of God in mankind. . . . Once humanity to a man renounces God (and I believe that period, analogous with the geological periods, will come to pass) the whole of the old out-look on life will collapse by itself without cannibalism and above all, the old mo-rality, too, and a new era will dawn. Men will unite to get everything life can give, but only for joy and happiness in this world alone. Man will be exalted with a spirit of divine, titanic pride, and the man-god will make his appearance. Extending his conquest over nature infinitely every hour by his will and science, man will every hour by that very fact feel so lofty a joy that it will make up for all his old hopes of the joys of heaven. Everyone will know that he is mortal, that there is no resurrection, and he will accept death serenely and proudly like a god. (763-64; XI,9)

Ivan's nihilism points beyond itself towards its overcoming in the "man-god," who is thereby revealed as the ultimate justification and guarantee of the future universal state.

In order to grasp the significance of the "man-god" for the problem of order, we must first understand how he signifies the overcoming of nihilism. This requires that we turn for the moment from Ivan to Kirilov (in *The Devils*). This solitary eccentric who "hates discussions" expresses his ideas with great reluctance.[32] Nevertheless, his disjointed and cryptic utterances, if properly interpreted, constitute the most sustained elucidation of the "man-god" to be found in Dostoyevsky's writings.

Kirilov shows the characteristic impatience for action of the generation of the 1860s. He claims that the nihilism which has appeared in the modern world is as yet merely a theory which has not been put into practice. The nihilist denies the existence of any over-arching limit or end to his willing: "If there is a God, then it is always His will, and I can do nothing against His will. If there isn't, then it is my will, and I am bound to express my self-will."[33] But the nihilist has not yet lived out his freedom from God; he has

32 *The Devils*, p. 106 (I,3,iv).
33 Ibid., p. 612 (III,6,ii).

merely expressed it in little things "like a schoolboy." Nihilism has not yet
been acted upon in the most important point—self-annihilation.[34] According
to Kirilov, the suicide which truly expresses the individual's new-found
self-will must be committed with the clear intention of expressing the conquest of the fear of death; of the "millions" of suicides, the only one of
significance would be the self-annihilation which intends only to annihilate
the fear of death. It is this fear which underlies the invention of the "next
world" or "God" (God and immortality being equivalent). With the help of
this deception we continue to live, even to love life, although "life is pain,
life is fear, and man is unhappy." So long as we are unable to accept the
essential finiteness of existence we will continue to console ourselves with
various sorts of religions which foster the illusion that life has some final
meaning. Even the minority of the strong, who think that they have dispensed
with God, continue to live in his shadow, for they still feel his absence. The
sense of God's absence may induce suffering, or a frenzied willing with no
other object than the satisfaction of base desires; but, whatever the case, its
presence in even the strongest nihilist indicates an inability to accept the
finiteness of existence. Because nihilism itself is thus implicated in the religious deception, the final overcoming of God will signify also the overcoming
of nihilism.[35]

The "annihilation" of God presupposes the overcoming of the need for
God, or the overcoming of the fear of death, so that "it makes no difference
whether to live or not to live." Kirilov's indifference, however, is "unhappy,"
for he is *bound* to demonstrate his indifference to death in the most decisive
manner because such indifference is not natural to him. Nonetheless,
Kirilov's unhappy putting into practice of nihilism prepares the way for the
happy indifference of the "new man." His annihilation of God is at the same
time the annunciation of the man-god, for we cannot dispense with God
without ourselves becoming gods (though mortal ones). Kirilov envisages the
man-god as a being to whom "it won't matter whether he lives or not," for he
is able to accept the transitoriness of his existence. But the man-god does not
merely resign himself to the vision of life as perpetual becoming; he affirms it,
in all of its manifestations, as "good." According to Kirilov, he will affirm
that "all's good"—the "spider crawling on the wall" as much as the "bright
green leaf"—because he refuses to judge life according to the distinction
between "good" and "evil" which has its basis in the religious lie. However,
the man-god's movement of affirmation will not have its ultimate source
merely in the sceptical refusal of moral categories, for this could only lead to
the less positive declaration that "all is what it is." The question of the
fundamental source of the man-god's "happy" affirmation of life leads us to
the mysterious centre of Kirilov's vision—his intuition of eternity. He at-

34 Cf. Alexandre Kojève's interpretation of Kirilov's suicide, in A. Kojève, *Introduction à la
lecture de Hegel* (Paris, 1947), pp. 517-18.
35 *The Devils*, pp. 124-26, 242-44, 586, 611-15 (I,3,viii; II,1,v; III,5,v,6,ii).

tempts to convey to Shatov one of these glimpses of eternity which have been vouchsafed him:

> There are seconds—they come five or six at a time—when you suddenly feel the presence of eternal harmony in all its fullness. It is nothing earthly. I don't mean that it is heavenly, but a man in his earthly semblance can't endure it. He has to undergo a physical change or die.... It is as though you suddenly apprehended all nature and suddenly said: 'Yes it is true—it is good.' God, when He created the world, said at the end of each day of creation: 'Yes it is true, it is good.'[36]

Apparently the man-god's happy affirmation that "all's good" will be possible by virtue of his participation in this eternity which Kirilov apprehends only briefly. This participation makes him a god, not only because he imitates God's affirmation of the goodness of creation, but because his affirmation of life is bound up with his power over life. The analogy with the God who creates is significant in this respect, as is Kirilov's statement that the attribute of our divinity is "Self-Will." The modern yearning to bring heaven down to earth seems to be intimately related to Kirilov's apprehension of eternity, for Kirilov understands eternity to be, not in a "future everlasting," but in "an everlasting life here" (just as Nietzsche, who also attempted to move through nihilism to the recovery of eternity, envisaged this eternity, not as timelessness, but as endless time).[37] According to Kirilov, the man-god will attain to this earthly eternity through that complete loyalty to the earth which is signified in the affirmation that "all's good."

We must now turn from the mystery of the earthly eternity at the centre of Kirilov's thought to the question of social order. Kirilov's vision of the man-god appears to have political implications. He regards the appearance of the man-god as an event of tremendous import for all, understanding his self-annihilation as an act which will save humanity: "I shall begin and end, and open the door. And I shall save." And he divides human history into two epochs: from the gorilla to the annihilation of God, and from the annihilation of God to the era of the man-god.[38] Although he calls for the transformation of humanity in accord with the man-god's affirmation of the earth, Kirilov says nothing about how this transformation will be wrought. Nor does he seem interested in questions concerning the nature of the social order which would ensue in the wake of the man-god's appearance. It is in *The Brothers Karamazov* that the question of the implications of the man-god for human order comes explicitly to the fore. The "Devil's" mention, almost in the same breath, of "The Geological Upheaval" and "The Grand Inquisitor" would

36 Ibid., pp. 586, 614-15, 242 (III,5,v,6,ii; II,1,v).
37 See F. Nietzsche, *Thus Spoke Zarathustra* (Harmondsworth, Eng., 1969), "The Convalescent," "The Seven Seals." Although Nietzsche was familiar with some of Dostoyevsky's writings (*Notes from Underground* and *Crime and Punishment*), it is almost certain that Dostoyevsky never read Nietzsche (whose major writings were published after Dostoyevsky's death).
38 *The Devils*, pp. 614-15, 126 (III,6,ii; I,3,viii).

indicate that they are meant to be seen together (763; XI,9). The latter can be considered as the political expression of the former.

Ivan's vision of the man-god requires a corresponding political teaching because the period in which "humanity to a man renounces God" has not yet come, and it may not be attained "even for a thousand years." There are, however, those who can and will achieve mangodhood now:

everyone who is already aware of the truth has a right to carry on as he pleases in accordance with the new principles. In that sense "everything is permitted" to him. What's more, even if that period never comes to pass, and since there is neither God nor immortality, anyway, the new man has a right to become a man-god, though he may be the only one in the whole world, and having attained that new rank, he may lightheartedly jump over every barrier of the old moral code of the former man-slave, if he deems it necessary. There is no law for God! Where God stands, there is his place! (764; XI,9)

The universal state of the Inquisitor, then, would serve as the instrument whereby the one, or the few, who have attained to mangodhood will transform others according to their truth. The fervid dream of a time when all people are loyal to the earth—when "men will unite to get everything life can give, but only for joy and happiness in this world alone"—would become a grandiose, yet perhaps practicable, political task. It is not clear from "The Geological Upheaval" whether Ivan envisages the possibility of mangodhood for all men-slaves. If so, then the Inquisitor's tyranny will conceivably wither away when it is no longer required for hastening the advent of the new era. However, the radical emphasis on human inequality which is so central to "The Grand Inquisitor" would seem to preclude the possibility of universal mangodhood. Presumably, there will always be people who need the comforting horizon of a religion. The universal state, then, will always be necessary; and its most subtle task will be to appease the need for worship of the weak in a manner which turns them towards joy in the earth, rather than away from it. The universal state of "The Grand Inquisitor" requires the man-god of "The Geological Upheaval" no less than the man-god seems to require the universal state. For the goal of mangodhood would provide the tyrants with a unifying end for their rule which will not contradict their nihilism, but will at once justify and overcome it. And the presence of the man-god would absolve them of the responsibility of providing an object of worship for the masses, who will share their veneration of the "happy and proud new man."

Questions still remain about the relationship between the man-god and the future universal state. It is not perfectly clear, for instance, why the man-god's affirmation of the earth would lead him to a sustained effort to bring into being others capable of his supreme affirmation, and thus why he would consent to stand at the head of a tyranny dedicated to himself. Such questions, perhaps necessarily, are left unanswered in Dostoyevsky's adumbration of a possibility only barely perceptible on the horizon of modernity. Nevertheless, a definite conclusion can be drawn from his analysis of the motives of the rulers of the future universal state: the modern Western attempt to actualize justice on earth by means of reason alone points to a tyranny which will be animated, not by love of man, but by love of the man-god. It is this love which ultimately underlies the Inquisitor's acceptance of the three temptations. Yet it underlies also his acceptance of "him" who offers the temptations: "And would I conceal our secret from you? . . . Well, then, listen. We are not with you but with *him*: that is our secret!" (301-302; V,5). This close association of the man-god with Satan takes us from Dostoyevsky's elucidation of the modern Western quest for order to his judgment of this quest.

FIVE

DOSTOYEVSKY'S JUDGMENT OF THE FINAL WESTERN SOCIAL FORMULA

The Silence of Christ

In the Inquisitor and in Ivan, the final Western social formula expresses itself with almost overwhelming power. Dostoyevsky once remarked that "even in Europe such force of atheistic *expression* does not now exist, *nor did it ever*."[1] This assessment may still hold true a century later. Yet the "force of atheistic expression" which Dostoyevsky achieved, while the indisputable mark of his greatness as an artist and a thinker, does pose a grave problem for the proper interpretation of his writing, for Dostoyevsky never intended to allow the argument of the Inquisitor to stand unchallenged. "The Grand Inquisitor" is not a monologue, but a dialogue in which one of the protagonists happens to remain silent. This silence, nevertheless, is meant to express a response to and a judgment upon the "force of atheistic expression" embodied in the Inquisitor. Dostoyevsky's acquaintance, K. P. Pobedonostsev (who was at the time Procurator of the Holy Synod of the Russian Orthodox Church) was probably reflecting the general reaction of readers of "The Grand Inquisitor" when he expressed his doubt that the Inquisitor's argument had been, or could be, effectively answered. Dostoyevsky apparently shared this concern, for in a letter to Pobedonostsev he confessed his anxiety that very few would grasp the reply to the Inquisitor contained in the chapter and in the next (sixth) book of the novel, "The Russian Monk," which he was working on with "fear and trembling."[2]

---

1 *UD*, III, p. 175.
2 Letter of 24 Aug. 1879.

Dostoyevsky's anxiety has proven to be justified. The subsequent response to "The Grand Inquisitor" has ranged from that of D. H. Lawrence, who interpreted Christ's kissing of the Inquisitor as acquiescence in his argument, to those who argue that Dostoyevsky affirms Christ against the Inquisitor through an "existential leap" in defiance of human reason. In the words of Camus, "having reached the end, the creator makes his choice against his characters."[3] Both Lawrence and Camus share the view that, whatever his intentions as a Christian, as an artist Dostoyevsky formulated an argument which could not be met effectively by a rational counter-argument. Such a view may well be correct in regarding Christ's silence as the most appropriate response to the Inquisitor's speech, but not because silence implies acquiescence in the Inquisitor's argument, nor because it implies that reason is one thing and religious faith something else altogether. This silence must be grasped in its positive meaning if Dostoyevsky is to be adequately understood. Greater theoretical clarity thus requires that some attempt be made to "explain" the silence of Christ, although any such attempt must plead at the outset the impossibility of formulating an "explanation" which will in any way correspond to the commanding beauty of the novel itself. As Versilov points out, "Silence is always beautiful and a silent man is always more pleasing to the eye than a talking man."[4]

Dostoyevsky's Critique of Reason

The silence of Christ before the Grand Inquisitor is not merely a negative admission of the inability of the eternal to defend itself convincingly by means of rational argument. This silence has for Dostoyevsky the positive significance of being the most appropriate possible response to the nihilist assertion of the finality of becoming. The presence of silence highlights, by contrast, the compulsion of the nihilist to subject to rational argument that which cannot

---

3 See D. H. Lawrence, "The Grand Inquisitor," *Selected Literary Criticism* (New York, 1956); A. Camus, *Essais* (Paris, 1965), pp. 186-88. The notion that the Inquisitor's argument is fundamentally unanswerable on the level of human reason is shared by many interpreters of "The Grand Inquisitor." This critical consensus is clearly expressed by Edward Wasiolek, in *Dostoevsky, The Major Fiction* (Cambridge, Mass., 1964): "The Grand Inquisitor's argument is not based on idle rhetoric or cheap tricks. Nor is it contradictory as some have claimed. Logic is on his side not Christ's, although the truth of each is finally subject to more than logic. Lawrence, Shestov, Guardini, Rozanov, and many other distinguished critics have taken the side of the Grand Inquisitor against Christ because his argument is powerful and indeed unanswerable . . . Dostoyevsky made the only case he could for Christ, and the truth of Christ he presents does not demolish the Grand Inquisitor's truth any more than the Grand Inquisitor's truth demolishes Christ's truth. We are concerned here with two ways of understanding man's nature, and they are discontinuous" (pp. 166-67). For a dissenting view concerning the "unanswerable" nature of the Inquisitor's argument, see R. L. Cox, "Dostoevsky's Grand Inquisitor," *Cross Currents* (Fall 1967), pp. 427-44; K. Mochulsky, *Dostoevsky, his Life and Work* (Princeton, 1967), pp. 617-22.

4 *The Adolescent*, p. 212 (II,1,iv).

be encompassed by such argument. The manner in which silence itself can be understood as a refutation of the nihilist insight is revealed in the following observation of Prince Myshkin (in *The Idiot*) concerning the nature of religiosity:

> "As to faith," he said, smiling. . . . "In the morning I was travelling on one of our new railways, and I talked for some hours with a man I met in the train. I had heard a great deal about him before and, incidentally, that he was an atheist. He really is a very learned man, and I was glad of the opportunity of talking to a real scholar. He is, moreover, an exceedingly well-bred person, and he talked to me as though I were his equal in knowledge and ideas. He doesn't believe in God. One thing struck me, though: he didn't seem to be talking about that at all the whole time, and this struck me particularly because before, too, whenever I met unbelievers and however many of their books I read, I could not help feeling that they were not talking or writing about that at all, though they may appear to do so. I told him this at the time, but I'm afraid I did not or could not express myself clearly enough, for he did not understand what I was talking about.
> . . . [T]he essence of religious feeling has nothing to do with any reasoning . . . it is something entirely different and it will always be so; it is something our atheists will always overlook and they will never talk about *that*."[5]

Dostoyevsky's view of the relationship between reason and "religious feeling" is often misunderstood. As already noted, he tends to be regarded as the proponent of a radical cleavage between reason and faith. But the notion that the silence of Christ before the Inquisitor signifies an appeal to an irrational "leap of faith" is mistaken. Dostoyevsky does not posit a fundamental opposition between reason and the human being's sense of God; rather, he asserts that the latter is dependent upon a faculty which is of a different order than reason, rather than simply opposed to it. Because it is so often misunderstood and yet so central to his silent judgment of the final Western social formula, Dostoyevsky's critique of reason requires some elucidation. His most explicit analysis of reason is to be found in a letter which he wrote to his elder brother Mikhail:

What do you mean precisely by the word *know*? Nature, the soul, love, and God, one recognizes through the *heart*, and not through the *reason*. Were we spirits, we could dwell in that region of ideas over which our souls hover, seeking the solution. But we are earth-born beings, and can only guess at the Idea—not grasp it by all sides at once. The guide for our intelligences through the temporary illusion into the innermost centre of the soul is called *Reason*. Now, Reason is a material capacity, while the soul or spirit lives on the thoughts which are whispered by the heart. Thought is born in the soul. Reason is a tool, a machine, which is driven by the spiritual fire. When human reason (which would demand a chapter for itself) penetrates into the domain of knowledge, it works independently of the feeling, and consequently of the heart. But when our aim is the understanding of love or of nature, we march towards the very citadel of the heart.[6]

5 *The Idiot*, pp. 251-53 (II,4).
6 Letter of 31 Oct. 1838.

Dostoyevsky was only eighteen years of age when he formulated this account
of human knowledge of "nature, the soul . . . and God," but his thought on
this matter appears to have remained essentially unchanged throughout his
life.

Fundamental to Dostoyevsky's account of human knowing is the distinction between "reason" and the "heart." The expression of this distinction
may lack philosophical precision (Dostoyevsky averred more than once that
philosophy was not his "specialty"),[7] but it is sufficiently clear to yield a
definite epistemological teaching. It is evident, first, that Dostoyevsky considers knowledge of God to be accessible. The human being owes the possibility of such knowledge, not to reason, but to a higher spiritual principle
within (which Dostoyevsky calls the "heart"). Reason, itself essentially
"material," cannot be the means of transcending the realm of material necessity. Only through cultivation of the spiritual principle within them can human
beings have access to that truth which is not subject to the finality of
becoming—that is, God.[8] And only through the "heart" can human beings
know themselves as something more than the mere product of that becoming,
as "soul." It must be emphasized that, for Dostoyevsky, the knowledge of
the heart need not contradict that of reason, for reason is the "guide" to the
spiritual principle within human beings, a "tool" capable of conforming itself
to that principle. Dostoyevsky advocates, not the renunciation of reason, but
its elevation, so that it becomes that "believing reason" which participates in
the "wholeness" of knowledge rooted in the spiritual principle.[9] Reason and

7 *UD*, III, p. 175.
8 "God" is used here in the Platonic sense of an unchanging "perfection," or "good." For
   the purpose of clarifying Dostoyevsky's meaning, especially in this chapter, I often use
   "good," in the Platonic sense, as a designation for God. This designation helps to bring
   out the crucial distinctions which Dostoyevsky makes in regard to the proper conception of
   God's relation to the world.
9 Although Dostoyevsky's youthful statement of the relationship between reason and the
   heart is perhaps most evidently indebted to Schelling's later religious thought (as well as
   to Pascal), his final understanding of this relationship is best clarified with reference to the
   thought of the Slavophiles. The magnitude of the debt which Dostoyevsky owes to the attempt of Khomyakov and Ivan Kireyevsky to restore the thought of the Greek Church
   Fathers is difficult to ascertain. Yet it is possible, without a complete answer to this question of intellectual history, to assert that the debt exists, and that it is particularly evident
   in Dostoyevsky's characterization of the relationship between reason and "religious feeling." Since this characterization is largely implicit in his art, it may be helpful to turn to
   the explicit prose of Kireyevsky's treatise "On the Necessity and Possibility of New Principles in Philosophy." Kireyevsky writes as follows of the ultimate accord of reason with
   "Divine truth": "the main difference in Orthodox thinking is precisely this: that it seeks
   not to arrange separate concepts according to the demands of faith, but rather to elevate
   reason itself above its usual level, thus striving to elevate the very source of reason, the
   very manner of reason, to the level of sympathetic agreement with faith.
   The first condition for the elevation of reason is that man should strive to gather
   into one indivisible whole all his separate forces, which in the ordinary condition of man
   are in a state of incompleteness and contradiction; that he should not consider his abstract
   logical capacity as the only organ for the comprehension of truth; that he should not consider the voice of enraptured feeling uncoordinated with other forces of the spirit as the

the heart enter into conflict only when one makes a total claim to knowledge which excludes the other. Yet, according to Dostoyevsky, this is precisely the tendency of reason, "which would demand a chapter for itself."

The claim of reason to an independent knowledge of human beings inevitably leads to the nihilist rejection of the existence of God. Because it is itself "material," reason by itself can ultimately know human beings only as the product of material necessity; it cannot know that in them which transcends necessity. It cannot know that highest principle or "essence" which animates and expresses itself through a person's psycho-physical being. Knowledge of a human being as an object of necessity is not knowledge of what it is to be a human being. To penetrate to another's essence, to know that person as he is "in himself," it is necessary to somehow "become" that person; it is necessary to love him. Only reason informed by love can penetrate to the highest principle within a human being, can truly "know" him. And, for Dostoyevsky, to know a human being truly is to know him as claimed by God. Thus, while he eschews any attempt to "prove" the existence of God by rational argumentation, he does offer the "proof" through love formulated by Father Zosima:

Strive to love your neighbours actively and indefatigably. And the nearer you come to achieving this love, the more convinced you will become of the existence of God and the immortality of your soul. If you reach the point of complete selflessness in your love of your neighbours, you will most certainly regain your faith and no doubt can possibly enter your soul. This has been proved. This is certain.[10]

The positive significance of Christ's silence before the Inquisitor should now be apparent. In the light of Dostoyevsky's understanding of "reason" and the "heart," the silent kiss of love would seem to constitute an appropriate response to the rational argumentation of the nihilist. Through this silence Dostoyevsky intimates that the Inquisitor's speech fails to grasp the essential point; it does not talk "about *that* at all."

The Self-Betrayal of the Man-God

Silence not only highlights the failure of the Inquisitor's nihilist "insight" to penetrate to the heart of the matter. It also encourages the Inquisitor to speak too much, thereby betraying himself. Dostoyevsky encourages the final Western social formula to express itself without hindrance, and even with unsurpassed eloquence and lucidity, in order that it might reveal its own emptiness.

faultless guide to truth; that he should not consider the promptings of an isolated aesthetic sense, independent of other concepts, as the true guide to the comprehension of the higher organization of the universe; that he should not consider even the dominant love of his heart, separate from the other demands of the spirit, as the infallible guide to the attainment of the supreme good; but that he should constantly seek in the depth of his soul that inner root of understanding where all the separate forces merge into one living and whole vision of the mind" (found in P. Christoff, *An Introduction to Nineteenth-Century Russian Slavophilism* [The Hague, 1972], pp. 357-58, 364-65).

10 *BK*, p. 61 (II,4).

As we have noted, the future universal state reveals itself as a tyranny destructive of humanity. Yet this tyranny, and the "destruction" or "overcoming" of humanity which it implies, receives its justification in the vision of mangodhood. The man-god is the corner-stone of the final Western social formula, and it is the vision of mangodhood therefore which must betray itself as an illusion if this formula is to be seen not as sober "realism" but as the product of *nosos*. Dostoyevsky's judgment of the future universal state therefore presupposes his judgment of the man-god. This judgment is expressed, above all, in the failure of even the most courageous of his nihilists—Stavrogin and Ivan Karamazov—to move through nihilism to the man-god's joyful affirmation of the finality of becoming.

Stavrogin refuses to judge life according to a perspective outside of life: he finds the "same sort of beauty and equal enjoyment" in all of life's manifestations, perceiving no difference in beauty "between some voluptuous and brutish act and any heroic exploit, even the sacrifice of life for the good of humanity." He regards the distinction between good and evil as "just a prejudice," and lives consciously in the absence of any over-arching meaning.[11] Life beyond good and evil is not merely a fashionable theory for Stavrogin: his nihilism expresses itself in the abuse of an innocent child, a deed which, from a perspective within good and evil, is one of the most ignominious of crimes. Stavrogin's nihilism appears to be so complete that he is able to play with convictions which could give some meaning to life, without himself being imprisoned by them. For instance, he inspires Shatov with a conviction of Russia's religious mission to the West, while at the same time remaining coolly aloof from any commitment to such a notion himself.[12]

There is, nevertheless, something in Stavrogin's preoccupation with ideas which betrays a profound need for a conviction. He, in fact, suffers from his nihilism as from a sickness, and he himself admits this. He is unable to move from the "disease of indifference" engendered by his nihilism to the man-god's joyful affirmation of life as meaningless. From Stavrogin, by his own admission, "nothing has come but negation—and not even negation." Whereas Kirilov's negation is "magnanimous," Stavrogin's suicide does not point beyond negation to any affirmation; and it does not do so perhaps because it is not a sufficiently radical negation.[13] Unlike Kirilov, he cannot affirm the goodness of that spider which symbolizes his violation of the innocent child, Matryosha. Stavrogin's suicide is, above all, motivated by the desire to avoid a public repentance to which he is being driven inexorably by a sense of guilt. He is finally kept from repentance, not by the magnificent and happy pride of the man-god, but by his inability to envelop himself within the Christian horizon. The absence of a conviction of the efficacy of the Christian way of repentance renders him inadequately "prepared" or "hardened" for

11 *The Devils*, pp. 260, 692 (I,1,vii; II,3,ii).
12 *NP*, p. 181.
13 *The Devils*, pp. 298, 522, 667, 682, 685 (II,3,iv; III,3,i,8; II,9,ii); *NP*, pp. 180, 183.

the humiliation which his pride would be required to undergo in the fact of public contempt and even derision.[14]

It would seem, from the dynamics of Stavrogin's movement to and away from Christian repentance, that he finally comes to embody the problem of, not so much overcoming nihilism in the man-god, as moving from nihilism back to Christianity. Seen in this light, Stavrogin's most extraordinary actions throughout *The Devils*—his endurance of Shatov's slap in the face, the duel with Gaganov, his marriage to the cripple, Maria Lebyadkin—become the self-punishment of a man striving to forgive himself—a man "looking for a burden"—rather than the demonstration of a magnificent indifference to merely conventional moral codes.[15] The failure of Stavrogin to affirm life beyond good and evil casts a grave doubt on Kirilov's hope for the man-god. If even Stavrogin, with his extraordinary courage and beauty, his intelligence and strength of will, is unable to move through nihilism to its overcoming, then is such a movement possible? This doubt is enhanced by the manner in which Dostoyevsky portrays the prophet of the man-god. Kirilov is absurdly eccentric, a semi-literate engineer, regarded by Stavrogin as "insane" and by the narrator as "mad as a hatter"; and the suicide which is to herald the annihilation of God takes on, in the final moments, all the appearance of a grotesquerie. It is intimated also that Kirilov's apprehension of an "everlasting life" here on earth may be the product of an incipient epilepsy.[16]

Ivan Karamazov's vision of the man-god is also associated with disease—in his case, "brain fever." And he too fails to move through nihilism to the realization of mangodhood. He fails because, like Stavrogin, he finds it impossible to be a perfect nihilist. He teaches that "everything is permitted," and yet he cannot live out this teaching fully. The lackey, Smerdyakov, notes with mingled surprise and contempt Ivan's inability to endure his responsibility for the murder of his father: "You was brave enough then, sir. Everything, you said, is permitted, and look how frightened you are now!"[17] Yet Ivan's inability to affirm the consequences of his nihilism is not due to mere cowardice. It is rooted in a dilemma far beyond the grasp of a lackey, a dilemma which is perceptible, however, to the "Devil" of Ivan's nightmare:

Oh, you're going to perform a great act of virtue! You're going to declare that you murdered your father, that the servant killed him at your instigation. . . . You're going to perform a great act of virtue and you don't believe in virtue—that's what makes you so angry, that's what worries you. . . .[18]

14 *The Devils*, pp. 671-704 (II,9,i); *NP*, pp. 371-72, 176-83.
15 *The Devils*, p. 295 (II,3,iii); *NP*, pp. 236-44.
16 *The Devils*, pp. 667, 127, 587 (III,8; I,3,viii; III,5,v). See also *The Idiot*, pp. 258-59 (II,5) for Prince Myshkin's doubts concerning the validity of an experience which has its source in a disease. As is well-known, Dostoyevsky himself suffered from epilepsy. It is likely that Myshkin expresses his views on the subject.
17 *BK*, p. 733 (XI,8).
18 Ibid., pp. 768-69 (XI,10).

The nihilist who was willing to countenance the devouring of one "reptile" by another is inexorably driven by a sense of guilt to sacrifice himself to save one of these "reptiles." Ivan still feels the claim of the moral good even though he knows that this claim is his own "invention."[19] The abiding presence of this claim and the knowledge that it is not sustained in the nature of things is the source of that "contradictoriness" which is Ivan's chief characteristic. His appearance in court sets him upon the way undertaken by Stavrogin, the way of returning to life within the confines of good and evil. Driven by an overwhelming sense of guilt into a way of repentance in which he cannot believe, Ivan will perhaps perish also, finding the resolution of his contradictoriness in madness or suicide.

The phenomenon of contradictoriness may be insufficient of itself to constitute a refutation of the man-god. For the question still remains as to how this contradictoriness is to be interpreted. Though suffering acutely from the contradiction between his nihilist insight and his moral conscience, Ivan nevertheless denies that this contradiction must be final:

Conscience! What is conscience? I invent it myself. Why, then, am I so unhappy? From habit. From the universal habit of mankind for the past seven thousand years. When we get rid of our habits, we shall become gods.[20]

If the guilty conscience which afflicts Ivan and Stavrogin is ultimately a matter of "habit," of however long a duration, then the evidence of contradictoriness adduced against the possibility of the man-god could not be considered conclusive. The nihilist insight into the nature of morality holds out the possibility of an eventual resolution of contradictoriness which will banish the moral conscience from human life, or at least reduce it to a salutary illusion for the weak. Habits may die hard, but they do finally die. The contradiction which besets Dostoyevsky's nihilists constitutes a decisive argument against the possibility of the man-god only if it is the manifestation, not of a peculiarly obstinate human habit, but of the exclusive claim of the moral good. It is thus that Alyosha interprets Ivan's contradictoriness: "He began to understand Ivan's illness: 'The agony of a proud decision—a deep-seated conscience.' God, in whom he did not believe, and truth had gained a hold over his heart, which still refused to give in."[21]

There is a clear corollary to Alyosha's interpretation of Ivan's agony: the nihilism which contradicts the claim of good reveals itself as evil. That which Ivan interprets as a struggle between the "universal habit of mankind" and scientific or "Euclidean" truth is thus transposed into a struggle between good and evil, between God and the Devil, in which "the battlefield is the heart of man."[22] Dostoyevsky points to such a transposition by inducing a

19 Ibid., p. 768 (XI,10).
20 Ibid., p. 768 (XI,10).
21 Ibid., p. 771 (XI,10).
22 Ibid., p. 124 (III,3).

shift of perspective, a sense of "a new and hitherto unknown reality," in the nihilist characters themselves. Raskolnikov finally comes to the realization that "it was the devil who killed the old hag, not I"; Stavrogin confesses to a belief in the devil, "a personal devil, not an allegory"; and Ivan's "Euclidean" mind eventually betrays an openness to the presence of Satan.[23] It must be emphasized, however, that Dostoyevsky does not impose such a shift of perspective upon his readers. He goes to some lengths, for instance, to introduce an ambiguity into the relationship between nihilism and the Devil by implying that the "Devil's" presence for Ivan and Stavrogin is attributable to the nervous disorder which afflicts both of them.[24] This ambiguity is an aspect of that larger silence through which Dostoyevsky encourages the vision of mangodhood to betray its own emptiness.

At the heart of this vision is the notion that the orientation towards the eternal has turned human beings away from loyalty to the earth. Now that the "other world" has once and for all been exposed by the nihilist insight as an illusion, it is possible for human beings to return to the earth, to affirm it as their true and only home.[25] In Dostoyevsky's art, however, the aspiration to mangodhood actually reveals itself as indifference to, and even hatred of, the earth. It thereby betrays itself in regard to the most fundamental question. This self-betrayal must be understood in the light of Dostoyevsky's critique of reason: the renunciation of eternity in favour of loyalty to the earth is rooted in a "knowledge" of life which is not really knowledge at all. The nihilist's rational "insight" into the finality of becoming—the theoretical basis of mangodhood—is an "insight" into life which fails to penetrate to the essence of life. The man-god cannot truly know the earth to which he declares his sole allegiance. His supposed knowledge of life moves in a circle on the threshold of life, effectively excluding him from that genuine communion with the earth which he is meant to embody. Dostoyevsky strives in his art to give concrete representation to this exclusion—most memorably in the figure of Stavrogin. The further Stavrogin moves through nihilism towards mangodhood the more he lapses into a condition of isolation from life which expresses itself in various ways. He becomes shut up within himself, moving constantly within the ever-constricting circle of his own consciousness; he becomes increasingly abstract, disembodied, cut off from living life; he is unutterably bored, a boredom from which he finds it ever more difficult to distract himself; everything has become "all the same" to him, and so overwhelming is his indifference to life that even self-annihilation seems too definite an act.[26] In Stavrogin the ascent to mangodhood betrays itself as a descent into nothingness.

23 *CP*, pp. 559, 433 (VII,2; V,4); *The Devils*, p. 677 (II,9,i); *BK*, pp. 746-65 (XI,9).
24 *BK*, p. 746 (XI,9); *The Devils*, pp. 676-77 (II,9,i).
25 See *NBK*: "Inquisitor: Why do we need the beyond? We are more human than you. We love the earth—Schiller sings of joy..." (p. 74).
26 See, for instance, Stavrogin's final letter to Dasha Shatov in *The Devils*, pp. 665-67 (III,8). Another of Dostoyevsky's memorable "case-studies" of the "descent into hell" is Svidrigailov in *Crime and Punishment*.

In betraying itself as an aspiration towards nothingness the final Western social formula betrays itself at the same time as a manifestation of that spirit of "self-destruction and non-existence" which is, for Dostoyevsky, the spirit of evil.[27] The manner in which Christ's silence before the final Western social formula nevertheless constitutes a judgment upon that formula should now be clear. It remains unclear, however, whether this implicit judgment is sufficient. "The Grand Inquisitor" and "The Geological Upheaval" may betray a concealed aspiration towards "self-destruction and non-existence"; but it must be remembered that these two writings evolve out of Ivan's attempt to find a solution to the problem of suffering and injustice posed in "Rebellion." The nihilist insight and the aspiration to mangodhood implied in it are consequences of Ivan's exclusive reliance on reason, not of his thirst for justice. The thirst for justice and the reliance on reason alone may, through Ivan, prove themselves incompatible. Yet the problem persists: the earth remains saturated "from its crust to its centre with human tears." The author of "The Geological Unheaval" and "The Grand Inquisitor" remains, in his "Rebellion," the most powerful witness to human suffering in Dostoyevsky's art. It may be that this witness is symptomatic of the good in that struggle between good and evil in which "the battlefield" is Ivan himself. Certainly it is difficult to understand how the condemnation of the final Western social formula can include the condemnation of that desire to wipe away the tears of human suffering with which it justifies itself. The question must be asked: Is Christ's silence a sufficient response to those tears of human suffering to which Ivan bears such powerful witness? Dostoyevsky apparently thought not, for the silence of Christ in "The Grand Inquisitor" is broken in the "Discourses and Sermons" of Father Zosima. The movement in *The Brothers Karamazov* from the silent figure of Christ to the teaching of the Russian monk may represent a descent,[28] but it is a descent which further illumines Dostoyevsky's judgment of the final Western social formula.

The Breaking of Christ's Silence

Through Father Zosima, Dostoyevsky voices explicitly the response to the modern Western project implied in the silent figure of Christ. Yet even this more explicit response remains highly indirect; rather than a point by point

27 *BK*, p. 295 (V,5). Cf. John of Damascus, *Exposition of the Orthodox Faith*: "For evil is nothing else than absence of goodness, just as darkness also is absence of light" (II,4).
28 Some commentators even regard Dostoyevsky's portrayal of Zosima as a failure—both artistically and philosophically. (See, for instance, J. Drouilly, *La pensée politique et religieuse de Dostoïevski* [Paris, 1971]). A proper judgment of this issue presupposes as complete an understanding as possible of what Zosima signifies for Dostoyevsky, in his teaching and his person. This is my chief concern in this study, for I would suggest that Book Six of *The Brothers Karamazov* has often not been read with as much attention as Book Five, and this has proven detrimental to a balanced interpretation of the novel.

refutation of Ivan and the Inquisitor, Zosima's teaching constitutes an opposing "world-conception... in an artistic picture." According to Dostoyevsky's own testimony, this Christian "world-conception" represents the whole of his own religious thought, although expressed in the "different form and different style" required in the artistic presentation of a Russian monk.[29] A discussion of Dostoyevsky's entire religious teaching is beyond the scope of this study, and we must thus undertake such a discussion only insofar as it clarifies his critique of the West. My approach to Zosima's Christian teaching will be determined by the requirement of discovering in it what most directly constitutes a response to the yearning for justice underlying the final Western social formula.

The Appeal to Eternal Justice

In response to Ivan's thirst for justice here and now Zosima appeals to the mystery of "eternal justice," as it is revealed in the Book of Job:

how could God give up the most loved of his saints to Satan to play with, take his children from him, smite him with sore boils so that he scraped the corruption from his sores with a potsherd, and why? Just to be able to boast to Satan: "See how much my saint can suffer for my sake!" But it *is* great—just because it is a mystery—just because the passing image of the earthly and eternal justice are brought together here. The act of eternal justice is accomplished before earthly justice... God raises Job again, gives him wealth again, and many years pass by and he has other children and he loves them... the old sorrow, through the great mystery of human life, passes gradually into quiet, tender joy; the fiery blood of youth gives place to the gentle serenity of old age... and over it all Divine Justice, tender, reconciling and all-forgiving![30]

The accomplishment of eternal justice, however, must ultimately be concealed for human reason, which is unable to encompass the eternal. The fundamental inaccessibility of eternal justice to reason implies that what seems unjust may actually be just. Injustice may be merely an appearance in that through it the mystery of eternal justice is fulfilled. Yet although eternal justice is a mystery for reason, the heart renders human beings open to acquiescence in it. Even from the depths of affliction human beings are able to consent to an eternal justice, and beyond this consent, even to love it. They are able to raise the hymn from under the ground of which Dmitri Karamazov speaks when contemplating his imminent penal servitude in the Siberian mines for a crime he did not commit:

Oh yes, we shall be in chains, and we shall not be free, but then, in our great sorrow, we shall arise anew in gladness, without which man cannot live nor God exist, for God gives gladness.... How can I be there under the ground without God?... If they banish God from the earth, we shall need him under the earth! A convict cannot exist without God, even less than a free man. And then shall we,

29 See Dostoyevsky's letter of 7 Aug. 1879 to N. A. Liubimov.
30 *BK*, pp. 342-43 (VI,2).

the men beneath the ground, sing from the bowels of the earth our tragic hymn to God, in whom there is gladness! All hail to God and his gladness! I love him!

... I shall overcome all things, all suffering, so that I may say, say to myself every moment: I am! In thousands of agonies—I am, writhing on the rack—but I am! I may sit in prison but I, too, exist, I see the sun; and if I do not see the sun, I know that it *is*. And to know that the sun is—that alone is the whole of life.[31]

The hymn from under the ground affirms the actuality of an eternal good—or God—and at the same time it distinguishes sharply between this good and the human condition. For the underground prison can be understood (as in Book VII of Plato's *Republic*) as an image of the realm of becoming, where chance and material necessity reign. The appeal to eternal justice, in response to the insistent demand for justice on earth, is in essence a denial that justice can be brought forth out of necessity.[32] Ivan's demand for justice on earth inevitably assumes such a bringing-forth when he ties this demand to a rejection of the eternal. His rejection of the other world implies that justice is to be rooted in this world—this world which he himself claims is nothing but meaningless chance and necessity, a world in which "no one is to blame," in which "effect follows cause, simply and directly."[33] As we have seen, for Dostoyevsky, the attempt to ground justice in the finality of becoming can issue only in the man-god tyranny. In response to the modern Western aspiration to justice on earth here and now, Zosima exhorts human beings to recollect their "living bond with the other world," with that eternal truth which is the genuine fount of justice.[34]

Dostoyevsky has increasingly been accorded recognition as one of the most profound critics of the modern attempt to bring heaven down to earth. Indeed, it could be argued that the critique of political utopianism embodied in his art signifies a magnificent restatement, in the context of modernity, of Plato's distinction between the necessary and the good. This emphasis on Dostoyevsky's negative view of modern political utopianism, however, cannot be considered the final word in the interpretation of his thought about human order. The final word of the silent figure who confronts the Grand Inquisitor is not the strict holding apart of good and necessity, of heaven and earth. For the interpreter of that silence, Zosima, repeatedly affirms that "life is paradise" if only people wish it. And no less inspired than Versilov's vision of the earthly paradise in *The Adolescent* is that of the Christian pilgrim, Makar Dolgoruky, who anticipates the day when "there will be no orphans, no beggars, everyone will be like one of my own family, everyone will be my brother... and our Earth will glow brighter than the sun and there will be no sadness, no sighs will be heard, and the whole world will be paradise."[35] The

31 Ibid., p. 695 (XI,4).
32 Cf. S. Weil, *Oppression and Liberty* (London, 1958), pp. 172-74.
33 *BK*, p. 285 (V,4).
34 Ibid., p. 377 (VI,3). The Western aspiration to bring forth good out of necessity is, for Dostoyevsky, epitomized in Hegel's thought. See *UD*, II, pp. 102-103.
35 *BK*, p. 356 (VI,2); *The Adolescent*, pp. 384-85 (III,3,ii).

silence of Christ seems to signify for Dostoyevsky the simultaneous affirmation of eternal justice *and* of justice on earth. The interpretation of his critique of the modern Western project must recognize this two-fold affirmation, and make some attempt to understand what underlies it.

It has been said that the contradiction between the Zosima who affirms eternal justice in the face of earthly injustice, and the Zosima who anticipates some sort of earthly paradise, is a reflection of Dostoyevsky's inability to face the implications of his own thought. Unable himself to accept the consequences of his radical distinction between heaven and earth, he tended, especially in the latter years of his life, to retreat from this distinction into a "utopian" or "rose-water" Christianity reminiscent of his youthful socialism.[36] There may indeed be a "contradiction" in Dostoyevsky's simultaneous rejection and affirmation of that yearning for an earthly paradise which he thought animates the modern West. But this "contradiction" takes us far beyond the problem of Dostoyevsky's personality to a reconsideration of the more fundamental problem posed by Ivan's "Rebellion."

Zosima's appeal to an eternal justice in the face of human suffering on earth is anticipated by Ivan. Ivan is not unwilling to "accept" God, or even to believe in "the eternal harmony into which we are all supposed to merge one day." But, even while accepting the existence of eternal justice, he returns his "ticket of admission" to the fulfillment of the mystery, for he considers the question of eternal justice to be irrelevant to his demand for justice here and now: "Please understand, it is not God that I do not accept, but the world he has created. I do not accept God's world and I refuse to accept it."[37] Ivan's willingness to admit that distinction between God and the world, between heaven and earth, which preserves the good from identification with the necessary is made explicit in the rough notes: "I will accept God all the more readily if he is the eternal old God who cannot be understood. And so let it be *that God*."[38] Yet for Ivan, the obverse of God's total transcendence of the world is God's total ineffectiveness within the world. And if goodness has no effective place within the world, then the world is indeed a prison. The prisoner would appear to have no choice but to escape from his bonds, or to become so thoroughly the master of his prison that he is able to transform it into a home. The former choice entails self-annihilation, and the latter the actualization of the final Western social formula. Ivan may "dash the cup to the floor," or he may join those who are "correcting" the world.[39] Neither choice, in his view, necessarily denies the existence of God or eternal justice.

36 See, for instance, K. Leontiev's remark, quoted by V. Solovyov, in "Tri rechi v pamyat Dostoyevskago," *Sobranie sochinenii* (Brussels, 1966), III-IV, pp. 219-23. See also J. Drouilly, *La pensée politique et religieuse de Dostoïevski* (Paris, 1971), p. 430.

37 *BK*, pp. 275, 287 (V,3,4). See also Dostoyevsky's letter of 10 May 1879 to N. A. Liubimov in which he asserts that Ivan's rebellion signifies "the denial not of God, but of the meaning of his creation."

38 *NBK*, p. 76.

39 *BK*, pp. 308-309 (V,v).

At this point it must thus be asked whether there is any fundamental difference between the assertion of the finality of becoming, and the assertion that what is not subject to becoming is utterly divorced from the realm wherein it holds sway. It is significant that there appears to be no fundamental contradiction for Ivan between his acceptance of the "eternal old God who cannot be understood"—the God who remains totally transcendent of the world—and his teaching that "everything is permitted." Is the insistence on the strict distinction between heaven and earth, between goodness and necessity, a sufficient response to the modern Western project? This is the question posed by Ivan's anticipation of Zosima's appeal to "Divine Justice." The question becomes even more compelling when the implicit parallel which Dostoyevsky draws between Ivan's rebellion and that of Job is recognized. The wise castigate Job for his reluctance to consent to the divine dispensation, but it is the rebellious Job who finally comes to "see" God, while the wise incur the divine wrath.[40]

In a letter written to N. Strakhov in the aftermath of the Paris Commune, Dostoyevsky speaks as follows of the quest for the earthly paradise:

Through the whole of the 19th century, that school has dreamed of the setting-up of earthly paradises... and then, directly it came to action (as in the years 1848, 1849, and now), has shown a contemptible incapacity for any practical expression of itself. At bottom, the entire movement is but a repetition of the Russian delusion that men can reconstruct the world by reason and experience.... Have we not sufficient evidence by this time to be able to prove that a society is not thus to be built up, that quite elsewhere lie the paths to the common good, and that this common good reposes on things different altogether from those hitherto accepted? On what, then, *does* it repose? Men write and write, and overlook the principal point.[41]

It is clear from this letter that Dostoyevsky does not reject the quest for the earthly paradise as such, but the quest for an earthly paradise which is founded exclusively on reason. The animating presence of the desire for justice on earth constitutes, for Dostoyevsky, the supreme worth of the original Geneva attempt to establish a human order of freedom, equality, and brotherhood. (And to the extent that this desire remains most fully alive in modern Western socialism, Dostoyevsky accords to it the moral leadership of the West).[42] But insofar as the quest for justice on earth has turned to reason and science alone for its satisfaction, Dostoyevsky rejects it as pointing towards a world-wide tyranny in bondage to the "spirit of self-destruction and non-existence." To repeat Dostoyevsky's own question: On what *does* the possibility of justice on earth repose? What is the "principal point" which has been overlooked by the modern West? The answer is contained in Zosima's most explicit enucleation of the modern Western project: "Following science, they wish to live a life based on justice by their reason alone ... without Christ. . . ."[43] The silent

40 Job 42:5.
41 Letter of 18 May 1871.
41 *DW*, p. 252 (March 1876).
43 *BK*, pp. 371, 373 (VI,3).

presence of Christ in "The Grand Inquisitor" not only signifies the condemnation of the modern Western attempt to attain to the earthly paradise through
reason alone; it also signifies an alternative way to this paradise, to "a life
based on justice." According to Dostoyevsky, Christianity possesses that
principle on which alone reposes the true reconciliation of heaven and earth.

The God-Man: The Bridging of the Gulf between Heaven and Earth

Dostoyevsky stated in his unpublished notes that any attempt to grasp the
essential meaning of Christianity must recognize that "what really matters is
the figure of Christ, from which any teaching must emerge...."[44] Theology
was not Dostoyevsky's "specialty," just as philosophy was not his "specialty." There is therefore little point in looking in his writings for a systematic teaching about the "figure of Christ." Nevertheless, Dostoyevsky's art
does reflect a profound and consistent (if not systematic) meditation on the
meaning of Christ. This meditation did not, of course, occur within a vacuum,
and the issue of Dostoyevsky's relationship to Christianity as an historical
institution, and particularly to Christian theology, is an important question of
intellectual history. As we shall see, it is also crucial for Dostoyevsky's own
final understanding of the confrontation between the Inquisitor and Christ
which he presents in "The Grand Inquisitor." Yet just as I have considered
the Inquisitor's argument initially in its timeless aspect, apart from its relation
to sixteenth-century Roman Catholicism, so I will at this point consider the
meaning of the "figure of Christ" apart from its relation to any particular
historical configuration of Christianity. My concern will be with the meaning
of Christ as it is actually articulated by Dostoyevsky in his writing, and
particularly in the "Discourses and Sermons" of Father Zosima.

The figure of Christ represents, according to Dostoyevsky in his rough
notes, "a conception of man so noble that one cannot grasp it without a sense
of awe," an image of goodness, truth, and beauty which is the "undying ideal
of mankind."[45] The potency of this ideal is evinced, for Dostoyevsky, in the
fact that those in the modern world who have rejected Christianity as a
religion have been singularly reluctant to include Christ himself in this rejection.[46] The willingness of the liberal-socialist tradition, at least in its pre-

---

44 NP, p. 218. See Dostoyevsky's letter of March 1854 to Mrs. N. D. Fonvizin, written
   while in Siberia shortly after his return to Christianity: "God gives me sometimes moments of perfect peace; in such moments I love and believe that I am loved; in such moments I have formulated my creed, wherein all is clear and holy to me. This creed is extremely simple; here it is: I believe that there is nothing lovelier, deeper, more sympathetic, more rational, more manly, and more perfect than the Saviour; I say to myself with
   jealous love that not only is there no one else like him, but that there could be no one."
   Dostoyevsky usually opposes this "undying ideal" to those "enlightened" intellectuals,
   like Belinsky, who would set themselves up as humanity's new "guides." See his letter
   of 16 Aug. 1867 to Apollon Maykov.
45 Letter of 16 Aug. 1867.
46 As we have seen in the first chapter, this evocation of the image of Christ would be

scientific phase, to regard Christ as an ally in its struggle for justice on earth testifies to the intimate relationship between Christianity and Geneva freedom, equality, and brotherhood. Yet for Geneva thought Christ is an inspiring ideal who is ultimately dispensable. The liberal-socialist quest for justice can finally "get along" without Christ because he is merely human, albeit an outstanding example of human rationality and goodness. Christ, while an extraordinary inspiration to others, can accomplish nothing which human reason and goodness themselves cannot accomplish. Christ is thus, for Geneva thought, ultimately reducible to the principle of human rationality.

Dostoyevsky, in his affirmation of the earthly paradise, also invokes the image of Christ. Yet, for him, the earthly paradise is impossible without Christ. To return to the problem posed by Ivan's rebellion: the quest for justice on earth is the quest for heaven on earth, for the ultimate reconciliation of goodness and necessity, God and the world. Neither the affirmation of a God who is totally transcendent of the world (as in Zosima's initial appeal to eternal justice) nor the immanentization of God within the world (as, for instance, in the scientific socialist's identification of goodness with necessity) constitutes a genuine resolution of the problem. Dostoyevsky thought that the figure of Christ himself, properly understood, did point to a genuine reconciliation of heaven and earth. For Dostoyevsky, Christ is fully human (the portrait in "The Grand Inquisitor" attests to his deep interest in Christ's humanity); and yet he is, at the same time, fully God—he is the God-man.[47] At the heart of Dostoyevsky's thought about the earthly paradise is this idea, signified by the figure of Christ, of the simultaneous transcendence *and* immanence of God in relation to the world. To express this idea in more strictly theological terms: God is totally beyond all finite determination, exempt from all relationship and multiplicity, all becoming; at the same time, God is present in all becoming, manifest in the multiplicity of finite things.[48] It should be noted that although Christ may thus signify something which is an impossible paradox for human reason alone, this does not necessarily violate that "believing reason" which is reason taken up into the knowledge of the heart. Dostoyevsky, however, does not explain how this is so, nor does he enter into any sustained consideration of the paradox of Christ. His primary concern appears to be with the implications of this paradox for the problem of the earthly paradise.

Dostoyevsky's own affirmation of the earthly paradise finds its most sustained expression in *The Dream of a Ridiculous Man*. The "Dream" has

characteristic of Geneva thought particularly as it is informed by French or "utopian" socialism. Dostoyevsky illustrates this tendency with reference to Ernest Renan; see *UD*, I, p. 96.

47 *PS*, p. 89; *The Devils*, p. 244 (II,1,v). In both instances the "God-man" (*bogochelovek*) is explicitly opposed to the concept of the "man-god" (*chelovekobog*).

48 Cf. Maximus the Confessor, *Mystagogia*, P.G., 91, 664, A, C; *Ambigua*, P. G., 91, 1257 B; V. Lossky, *The Mystical Theology of the Eastern Church* (London, 1957), chaps. 2, 3, 4; P. Sherrard, *The Greek East and the Latin West* (London, 1959), chap. 2.

been interpreted as a parody of modern political utopianism.[49] But if, as I have argued, the strict divorce of heaven and earth is not Dostoyevsky's final word, then the "Dream" must be considered a serious attempt to portray perfect justice on earth. It represents also an attempt to portray human beings as they are in essence, or as they are by nature; it is Dostoyevsky's version of the original state of nature. His natural humanity is in possession of a knowledge of life higher than that of modern science:

Their understanding was of a higher order and deeper than that provided by our science. Science tries to explain what life is in order to teach us how we should live; they didn't need science to tell them how to live—they knew by themselves ... They pointed at their trees, and I couldn't comprehend the intensity of the love with which they looked at them; it was as if they were communicating with beings like themselves. In fact, I don't think I'd be wrong in saying that they talked to them! Yes—they'd found the language of the plants, and I'm sure they could understand them. And these people were like that with all nature. The animals lived in peace with them, never attacked them, loved them; they were subdued, as it were, by love.

The people pointed out stars to me and spoke to me about them. I couldn't understand what they said, but I'm certain they had some sort of communion with the stars, a live, direct knowledge of them rather than a rational, scientific understanding.[50]

By virtue of this knowledge they are by nature fully human, inwardly as well as outwardly: "The eyes of these happy people were radiant and their faces were intelligent, expressing the serenity of those who have supremely fulfilled themselves."[51] Moreover, they are by nature fully social, living in a harmonious, complete order that has no need of civil institutions.

The theoretical basis of the paradise on earth depicted in the "Dream" is set forth in Zosima's teaching about the relation between this world and the "other world":

Many things on earth are hidden from us, but in return for that we have been given a mysterious, inward sense of our living bond with the other world, with the higher, heavenly world, and the roots of our thoughts and feelings are not here but in other worlds. That is why philosophers say that it is impossible to comprehend the essential nature of things on earth. God took seeds from other worlds and sowed them on this earth, and made his garden grow, and everything that could come up came up. . . .[52]

These words of Zosima—Dostoyevsky's only explicit account of God as creator—do not constitute a systematic doctrine of creation. It is not abso-

49 See, for instance, L. Grossman, *Dostoevsky* (London, 1974), p. 537; E. Wasiolek, *Dostoevsky, the Major Fiction* (Cambridge, Mass., 1964), pp. 144-48.

50 *DRM*, pp. 216-17. "The Dream of a Ridiculous Man" first appeared in the April 1877 issue of *The Diary of a Writer*. My references throughout are to the English translation by A. R. MacAndrew (New York, 1961).

51 *DRM*, p. 216.

52 *BK*, p. 377.

lutely clear, for instance, whether God created this world *ex nihilo* or by giving form to pre-existent and formless matter. Nevertheless, definite conclusions can be elicited from Zosima's words about creation. Of particular significance is his assertion that humanity's "living bond with the other world" is at the same time a bond with the earth. The knowledge of the eternal, accessible to human beings by virtue of the spiritual principle within them, is knowledge also of the "seeds"—that is, the "essences," "ideas," or *logoi*—of everything which "lives and is alive" on earth.[53] (It is noteworthy that Dostoyevsky thus denies to reason operating independently of the heart a genuine knowledge even of non-human nature).[54] Although Dostoyevsky does not elucidate the philosophical basis of this conviction that knowledge of the eternal is at the same time knowledge of the "seeds" of everything which "lives and is alive" on earth, the conviction itself is nonetheless clearly expressed, and it points to the human being as the "mediator" between this world and the "other world," between the realm of becoming and eternity. This mediation is realized in Alyosha's "ecstasy":

He did not stop on the steps, but went down rapidly. His soul, overflowing with rapture, was craving for freedom and unlimited space. The vault of heaven, studded with softly shining stars, stretched wide and vast over him. . . . The fresh, motionless, still night enfolded the earth. The white towers and golden domes of the cathedral gleamed against the sapphire sky. The gorgeous autumn flowers in the beds near the house had gone to sleep till morning. The silence of the earth seemed to merge into the silence of the heavens, the mystery of the earth came in contact with the mystery of the stars. . . . Alyosha stood, gazed, and suddenly he threw himself down flat upon the earth.

He did not know why he was embracing it. He could not have explained to himself why he longed so irresistibly to kiss it, to kiss it all, but he kissed it weeping, sobbing and drenching it with his tears, and vowed frenziedly to love it, to love it for ever and ever. . . . What was he weeping over? Oh, he was weeping in his rapture even over those stars which were shining for him from the abyss of space and "he was not ashamed of that ecstasy." It was as though the threads from all those innumerable worlds of God met all at once in his soul, and it was trembling all over "as it came in contact with other worlds."[55]

The notion of humanity's two-fold relation to the eternal and the earthly is the basis of Dostoyevsky's rejection of Kirilov's claim that it is the man-god who embodies loyalty to the earth. The affirmation of the earth is inseparable from the affirmation of "other worlds." To refer once more to Zosima's words about creation:

God took seeds from other worlds and sowed them on this earth, and made his garden grow, and everything that could come up came up, but what grows lives and is alive only through the feeling of its contact with other mysterious worlds; if that feeling grows weak or is destroyed in you, then what has grown up in you will also

---

53 Cf. V. Lossky, *The Mystical Theology of the Eastern Church* (London, 1957), chap. 5.
54 See, for instance, *The Adolescent*, pp. 354-55 (III,1,iii).
55 *BK*, pp. 426-27 (III,4).

die. Then you will become indifferent to life and even grow to hate it. That is what I think.[56]

Since, according to the *Dream of a Ridiculous Man*, the earthly paradise belongs to human beings by nature, the transition from the state of nature to civil society cannot be understood as the first step in human progress towards an as yet unrealized justice on earth. Rather, humanity's egress from the womb of nature into the process of history signifies a "fall" from paradise. According to the "Dream," political order itself is a consequence of this fall; human beings are compelled to "invent" justice and to enter into civil unions for mutual protection against the passions of "voluptuousness," "jealousy," and "cruelty" which have come to dominate them. The movement of humanity from its present state of unsocial sociability to a final union in a "harmonious society" would be, for progressivist Geneva thought, the vindication of the fall from nature. But, for Dostoyevsky, such a hope merely reflects the potency of our yearning for paradise. His rejection of the Hegelian teaching that the fall into history is a fall "upward" could not be more explicit:

"But then, we have science, and with its help we shall discover Truth once more; then we shall accept it in full knowledge. Knowledge is of a higher order than feeling; awareness of life is of a higher order than life. . ." That's an adage that we must fight.
And I shall fight it.[57]

The single most important consequence of the fall, as it is portrayed in the "Dream," is the obscuring of the spiritual principle within humanity. Dostoyevsky affirms the earthly paradise apparently only to interpose between it and humanity the insurmountable barrier of "sin."[58] The failure to live by the heart—and hence in the right relation to God, to each other, and to nature—renders human beings entirely subject to the laws of necessity. And once they become the slaves of necessity, they become incapable of recovering the spiritual principle or "image of God" within them. They cannot recover what is beyond material necessity by means of faculties which are themselves material, any more than one can extricate oneself from quicksand by pulling at one's own hair. Yet Zosima speaks of the "living bond with the other world" as though it were still an effective presence within humanity. And both Zosima and the "ridiculous man" insist that "life is paradise" if only people want it.[59]

For Dostoyevsky, paradise remains accessible to humanity through that ultimate bridge between the other world and this world—the God-man. The descent of God himself into the realm of necessity effects the "salvation of all men from despair" by restoring to them the spiritual principle of their being, which otherwise is an "unattainable ideal":

56 Ibid., p. 377 (VI,3).
57 *DRM*, pp. 216, 220-22, 226.
58 Ibid., p. 216.
59 Ibid., pp. 225-26; *BK*, pp. 352, 356 (VI,2).

Isn't this precisely why Christ came down to Earth, to tell mankind that . . . the nature of the human spirit as they knew it might . . . appear in such heavenly brilliance, and . . . indeed in the flesh, and not only in a mere daydream or ideal, this being both natural as well as possible.[60]

Because he is God also, the humanity of Christ is able to show forth that life in the spirit which is the fulfillment of the original human nature. This restitution of humanity is realized conclusively in the crucifixion: the subordination of the material psycho-physical self (or the "I," to use Dostoyevsky's word) to the spiritual bond with the eternal is accomplished in Christ's "obedience unto death"—an obedience rendered even when, as the "terrible cry" of dereliction on the cross signifies, he could no longer see the sun.[61] The crucifixion calls people to obedience to eternal justice, whatever the consequences for their earthly life; for in the crucifixion, God himself suffers the separation between goodness and necessity which was inaugurated by human beings. Alyosha thus responds to Ivan's rebellion against divine justice by pointing to Christ as that being who has the right to "forgive everything everyone and everything and *for everything*," even for the suffering of the innocents, because "he gave his innocent blood for all and for everything." Ivan concedes (in the rough notes) that the crucifixion may be "something big enough to equal" the suffering which he catalogues. And the Inquisitor acknowledges that Christ on the cross constitutes a "frightfully strong argument, an eternal argument."[62]

Yet the Inquisitor holds fast to his idea, and Ivan with him. They are apparently able to entertain the "eternal argument" of the crucifixion without renouncing their rebellion. For Ivan, persistence in rebellion is justified by the realization that heaven and earth are not ultimately reconciled in the crucifixion. Indeed, the death on the cross appears to constitute shattering evidence of the final exclusion of good from the world. This interpretation of the crucifixion is expressed at length in Ippolit Terentiev's vivid commentary (in *The Idiot*) on Holbein's painting of "The Dead Christ in the Tomb":

I know that the Christian Church laid it down in the first few centuries of its existence that Christ really did suffer and that the Passion was not symbolical. His body on the cross was therefore fully and entirely subject to the laws of nature. In the picture the face is terribly smashed with blows, swollen, covered with terrible, swollen, and blood-stained bruises, the eyes open and squinting; the large, open whites of the eyes have a sort of dead and glassy glint. But, strange to say, as one looks at the dead body of this tortured man, one cannot help asking oneself the peculiar and interesting question: if such a corpse (and it must have been just like that) was seen by all His disciples, by His future chief apostles, by the women who followed Him and stood by the cross, by all who believed in Him and worshipped Him, then how could they possibly have believed, as they looked at the corpse, that that martyr would rise again? Here one cannot help being struck with the idea

60 *NP*, pp. 238, 147.
61 *NI*, p. 106.
62 *BK*, p. 288 (V,4); *NBK*, pp. 75-77.

that if death is so horrible and if the laws of nature are so powerful, then how can they be overcome? How can they be overcome when even He did not conquer them, He who overcame nature during His lifetime and whom nature obeyed, who said *Talitha cumi*! and the damsel arose, who cried, *Lazarus come forth*! and the dead man came forth? Looking at that picture, you get the impression of nature as some enormous, implacable, and dumb beast, or, to put it more correctly, much more correctly, though it may seem strange, as some huge engine of the latest design, which has senselessly seized, cut to pieces, and swallowed up—impassively and unfeelingly—a great and priceless Being, a Being worth the whole of nature and all its laws, worth the entire earth, which was perhaps created solely for the coming of that Being! The picture seems to give expression to the idea of a dark, insolent, and senselessly eternal power, to which everything is subordinated, and this idea is suggested to you unconsciously.[63]

However it is finally to be understood, the crucifixion itself seems to effect no mitigation of humanity's enthralment to the "dark, insolent" power of material necessity. The human being seems still to be an involuntary participant in "a lie and a stupid mockery," a mockery evinced, for instance, in the stench of corruption which emanates from the body of Father Zosima after his death. Confronted with this cruel evidence of the exclusion of justice from the world—of the untrammelled reign of "blind, dumb, and pitiless laws of nature"—Alyosha himself moves towards the same rebellion which he had censured in Ivan.[64] If the "image of Christ" is identified solely with the crucified Christ, if Christ thus becomes exclusively the symbol of unconsoled human suffering, then for Ivan, and for Alyosha too, rebellion against that "eternal old God who cannot be understood" remains justified.

Alyosha's movement towards rebellion is quelled when he is bidden by the deceased Zosima to the eternal wedding-feast presided over by the living God-man:

It was his voice, the elder Zosima's voice. And who else could it be, since he called? The elder raised Alyosha by the hand, and he rose from his knees.

"Let us make merry," the dried-up old man went on. "Let's drink new wine, the wine of new gladness, of great gladness. See how many guests there are here? And there's the bride and the groom, and there's the ruler of the feast, tasting the new wine ... And do you see our Sun, do you see him? ... Do not be afraid of him. He's terrible in his majesty, awful in his eminence, but infinitely merciful. He became like one of us from love and he makes merry with us, turns water into wine, so as not to cut short the gladness of the guests. He is expecting new guests, he is calling new ones unceasingly and for ever and ever."

Zosima's appeal to the "image of Christ" is finally an appeal to the Christ who "overcomes" the world and its suffering in the resurrection.[65] An attempt must now be made to grasp what is signified for Dostoyevsky in this

---

63 *The Idiot*, pp. 446-47 (III,6).
64 *The Devils*, p. 614 (III,6,ii); *BK*, p. 398 (VII,2).
65 *BK*, pp. 425-26 (III,4). Cf. John 16:3. For an interesting interpretation of the deceased Zosima's "visit" to Alyosha, see V. Ivanov, *Freedom and the Tragic Life, a Study in Dostoevsky* (New York, 1971), pp. 161-62.

"overcoming." For him the "salvation" of humanity entails humanity's ultimate liberation from the rule of necessity—a rule epitomized in the phenomenon of death. It is crucial to note, however, that this liberation signifies, not a final escape from material necessity (as in Gnosticism), but its transformation or "transfiguration." The psycho-physical self becomes the "spiritual body" which is no longer subject to death. Dostoyevsky, however, does not pretend to a clear grasp of the nature of this personal immortality: "But if man is not man—what will his nature be? It is impossible to understand this on earth, but all humanity can have a presentiment about its law in direct emanations. . . ."[66]

Ivan states his willingness to "accept" the possibility of God, and even God incarnate and crucified, for, as we have seen, such an "acceptance" would not necessarily be incompatible with the argument put forward in "Rebellion" and "The Grand Inquisitor." But Ivan will not accept the resurrected God. This is made explicit in the declaration which Dostoyevsky attributes to him in the rough notes: "those who suffer his cross will not find anything that has been promised exactly as he himself had found nothing after his cross." For Dostoyevsky, Ivan's rebellion stands condemned finally by that transfiguration of material necessity which is accomplished in the resurrection of Christ. From the perspective of the resurrection, those who attempt to reconcile heaven and earth by means of the Inquisitor's social formula must be judged to have "joined Satan and his proud spirit entirely."[67]

The point at which the silent presence of Christ in "The Grand Inquisitor" signifies the condemnation of Ivan's argument has now been more precisely indicated. Yet a lack of clarity remains as to what, precisely, the God-man's "overcoming" of the world entails for the human yearning for paradise. In response to this question it must be emphasized, first, that for Dostoyevsky the final reconciliation of goodness with necessity is realized for human beings, not in a paradise on the present earth, but in the paradise of that "final . . . eternal life" which has been opened up to them by the God-man. Because their final end is eternity, human beings are in a "transitory state" while on earth.[68] This explicit avowal of the transitory nature of human life on earth would seem to rule out attributing to Dostoyevsky a chiliastic hope for heaven on earth. Dostoyevsky looks for the final satisfaction of the thirst for justice, not in the realization of heaven on earth, but in a "new heaven and a

---

66 *UD*, I, pp. 39-41. These words, written while Dostoyevsky kept a vigil by the dead body of his first wife, constitute his most sustained and explicit consideration of the nature of personal immortality—a consideration to which he sets limits by the words which have been quoted. For an exposition of the conception of personal immortality as the "transfiguration" of man into a "spiritual body," or "deification," see V. Lossky, *The Mystical Theology of the Eastern Church* (London, 1957), chaps. 7, 8, 12; P. Sherrard, *The Greek East and the Latin West* (London, 1959), pp. 41-47; V. Solovyov, *The Meaning of Love* (London, 1945).

67 *NBK*, p. 82; *BK*, p. 381 (VI,3).

68 *UD*, I, pp. 39-41.

new earth.''[69] Nevertheless, his appeal to the eternal life of the ''spiritual body'' has immediate implications for the question of a just order here and now. Turning away from the ''impossible'' task of illumining the nature of the ''final . . . eternal life,'' he devotes his attention to these implications.

The Church Idea

The explication of that silent presence with which Dostoyevsky confronts the final Western social formula entails finally the teaching that people are called to live within an order oriented towards the eternal, and thus to attain ''paradise'' insofar as the present earth is capable of containing it. For Dostoyevsky, the laying of the foundations of such an order was a central concern of the activity of the God-man. As Father Paissy (in *The Brothers Karamazov*) declares in the language of the Russian monk: ''Our Lord Jesus Christ came for the sole purpose of setting up the Church upon earth. The Kingdom of Heaven, of course, is not of this world, but in Heaven; but you enter Heaven only through the Church which has been founded and established on earth.''[70] Dostoyevsky offers no elucidation of the mystagogical or sacramental functions of the church. He is apparently concerned less with the church as the initiator into the way of personal immortality than with the church as the prototype of the best social order attainable on earth. Indeed, the church is present in his writing as the genuine realization of that freedom, equality, and brotherhood to which the modern West originally aspired in the Geneva idea. It is important to emphasize, however, that this realization is not associated with the church as an historical institution, but with the original ''church idea'' rooted in the God-man.

Although it tends to be neglected by Western commentators, the church idea is one of the central themes of *The Brothers Karamazov*. The novel as a whole can be interpreted as an extension of the debate ''*pro and contra*'' between the Grand Inquisitor and Christ. If this debate is to be comprehended fully it must not be seen simply from the perspective of the Inquisitor—that is, as a conflict between totalitarian order and anarchic individual freedom. For Dostoyevsky the two protagonists offer not so much a choice between freedom and order as a choice between alternative ideas of order—those of the church and the state. The former, in his view, preserves and enhances the freedom of the person, while the latter would abolish it. The state idea is developed in detail in Dostoyevsky's writings, and particularly through the characters of the Grand Inquisitor and Ivan in his final novel. The church idea, however, makes its appearance only in the final novel and only in rudimentary form. Its expression, moreover, is restricted by the requirements of art to the rather archaic speech of Russian monasticism. One can justifiably speculate

---

69 Cf. Revelation 21:1-4. The nature of Dostoyevsky's interest in the Revelation to John will be discussed in the next chapter.
70 *BK*, p. 68 (II,5).

that, had Dostoyevsky lived to complete the two-part novel of which *The Brothers Karamazov* was the first part, the church idea would have received a more complete and perhaps more contemporary expression.[71] The main features of the idea, however, are discernible in the novel, and can therefore be at least briefly indicated.

Freedom

The freedom of the God-man order is that freedom from subjection to material necessity which is dependent upon the recovery of the spiritual principle within humanity. In its attempt to find human freedom in the conscious will, the Geneva idea condemns human beings to the "tyranny of material things and habits," for reason and will are themselves rooted in material necessity. To the "slavery" inherent in the modern Western notion of freedom, Zosima opposes the "real, true" understanding of freedom: "I cut off all superfluous and unnecessary needs, I subdue my proud and ambitious will and chastise it with obedience, and, with God's help, attain freedom of spirit and with it spiritual joy!"[72] Because the recovery of the spiritual principle is equivalent to the recovery of one's true or essential being, the attainment of freedom can be expressed as the finding of oneself within oneself. Yet this self-discovery implies also a self-renunciation, for the spiritual principle is overlaid by the material principles of reason, will, and desire, which together constitute a false self or "ego." The overcoming of the ego presupposes a hard discipline, a discipline which Dostoyevsky calls "self-mastery" or "self-conquest."[73]

As we have seen, the Geneva idea of freedom also entails self-discipline, but because it locates the source of this discipline in the conscious will, it is doomed to failure. The disciplining of material needs in Geneva thought becomes that "right of multiplication of needs" characteristic of bourgeois liberalism and scientific socialism.[74] While Versilov starts "straight from himself" in his quest for moral perfection, Zosima knows that such perfection is possible for fallen humanity only because of the descent of perfection itself into the world. That "self-conquest" which true freedom requires is possible only through humanity's participation in the God-man. Although the consummation of this participation is an eternal matter, the means of a partial participation are available to people here and now in the God-man order. The church can be the source of a discipline enabling the person, while not yet a "spiritual body," to achieve an image of that complete overcoming of material necessity which is true freedom.[75]

71 See Dostoyevsky's foreword to *The Brothers Karamazov*.
72 *BK*, p. 370 (VI,3).
73 *PS*, p. 46; *BK*, p. 28 (I,5).
74 *BK*, p. 369 (VI,3).
75 "Self-control amounts to discipline and discipline is in the Church." *NP*, p. 163.

Equality

Self-discovery is the discovery also of the true basis of each person's equality with others. The attempt of the Geneva idea to overcome the distinction between master and slave finally issues in the Inquisitor's radical reassertion of this distinction. The God-man order, while concurring in the Geneva assertion of the fundamental equality of human beings in their capacity for goodness, grounds this capacity in the common possession of the spiritual principle rather than in the common possession of reason and will (for in regard to reason and will human beings prove themselves to be unequal). Dostoyevsky asserts that within the church there can be no masters and slaves, for such a distinction presupposes that some human beings can be more fully human than others. He does acknowledge, however, an inessential inequality among human beings, and hence the distinction between masters and servants.[76] In the God-man order, human beings are able to affirm the contingent psychophysical differences among themselves, without permitting this recognition of natural inequality to obscure their spiritual equality.

Brotherhood

The Geneva idea sought to resolve the contradiction between individual freedom and social unity (or brotherhood) through the mediation of love. Yet because it made this love dependent on the renunciation of eternity, it ended by grounding brotherhood in the realm of material necessity and, concomitantly, in human reason. For Dostoyevsky, the Inquisitor's social formula is the final outcome of the attempt to reconcile the individual to society by means of reason alone. The God-man order, however, promises the reconciliation of individuality with brotherhood through a love which is dependent on the descent of God into the realm of necessity. Moved by love for humanity, the God-man offers himself as the supreme model for the reconciliation of the "I" and the "all":

after the appearance of Christ, as the *idea of man incarnate*, it became as clear as day that the highest, final development of the individual should attain precisely the point (at the very end of his development, at the very point of reaching the goal) where man might find, recognize and with all the strength of his nature be convinced that the highest use which he can make of his individuality, of the full de-

---

76 See *PS*: "In Christianity, in true Christianity, there are and there will ever be, masters and servants, but a slave can never be even conceived. I speak of a true and perfect Christianity. Servants are not slaves. The pupil Timothy served Paul when they journeyed together; but read Paul's epistle to Timothy. Is it written to a slave, to a servant even? He is in truth his 'child Timothy,' his beloved son. These, these are indeed the relations that will be between master and servant, if master and servant become perfect Christians! Servants and masters there will be, but masters will be no longer lords nor servants slaves" (*PS*, p. 81). For Dostoyevsky's account of the incompatibility of serfdom with Christianity, see *PS*, pp. 78-80. This passage demands the attention particularly of those who speak of Dostoyevsky's "reactionary" politics. In this regard, see also *UD*, I, p. 106; II, pp. 64, 115; III, p. 16.

velopment of his *I*, is to seemingly annihilate that *I*, to give it wholly to each and every one wholeheartedly and selflessly. And this is the greatest happiness. In this way the law of the *I* merges with the law of humanism, and in the merging both, both the *I* and the *all* (in appearance two extreme opposites) mutually annihilated for each other, at that same time each apart attains the highest goal of his individual development.

This is indeed the paradise of Christ.[77]

The possibility of finding oneself in giving oneself to others is rooted in the essential unity of human beings and, indeed, of all life. This fundamental unity, which people can apprehend only through reason taken up into love, is expressed by Zosima as follows: "everything, like the ocean, flows and comes into contact with everything else: touch it in one place and it reverberates at the other end of the world."[78] Because the unity of the whole has its basis in the inherence of the "seeds" or *logoi* of all things in the eternal Logos which is God, it is a unity which preserves rather than consumes particularity. Within the God-man order, individuals are able to find in their unity with others at the same time the highest development of their own "personality."[79]

The simultaneous affirmation of human beings as unique "persons" and as manifestations of a common humanity is evident in the "brotherhood" of boys founded by Alyosha at the end of *The Brothers Karamazov*. This brotherhood, having its basis in a shared devotion to the memory of the little boy, Ilyusha, is a microcosm of that order which has its basis in the God-man:

"I give you my word, boys, that I will never forget any one of you. I shall remember every face that is looking at me now, even after thirty years. You're all dear to me from now on boys. I will find a place for you all in my heart and I beg you to find a place for me in your heart also! Well, and who has united us in this good and kind feeling which we shall remember and intend to remember all our lives? Who did it, if not Ilyusha, the good boy, the dear boy, dear to us for ever and ever! Don't let us, then, ever forget him, may his memory live in our hearts for ever and ever!"

"Yes, yes, for ever and ever!" all the boys cried in their ringing voices, looking deeply moved . . . .

"Karamazov", cried Kolya, "is it really true that, as our religion tells us, we shall all rise from the dead and come to life and see one another again, all, and Ilyusha?"

"Certainly we shall rise again, certainly we shall see one another, and shall tell one another gladly and joyfully all that has been", Alyosha replied, half laughing, half rapturously.[80]

77 *UD*, I, pp. 39, 96.
78 *BK*, p. 376 (VI,3).
79 Cf. V. Lossky, *The Mystical Theology of the Eastern Church* (London, 1957), pp. 164-71.
80 *BK*, pp. 911-13 (XIII,3). For a similar interpretation of the "Ilyusha brotherhood," see
    V. Ivanov, *Freedom and the Tragic Life, a Study in Dostoevsky* (New York, 1971), pp.
    150-52.

The final consummation of human freedom, equality, and brotherhood is enfolded in the mystery of eternal life. Yet insofar as our transitory life on earth can contain it, the God-man order constitutes for Dostoyevsky an alternative to the Geneva idea of order—and at the same time the redemption of that idea.

SIX

RUSSIAN SOCIALISM AND
THE WESTERN CRISIS

The Grand Inquisitor avers that the human yearning for order will ultimately be satisfied with nothing less than the actualization in practice of his social formula. His entire enterprise, as we have seen, requires not merely that his teaching about order be the best in theory, but that it be realizable also. It is this requirement, above all, which determines his interpretation of the third temptation posed to Christ in the wilderness. For Dostoyevsky this emphasis on practice is an essential ingredient of the modern Western project. The modern rebellion against "divine justice" is rooted in an impatience with apparently unfulfilled promises, in an urge to *do* something *now* to wipe away the tears of human suffering. A primary consequence of this urge has been a lowering of the sights, a reduction of the distance between the "is" and the "ought," for the sake of practical certainty. Modern science and technology owe their immense success to this favouring of the "is" over the "ought," and the tangible alleviation of human suffering thereby achieved is one of the principal reasons for the world-wide influence of the Western social formula. In the face of this influence, the silent figure of "The Grand Inquisitor" must embody a response not merely in theory but also in practice. It was in an attempt to meet this requirement that Dostoyevsky developed, at least in bare outline, a "theory of practical Christianity," a doctrine of Christian work which calls people to devote themselves to the actualization in practice of the church idea insofar as the earth can contain it.[1]

The "first step" towards the actualization of the God-man order is, for Dostoyevsky, the regeneration of the spiritual principle within the individual. This regeneration cannot be accomplished in one heroic leap. It must be a gradual process involving that relentless self-discipline for the sake of genuine

1 *NI*, p. 222; *PS*, p. 47; *DW*, pp. 605, 622, 624 (Feb. 1877); *NP*, pp. 216, 226, 366.

163

freedom which has become so foreign to modern individuals. In response to those who work for the transformation of the political or socio-economic structure, Dostoyevsky calls for a different sort of transformation: "It is my idea that the world must be refashioned, but that the first step ought to consist of . . . starting with one's self." There can be no genuine brotherhood unless men first become brothers, and this presupposes that they become fully human.[2] Yet Dostoyevsky's teaching concerning the "first step" does not issue in a call for a monastic retreat from the world, or for a merely private asceticism. His doctrine of "practical Christianity" advocates a monasticism within the world rather than out of the world. Zosima's teaching of the identity of the most selfless love of others with the most certain apprehension of the spiritual principle within one's self is the theoretical basis of this worldly monasticism.

The "new type of man" who will "live in the world like a monk" is Dostoyevsky's answer to the "enlightened" intellectual who works for the actualization of the universal state. This "new man" is embodied in Alyosha, the "hero" of *The Brothers Karamazov*: he is eccentric and chaste, even morbidly so, and he resembles to some extent a "saintly fool"; but his saintliness is characterized by health rather than sickness, by intelligence and commonsense rather than fanaticism, and by a yearning for truth rather than an impulse towards mystification. In Alyosha, Dostoyevsky attempts to re-claim for the Christian worker some of the virtues which have been arrogated to the secular intellectuals.[3] Alyosha's chief activity within the world is to be the education of others to the "first step." Dostoyevsky speaks of education, in the broadest sense, as the scattering of "seeds," either by means of the written word or through direct example. His employment of this image em-phasizes that the imparting of ideas to others has an effect which is not susceptible of any certain measurement. Because the "tiniest fire" can ignite a "universal conflagration," Dostoyevsky affirms education as one of the most significant of human activities.[4] Education is of paramount importance also to the builders of the future universal state. It is here in particular, therefore, that the Christian educator must confront the secular intellectual: Alyosha is to go to the university as Ivan did, but in service to the God-man order rather than that of the man-god.[5]

Although there would appear to be a vast gulf between the education of others to the "first step" and the universal actualization of the church idea, Dostoyevsky envisages a bridging of this gulf in the possibility that the rare worker who inspires others to the "first step" may unite them also in a common orientation towards his teaching or his example. The Christian worker may be unable to discern the final fruit of the seeds which he scatters,

2 *NRY*, p. 480; *DW*, p. 605 (Feb. 1877); *WNSI*, pp. 112, 114 (6).
3 *BK*, pp. 334, xxv, 17-21, 25-27, 65, 86 (VI,1; foreword; I,4,5; II,5,7).
4 *The Idiot*, pp. 442-43 (III,6); *NRY*, p. 380.
5 See V. Ivanov, *Freedom and the Tragic Life, a Study in Dostoevsky* (New York, 1971), p. 153.

but through his activity he can sometimes bring into immediate existence a community which points towards the God-man order. The immediate outcome of Alyosha's mission of work in the world is the formation of the "Ilyusha brotherhood." Dostoyevsky himself hoped that the immediate practical outcome of his work as a writer would be the formation of a community, which he designates as "Russian socialism."[6] His understanding of such a community, and his hope for its actualization, is dependent primarily on a particular interpretation of the history of both Russia and the West.

Dostoyevsky's Philosophy of History

The Grand Inquisitor's need for practical certainty turns him towards history as the realm of the appearance and development of the prime instrument for the actualization of his theory—the universal state. As we have seen, his discourse on the three temptations is permeated by a particular interpretation of history, amounting almost to a full-blown philosophy of history. This concern with meaning in history is for Dostoyevsky another of those elemental tendencies which have given shape to Western modernity. It is a concern which no complete response to the final Western social formula can ignore. The need to formulate a "theory of practical Christianity" in the face of this formula leads Dostoyevsky too towards history—as the realm of the appearance and development of the church idea. Dostoyevsky's interest in the problem of meaning in history is evident as early as his Siberian exile, and it remained a consistent subject of his reading in philosophy, theology, and history throughout his life.[7] Yet the results of his meditation on history did not become manifest in his art in any sustained way until *The Brothers Karamazov*, and even here in merely embryonic form. It is to Dostoyevsky's journalistic writings that we must turn for a more complete outline of his interpretation of history, an interpretation amounting to a "kind of 'meta-history,' into which are gathered all historical empires . . . all cultural, political, and economic history."[8]

Two points should be made prior to consideration of Dostoyevsky's "meta-history." First, it bears repeating that the chief tension informing his interpretation of history is not, as for the Inquisitor, the tension between order and freedom. The Inquisitor's philosophy of history presupposes a basic in-

---

6 This motivation is most explicitly evident in Dostoyevsky's work on *The Diary of a Writer*. See K. Mochulsky, *Dostoevsky, his Life and Work* (Princeton, 1967), pp. 536, 544. For his use of the term "Russian socialism," see *DW*, p. 1029 (Jan. 1881).

7 Dostoyevsky's interest in philosophy of history, and the history of Christianity, is first apparent in a letter of 22 Feb. 1854 written to his brother Mikhail (from his exile in Omsk, Siberia) in which he requests that various books concerned with these subjects be sent to him. See also V. V. Zenkovsky, "Dostoevsky's Religious and Philosophical Views," *Dostoevsky, a collection of critical essays* (Englewood Cliffs, N.J., 1962), pp. 142-44.

8 F. Stepun, *Dostojewskij und Tolstoj: Christentum und soziale Revolution: Drei Essays* (Munich, 1961), pp. 21-22, 48.

compatibility between freedom and order. Freedom and order can co-exist, but not coincide. Order thus exists for the many who are thereby "happy," while freedom exists only for the few who are "unhappy." Dostoyevsky's enucleation of the church idea denies this incompatibility between order and freedom, presenting the church instead as the order in which the "I" and the "all" are mutually preserved and enhanced. The central tension informing his interpretation of history is that between two ideas of order—the church and the state. In *The Brothers Karamazov* the universal church, oriented towards the final deification of man through the God-man, is explicitly opposed to the universal state, which is oriented towards the self-deification of man in the man-god. Because the ideas of church and state represent for Dostoyevsky antithetical religious conceptions, there can be no final accommodation or compromise between them. There is a fundamental and direct opposition of the "essential principles underlying Church and State":

it is not the Church that ought to seek for itself a definite place in the State like 'any other social organization' or like 'an organization of men for religious purposes'. . . but, on the contrary, every State on earth must eventually be entirely transformed into a Church, and become nothing but a Church, renouncing those of its aims which are incompatible with the principles of the Church. All this will in no way lower its prestige or deprive it of its honour and glory as a great State . . . but will merely turn it away from the false, still pagan and mistaken path to the right and true path which alone leads to the eternal goal.[9]

The human yearning for order will not tolerate a perpetual condition of divided or confused reverences. To advocate the permanent separation of church and state is, in Dostoyevsky's view, merely to delay the final resolution of the problem of order.

It must be emphasized, secondly, that Dostoyevsky does not identify the church or the state exclusively with any actual historical configuration of ecclesiastical or political power. His ultimate concern is with the "essential principles underlying Church and State," that is, with the church idea and the state idea. These ideas are capable of adopting diverse and even unlikely empirical attire. Indeed, as we shall see, what appears outwardly to be the church can, for Dostoyevsky, be animated at its heart by the state idea. He does not assume any easy identification of the church idea rooted in Christ with the organized Christianity of history.

The History of Church and State in the West

Although there are references to various ancient civilizations in his writing, Dostoyevsky's attention focuses upon Rome as "the outcome of the moral aspirations of the whole ancient world." According to him, the idea which chiefly animated ancient Rome was that of the universal "*compulsory* com-

9 *BK*, pp. 67-69 (II,5).

munion" of humanity.[10] This world-wide communion to which Rome aspired was compulsory because the boundaries of the communion were expanded by means of the sword. But more significantly, the communion was compulsory because it was rooted in the attempt (epitomized in the classical humanism of Cicero) to order human life exclusively on the basis of rational categories. The prodigious effort to submit all facets of life to the principle of "right reason" led increasingly to the subjection of human beings to material necessity (and, concomitantly, to chance or "Fortuna"—that in nature which would not submit to the control of reason).[11] The compulsion which came to characterize Roman order achieved appropriate outward expression during the rule of the emperors. For Dostoyevsky, the Eternal City of the Caesars is edifying only because in it the state idea has revealed itself with the minimum of concealment. Although there were gods in ancient Rome behind which the state could hide, little attempt was made to conceal the reduction of all theology to civil theology. In its adornment of Caesar's sword with an elaborate civil theology (or "miracle, mystery, and authority"), Rome was the first great historical embodiment of the Inquisitor's social formula. According to Dostoyevsky, the end to which this formula is dedicated was also discernible in ancient Rome. That quintessential article of the imperial civil theology—the divinity of the emperor himself—betrays the orientation of ancient Rome towards the man-god.[12] The Eternal City ultimately aspired to be the vehicle of human self-deification.

Rome was opposed by those peoples who wished to retain their gods, not as members of the Roman pantheon, but as guarantors of their own particularity. In the forefront of this opposition were the northern Germanic peoples, who stubbornly resisted the Roman sword and the Roman civil theology. A far more profound opposition to Rome, however, appeared within its own borders. The Eternal City was confronted by an antithetical religious idea: "Then occurred the collision of the two most opposite ideas that could exist in the world. The Man-God met the God-Man, the Apollo Belvedere met the Christ."[13] The advent of Christianity in the ancient world is, for the Inquisitor, equivalent to the advent of disorder because it fostered the development of the personal conscience. For Dostoyevsky, however, the appearance of Christianity signifies the possibility of an alternative universal order in which the personal conscience is reconciled with social unity, and particularity with universality:

remember what was the ancient Christian Church and what it aspires to be. It began immediately after the death of Christ, with a handful of people, and instantly, almost in the very first days after the death of Christ, it attempted to discover its

10 *PS*, p. 88; *DW*, pp. 256, 563, 728 (March 1876; Jan., May-June 1877); *The Devils*,
   p. 258 (II,1,vii).
11 Cf. C. N. Cochrane, *Christianity and Classical Culture* (Oxford, 1957), pp. 112-13;
   P. Sherrard, *The Greek East and the Latin West* (London, 1959), pp. 13-18.
12 *PS*, pp. 88-89.
13 Ibid., pp. 88-89.

"civic formula," which was wholly based upon the moral expectation of satisfying the spirit by the principles of personal self-perfection. Then arose the Christian communities—Churches; then speedily began to be created a new and hitherto unheard-of nationality, a nationality of universal brotherhood and humanity, in the shape of the catholic oecumenical Church. But the Church was persecuted, and the ideal grew beneath the earth, and above it, on the face of the earth, an immense building was also being formed, a huge ant-hill, the old Roman empire, which was also the ideal and the outcome of the moral aspirations of the whole ancient world. But the ant-hill did not fortify itself; it was undermined by the Church.[14]

The Roman state, however, was not completely overcome by the church. It succeeded in preserving itself by means of a compromise: the Empire accepted Christianity, while the church accepted the temporal jurisdiction of Roman law and the Roman state. Under the Emperor Constantine in the third century A.D. Christianity became the official religion of the Roman Empire; it permitted itself to become, in effect, the new civil theology of the Empire.[15] Rome perhaps hoped that its acceptance of Christianity as a civil theology would help to combat that moral exhaustion which was undermining its will to preserve itself against the encroaching barbarians. And the church perhaps sought in the compromise a respite from persecution, as well as a prodigious instrument for the accomplishment of its work. Yet, whatever the motives for the compromise effected between the church and the state under Constantine and his successors, this compromise could not, according to Dostoyevsky, be permanent—for Christianity is by its very nature unsuited to fulfill the function of a civil theology.[16] The clear-sighted among the devotees of the Eternal City perceived the absurdity of a compromise with the church. The futile effort of Julian the Apostate, for instance, to find within the antique world itself the spiritual resources necessary for its preservation may have stemmed from his recognition of the fundamental antithesis between Rome and Christianity.[17] Those within the church who recognized the ultimate impossibility of compromise "went into the desert," and there continued to work for the actualization of the universal God-man order: "Christian communities once more appeared, then monasteries; and these were only attempts, attempts which have lasted even unto our day."[18] Dostoyevsky does not maintain that the church simply ceased to be the church wherever it came to terms with Rome. The church ceased to be the church only when it finally sacrificed its essential principles in favour of those of the state. According to Dostoyevsky, this overcoming of the church by the state occurred first in the Western part of the Roman Empire.

The triumph of the state over the church in the West coincides, for Dostoyevsky, with the first great schism within the church. The mutual ex-

---

14 Ibid., p. 88.
15 Ibid., p. 89. Cf. E. Voegelin, *The New Science of Politics* (Chicago, 1952), pp. 100-106.
16 *BK*, p. 68 (II,5).
17 *DW*, p. 256 (March 1876). See C. N. Cochrane, *Christianity and Classical Culture* (Oxford, 1957), chap. 7.
18 *PS*, p. 89.

communication pronounced in Constantinople in 1054 by the Patriarch of Constantinople, Michael Cerularius, and the papal legate, Cardinal Humbert, is generally considered to be the decisive moment in the rupture between Western and Eastern Christianity. Yet Dostoyevsky implies, in "The Grand Inquisitor," that this event represented merely the explicit acknowledgment of a division which had become critical as much as three centuries earlier.[19] It was towards the end of the eighth century that the addition of the *filioque* clause to the Nicene Creed became common practice throughout the Western church (although the altered Creed was not used in the papal chapel itself until the early eleventh century). In accord with his conviction concerning the primacy of ideas in determining the course of human affairs, Dostoyevsky attributes the great schism within Christendom to a differing interpretation of credal truth, rather than to political, economic, or cultural differences.[20] He apparently thought that an event of such significance could not be attributed to merely material causes such as the economic rivalry between the Italian maritime cities and Byzantium, or the resentment of the East towards the military aggression of the Latin crusaders. Nor could it be reduced to a squabble over the use of unleavened bread or the wearing of beards. Such matters were merely peripheral to the essential source of the schism: the alteration by the Bishop of Rome of the Christian representation of truth without the consent of the whole church. The question which must now be considered is this: What, for Dostoyevsky, is the relation between the Bishop of Rome's alteration of the Creed—with the concomitant assertion of his primacy within the church—and the acceptance of the "sword of Caesar" by Western Christianity?[21]

The enthusiastic support accorded to the *filioque* clause by the Emperor Charlemagne was decisive in persuading the Western church to alter the Creed. The Latin church was doubtless motivated to accept the *filioque* in part by the hope of gaining Charlemagne's help in extending its influence over the barbarian peoples of Europe. Yet for Dostoyevsky the relationship between the *filioque* and the "sword of Caesar" is of a more fundamental nature. The church's acceptance of the new clause was not simply a matter of policy, or, if it was, this policy was the appropriate expression of a deeply rooted theological tendency. In Dostoyevsky's view, the *filioque* had its ultimate source in the tendency of the Western church to conform the Christian truth to human reason.[22] The alteration of the Creed was the outcome of a propensity for rationalization which the Latin church was unable to resist. Unfortunately, Dostoyevsky does not indicate why the Latin West, unlike the

19 *BK*, p. 302 (V,5).
20 Cf. P. Sherrard, *The Greek East and the Latin West* (London, 1959), pp. 49-51.
21 *BK*, p. 302 (V,5).
22 The reliance of the Grand Inquisitor on reason alone has been discussed in the fourth chapter. See also Father Zosima's assertions that this reliance is at the centre of Western civilization, in *BK*, pp. 371, 374 (VI,3).

Byzantine East, succumbed to this propensity. Nor does he indicate explicitly how the addition of the *filioque* clause to the Nicene Creed constitutes a rationalization of the Christian truth. Here note can only be taken of his conviction, which reflects the Eastern side of the controversy, that such a rationalization did take place in the West. According to the Eastern view, this rationalizing of the Christian principle entailed the overcoming of the paradox of God's simultaneous transcendence and immanence in relation to the world, the paradox which is at the heart of Godmanhood. This paradox was overcome, however, only through the exclusion of one of its poles. Western Christianity had come increasingly to conceive God as transcendent only, and not at the same time immanent within the world.[23]

It would seem to be Dostoyevsky's view, then, that the Western church effectively took up "Caesar's sword" when it attempted to organize Christendom on the assumption of God's absence from the world. The alliance with Charlemagne, and the adoption of much of the civic and legal apparatus of the Roman state, therefore represented merely the outward confirmation of an inner attitude. This attitude was not a denial of the God-man so much as a denial that the world is effectively overcome by him. As we have noted in the preceding chapter, it is the *resurrected* God-man whom the Inquisitor will not accept. Not believing in the God-man who has overcome necessity, the Inquisitor accepts the offer of the universal state held out in the third temptation as the only order which renders human happiness possible. We have seen the manner in which, according to Dostoyevsky, this state ultimately achieves its order. Insofar as Western Christianity succumbed to the temptation of organizing itself as a "continuation of the Holy Roman Empire," it too depended for the realization of its order on "compulsion" or "coercion." Its unity was a fundamentally material or mechanical unity, having its source of power in the visible presence of the Pope in Rome rather than in the invisible presence of the resurrected God in each local church.[24] The reliance upon compulsion in the service of the God-man is, for Dostoyevsky, a tacit admission of the ultimate impotence of goodness in the face of chance and necessity—an admission which constitutes the "essence" of Roman Catholicism.[25] In his view the most typical empirical expression of this admission is the Jesuit order, with its implicit affirmation of "the righteousness of every means for Christ's cause." Such an affirmation achieved final explicitness when Pope Pius IX proclaimed his infallibility, and at the same time the thesis that without temporal power Christianity cannot survive on earth; that is, "strictly speaking, he proclaimed himself Sovereign of the world." In its struggle during the 1870s to defend the last remnant of its earthly sovereignty against the Italian liberal movement, the papacy had revealed its animating idea to be

23 See the Appendix for further discussion of the *filioque* issue.
24 *The Idiot*, pp. 585-86 (IV,7); *The Devils*, p. 255 (II,1,vii); *DW*, pp. 563, 728-29 (Jan., May-June 1877).
25 *The Idiot*, pp. 585-86 (IV,7).

"political" rather than "spiritual"—to be, in fact, a reformulation of the ancient Roman idea of universal unity.[26]

Dostoyevsky does not maintain that the image of Christ became obscured for all Christians in the West. He declares in his unpublished notes that he would never say "such a stupid thing." Because he is often misunderstood in this regard, attention should be drawn to his clear distinction between the papal principle informing the mainstream of Western Christianity, and the God-man principle which has continued to live within particular Westerners.[27] Inadequate or false representations of the truth do not alter the truth itself. The church cannot "disappear entirely." Dostoyevsky's historical account of Western Christianity is not, however, concerned with those "individual representatives" of Western Christianity, in whose hearts the image of Christ unquestionably remains in all its "original truth and purity." He is concerned, rather, with the fundamental meaning of Roman Catholicism as a form of human order.[28]

Roman Catholicism finally failed to organize the West in Christ's name. It failed because there were too many Europeans whose "sacred, truthful, innocent, ardent feelings" were outraged by the distortion of Christ's image represented by the papal principle.[29] This outrage first erupted into historical effectiveness in the sixteenth century when it was given direction by the German monk, Luther. The Protestant attempt to recover the obscured essence of Christianity was, however, seriously limited by historical circumstance. Cut off from the East by eight centuries of cultural prejudice and political conflict, and by the approaching tide of Islam, Protestantism declined to seek in Eastern Christianity the original church idea. Yet in the absence of a sufficient spiritual tradition of its own, Protestantism could only refuse the "compulsory communion" held out in the papal idea, while being unable to offer as a living alternative the "spiritual communion" of the original church idea. The Protestant churches which were established therefore tended to be little more than vehicles of the desire for individual and national "segregation" which had been fostered by the coercive unity of Roman Catholicism. Despite its "good beginnings," Protestantism only contributed, in Dostoyevsky's view, to the further "segregation" and "isolation" of Western people. The limitations inherent in Luther's rejection of the papal idea inevitably entailed a proliferating sectarianism:

A vessel is carried with some precious vivifying liquid. But presently people get up on their feet and begin to shout: "Blind men! Why do you kiss the vessel?—It is only the content, and not the container, that is precious; you are kissing glass, mere glass; you are adoring a vessel; you are attributing all the holiness to glass, so that

26 *DW*, pp. 911, 735-36, 728 (Oct., May-June 1877); *UD*, I, pp. 94-95; *BK*, pp. 305-306 (V,5).
27 *UD*, III, pp. 151, 153; *DW*, p. 736 (May-June 1877).
28 *The Idiot*, p. 586 (IV,7).
29 Ibid., p. 585 (IV,7).

you are forgetting its precious content! Idolaters! Throw away the vessel! Break it! Worship only the liquid, and not the glass!" And they break the vessel and the vivifying liquid, the precious content, is spilled on the earth and, of course, vanishes there. The vessel is broken and the liquid is lost. However, while the liquid has not yet entirely vanished in the soil, there ensues a hubbub: . . . men break up in antagonistic groups, and each group carries away for itself a few drops of the precious liquid in special multiformed cups picked up at random, and the groups no longer communicate one with the other.[30]

Unable to replace the corrupt vessel of Roman Catholicism which it had broken, the Protestant movement was consigned to the fundamentally negative stance indicated by its name.[31] For this reason it could be no more than a by-product of the papal idea, radically dependent on this idea for its very existence.

In Dostoyevsky's view, the close dependence of the Protestant movement upon the very papal principle which it rejects is particularly evident in its rationalism. In their quest for a new vessel, Protestants turned to the only indisputable criterion available to them—the Bible. Yet in the absence of a universally recognized authority for the interpretation of this criterion, it was inevitable that the final "banner" of Protestantism would become the individual's right to "freedom of inquiry."[32] This right to inquire into the meaning of Scripture in freedom from the pronouncements of any external authority was to be transformed eventually into the right to inquiry for its own sake, an inquiry increasingly conducted on the basis of reason alone. Dostoyevsky does speak of the "sad and rapturous music" of northern Protestantism, of "the illimitable mystic with his dull, sombre, invincible aspiration, and the impetuous power of his mystical dreaming." But he discerns the most characteristic outcome of Luther's protest in the philosophy of Hegel. Through its intensification of the rationalizing tendency already present in Roman Catholicism, the Protestant movement had prepared its own grave, and that of Western Christianity as a whole.[33]

The dimming of the church idea in the West was most clearly evident for Dostoyevsky in the fact that the two poles of the idea—freedom and unity— had become antithetical. They had been placed in mutual opposition through their embodiment in the two great divisions of Western Christendom.[34] Threatened with the perpetual disorder consequent upon such an opposition, the West had turned to the promise of a new order held out in the Geneva idea.

30 *DW*, pp. 567-68 (Jan. 1877). Dostoyevsky's understanding of Protestantism was probably derived largely from his reading of Khomyakov. See A. Khomyakov, *L'Eglise Latine et le Protestantisme* (Lausanne, 1872); W. J. Birkbeck, ed., *Russia and the English Church* (London, 1969).

31 *DW*, p. 193 (Jan. 1876).

32 Ibid., p. 730 (May-June 1877).

33 *PS*, p. 56; *NP*, p. 355. For an allusion to the intrinsic relation between Lutheranism and Hegelianism, see *BK*, p. 72 (II,5). Cf. V. Solovyov, *Lectures on Godmanhood* (London, 1948), p. 202. Solovyov's account of Protestantism is very similar to that of Dostoyevsky.

34 *DW*, pp. 562-64 (Jan. 1877); *PS*, p. 64.

The Geneva idea purported to reconcile the individual freedom of Protestant-ism with the universal unity of Roman Catholicism, and to do so on the basis of a reason liberated from the accumulated tradition of centuries. Yet despite its rejection of the past, the Geneva idea is actually the most recent metamor-phosis of the old state idea—"an idea which dates back to ancient Rome and which was fully conserved in Catholicism."[35] The state idea, however, has a further metamorphosis to undergo before it becomes the final Western solu-tion to the problem of order expressed in the formula: "The Pope—leader of communism." Our earlier exploration of this formula raised a fundamental question which was left without a complete answer. In the light of Dostoyev-sky's interpretation of Western history it should now be clearer why he thought it possible that Roman Catholicism would consent to the alliance expressed in the Inquisitor's social formula. This consent had, in essence, been granted centuries before communism made its appearance in the West. In the Inquisitor's words:

It's a long time—eight centuries—since we left you and went over to *him*. Exactly eight centuries ago we took from him what you rejected with scorn, the last gift he offered you . . . we took from him Rome and the sword of Caesar and proclaimed ourselves the rulers of the earth . . . .[36]

The History of Church and State in Russia

Dostoyevsky's outline of the history of Western civilization constitutes his justification for identifying the state so closely with the West. While associat-ing the state idea with the West, he at the same time associates the church idea with Russia. In order to grasp this latter association more clearly we must turn to his account of the "collision" between church and state in the Eastern part of the Roman Empire.

Dostoyevsky revered Byzantine Orthodoxy as the preserver and prop-agator of the "Divine image of Christ . . . in all its purity."[37] The modern Western tendency to dismiss Byzantine civilization as, in Hegel's words, "a disgusting picture of imbecility . . . and consequently a most uninteresting picture"[38] is for Dostoyevsky merely symptomatic of the Western distance from the "Divine image." Yet his admiration for the marvellous expression of the church idea attained by Byzantine thought does not preclude scepticism concerning Byzantine practice. He concurs in the usual Western judgment of the relation between church and state in Byzantium as one of "Caesaropapism." In his view the Byzantine church had already become separated from the true image of Christ long before the Byzantine Empire was

35 *DW*, pp. 563, 721, 729 (Jan., May-June 1877); *The Idiot*, pp. 585-86 (IV,7); *UD*, I, p. 94.
36 *BK*, p. 302 (V,5).
37 *DW*, p. 63 (1873).
38 G. W. F. Hegel, *The Philosophy of History* (New York, 1956), pp. 336-40.

destroyed by the "sword of Mahomet."[39] And the destruction of the Byzantine state did not free the Byzantine church for the attempt at a genuine realization of its idea, for under the rule of Islam the church increasingly became little more than a vehicle for the national aspirations and "national antagonisms" of Greeks, Bulgars, Serbs, and other subject peoples. Even where it did not confuse Christianity with nationality, the Eastern church was in no position to do more than preserve the theoretical purity of the "Divine image" bequeathed to it by Greek theology. This task it accomplished largely through its monastic tradition. Yet, while Dostoyevsky venerates Mount Athos as the place where, in the words of Father Joseph (in *The Brothers Karamazov*), "the Orthodox doctrine has been preserved since olden times inviolate and in its brightest purity," he looks elsewhere for the actualization of the church idea.[40]

The Eastern church did not engage in missionary activity with the same zeal or success demonstrated by the Western church in its mission to the barbarian peoples. Yet the activity of two Greek missionaries, Cyril and Methodius, kept the greater part of the Slavic people outside the Roman fold. When the Russian Slavs finally renounced paganism in the tenth century and "accepted and exalted Christ anew," it was the Christ brought to them by Byzantium whom they embraced with such ingenuous devotion.[41] So fervent was their adoption of Eastern Christianity that they reacted with bewildered dismay to the accord between the Latin and Byzantine churches reached at the Council of Florence in 1439. No longer able to stand alone against Islam, Byzantium had finally been compelled to make overtures to the West. In return for Western military aid the Byzantine Emperor was required to secure the Eastern church's acceptance of the principle of papal supremacy. Although the accord of Florence was eventually rejected by the entire body of the Eastern church, it had a profoundly disturbing effect upon the Russians. The fall of Constantinople to the Turks fourteen years after the Council of Florence was interpreted by the Russian church as a judgment upon Byzantine Christianity, and by the Russian state as an opportunity to take up the Byzantine Emperor's fallen sword. The Grand Duke of Moscow, Ivan III, married Constantine XI's niece, adopted the double-headed eagle of Byzantium, and styled himself "Tsar" (Caesar), thereby proclaiming the succession of Moscow to Constantinople. The pretensions of the young Russian state found definitive expression in the doctrine of the "Third Rome" enunciated by Filofey of Pskov:

The Church of old Rome fell for its heresy; the gates of the second Rome, Constantinople, were hewn down by the axes of the infidel Turks; but the Church of Mos-

39 *PS*, p. 89.
40 *DW*, pp. 632-37 (March 1877); *BK*, p. 390 (VII,1). Dostoyevsky once planned to visit Athos. See his letter of 2 July 1870 to his niece, Sofya Ivanova.
41 *PS*, p. 89. For further discussion about the conversion of the Russians to Orthodox Christianity, and about the history of Russian Orthodoxy, see G. P. Fedotov, *The Russian Religious Mind* (Cambridge, Mass., 1946); N. Zernov, *The Russians and their Church* (London, 1945).

cow, the Church of the new Rome, shines brighter than the sun in the whole universe . . . Two Romes are fallen, but the third stands fast; a fourth there cannot be.[42]

The Muscovite Tsardom attempted to transform the church into its instrument, to employ Christianity as a civil theology. Insofar as Russian Christianity acquiesced in this, it came to be characterized by that same "Caesaropapism" which marked the official Christianity of Byzantium. For Dostoyevsky this trend was to culminate finally in the explicit subordination of the Russian church to the state under Peter the Great, who "practically turned priests into government functionaries."[43] Those "government functionaries" evinced an increasing concern with the material rather than the spiritual, a concern which had become shamelessly blatant by the latter part of the nineteenth century. The transformation of the Russian church into a department of the state bureaucracy had, moreover, divorced it from the deepest religious needs of the people. Dostoyevsky's scathing criticism of the Russian Orthodox Church underlies his explicit assertion that the "real social formula" of the God-man order "has not yet been evolved" in Russia.[44] In Russia, no less than in the West, the state had apparently achieved complete hegemony. (In this regard it is worth noting that the Procurator of the Holy Synod of the Russian church, Konstantin Pobedonostsev, may have served in part as a model for the Grand Inquisitor.) Yet Dostoyevsky's criticism of Russian Orthodoxy does not preclude the notion that Russia may be the bearer of the church idea, for he does not identify Russian Christianity primarily with the official ecclesiastical structure. Dostoyevsky justifies his close association of the church idea with Russia by pointing to the unofficial Christianity of the Russian monk and the Russian peasant.

Father Zosima's role as the interpreter of Christ's silence takes on its full significance in his words about the Russian monks:

they are verily prepared in peace and quiet "for an hour, and a day, and a month, and a year." In their solitude they keep the image of Christ pure and undefiled for the time being, in the purity of God's truth, which they received from the Fathers of old, the apostles and martyrs, and when the time comes they will reveal it to the wavering righteousness of the world. That is a great thought. That star will shine forth from the East.[45]

The monk, Zosima, speaks from within a Russian spiritual tradition which had its beginning in the fifteenth century, in the struggle between the rival monastic orders of Nil Sorsky and Joseph, Abbot of Volokolamsk. Nil op-

---

42 Found in N. Zernov, *The Russians and their Church* (London, 1945), p. 51.
43 *UD*, II, p. 6. For a general account of Peter's subordination of the Russian church to the state, see N. Zernov, *The Russians and their Church* (London, 1945), chap. 13.
44 *PS*, p. 89. Because there has been a tendency to regard Dostoyevsky as an uncritical proponent of the Russian Orthodox Church, attention should be accorded to the criticism which he levelled against it. See, for instance, *BK*, p. 343 (VI,2); *NBK*, p. 101; *DW*, p. 754 (July-Aug. 1877).
45 *BK*, p. 368 (VI,3).

posed the attempt of the Moscow Tsardom to transform Russian Orthodoxy into a civil theology, while Joseph lent the support of his monastic order to this attempt. Nil and his followers (called the "non-Possessors") emphasized the primacy of the task of recovering the inner spiritual principle through disciplined contemplation. This discipline entailed the renunciation of a concern with material possessions, and with worldly activity as a whole—particularly the activity implied in that alliance of church and state proclaimed by Filofey. Joseph and his followers (the "Possessors") maintained that it was permissible for the church to possess large landed estates, and otherwise to employ the instruments of the world for the realization of Christian truth. This tendency brought them into a close alliance with the state. In return for the church's moral sanction, the state was willing to guarantee its economic prosperity and to promote its spiritual monopoly by persecuting heretics. Although the victory of the Possessors was to be decisive for the external structure of the Russian church, it did not determine completely the future of the church idea in Russia. For the followers of Nil Sorsky established an "underground" spiritual tradition which bore fruit with the appearance of the "*startsy*" ("elders" or "spiritual directors") in the nineteenth century. This tradition was to bear fruit also in the art of Dostoyevsky, for it is the primary source of that response to the Grand Inquisitor which is embodied in the "Discourses and Sermons" of Father Zosima.[46]

Father Zosima represents the outcome of Dostoyevsky's effort to give artistic form to the thought and practice of the Russian *startsy*. The ultimate theoretical source of the spirituality of the *startsy* was the patristic theology of the Eastern church, as well as the later "hesychast" (or "mystical") teaching of St. Symeon the New Theologian (949-1022) and Gregory Palamas (1296-1359). This teaching represented the height of the Eastern church's attempt to appropriate Christianity not merely as dogma to be believed, but as the living "way" of freedom from the bondage of material necessity. Symeon and Gregory strove to communicate the way in which human beings are able to realize the spiritual principle within themselves, to attain to the vision of "fire truly divine . . . fire uncreated and invisible, without beginning and immaterial."[47] Although this knowledge of the way to participation in the eternal was incorporated to some degree within the normal sacramental life of the Eastern church, it did come to be associated particularly with the monasticism of Mount Athos. The continuous pilgrimages made by Russian monks to Athos were responsible for the transmission of the hesychast teaching to the Russian church, especially to that part of the church which followed Nil Sorsky. The heart of the hesychast movement in post-Petrine Russia was to be found in the succession of *startsy* at the monastery of Optina Pustyn. Dostoyevsky himself once spent two days at Optina Pustyn; and the monastery and its *starets*, Father Amvrosy, undoubtedly served as a major inspiration for his account of

46 See Dostoyevsky's letter of 7 Aug. 1879 to N. A. Liubimov; *BK*, pp. 25-30 (I,5).
47 T. Ware, *The Orthodox Church* (Harmondsworth, Eng., 1963), p. 75.

Russian monasticism in *The Brothers Karamazov*.[48] This account, and indeed the novel as a whole, is his testimony to the living knowledge of the church idea still present within Russian Christianity in the latter part of the nineteenth century. It was his hope that this idea would achieve practical realization in that new order which he designates as "Russian socialism."

Russian Socialism

According to Dostoyevsky, it is through the Russian peasant that the church idea must find a life beyond the solitude of the Russian monk. Without the Russian common people to serve as its "raw material," the community of "Russian socialism" can be nothing more than a dream. We must thus turn to Dostoyevsky's assessment of this "raw material."

Although he does not ignore the notorious "bestiality" of the Russian people, Dostoyevsky insists on the necessity of distinguishing between their "alluvial barbarism" and their "beauty."[49] The former is, in his view, a transient phenomenon attributable largely to historical circumstance, and in particular to the binding of the people in serfdom so that the gentry could have the leisure to acquire their "European enlightenment." The beauty of the people is manifest in the fact that they are still able to long for truth and goodness in the midst of the "stench" of sin. They refuse to affirm their own "likeness of the Beast" as the standard for human beings, to confuse the "is" with the "ought."[50] According to Dostoyevsky, the consciousness of the Russian people that they are not what they ought to be is evinced particularly in their reverence for the holy, a reverence which says to itself:

If there is sin, injustice, and temptation among us, then there is at any rate some-one somewhere on earth who is holier and superior; he has the truth, he knows the truth, which means that it is not dead on earth and will therefore come to us, too, one day, and rule over all the earth, as it was promised.[51]

Dostoyevsky maintains, however, that the people suffer from their thirst for truth as from a painful affliction, for this thirst has never been satisfied. Living since Peter the Great without the guidance, or even the sympathy, of the educated gentry, many among the Russian people had attempted to slake their thirst with narrow, rigidly exclusive interpretations of truth. Just as Dostoyevsky's writings attest to the bestial likeness of the Russian people, so they attest also to their predilection for a morbid sectarianism.[52] He argues,

48 See A. Dostoyevsky, *Reminiscences* (New York, 1975), pp. 292-94. Father Zosima has his source also in a Russian monk of the eighteenth century; see N. Gorodetzky, *Saint Tikhon of Zadonsk: Inspirer of Dostoevsky* (New York, 1976), pp. 215-29.
49 *DW*, pp. 202-205 (Feb. 1876).
50 *PS*, pp. 65-66. See also V. Solovyov, "Tri rechi v pamyat Dostoyevskago," *Sobranie sochinenii* (Brussels, 1966), III-IV, pp. 202-203.
51 *BK*, p. 31 (I,5).
52 *DW*, pp. 1025-30, 567-68 (Jan. 1881; Jan. 1877). For a discussion of Dostoyevsky's concern with Russian sectarianism, see E. Sandoz, *Political Apocalypse, a Study of Dostoev-*

however, that the majority of the Russian people have long aspired, in the midst of their suffering and moral confusion, to a truth of more universal scope—that of the brotherhood of man.[53] For Dostoyevsky the most tangible evidence of this Russian aspiration to brotherhood is the peasant commune (*obschina*), in which a remarkable degree of reconciliation between individual freedom and social unity has been achieved.

In a public letter to the French historian, Michelet, Alexander Herzen defended the Russian people against the charge that centuries of oppression had reduced them to a merely inert, unconscious mass with no thought or life of its own. In this letter he pointed to the existence of the commune as evidence that the Russian people had by themselves evolved a rudimentary socialism. They would thus prove particularly receptive to the theoretical socialism of the West, which would crown their instinctive, practical socialism with self-consciousness.[54] This appeal to the innate socialism of the Russian people came to constitute a leading idea of the ''populist'' movement which achieved particular prominence during the 1870s. Populism called upon Westernized Russians to return to the people, and there to discover the concrete beginnings of an answer to their quest for a new order. What the populists sought especially in the Russian people was that commune described by the Slavophile author, Konstantin Aksakov:

An *obschina* . . . represents a moral choir, and even as in a choir one voice is not lost but follows the notes of music and is heard in the harmony of all the voices: so in an *obschina* the individual is not lost, but renounces his exclusivity in regard for the common accord, and there emerges the noble phenomenon of a harmonious, shared existence of rational minds; there emerges a brotherhood, an *obschina*—a triumph of the human spirit.[55]

Dostoyevsky also regarded the Russian commune as an immensely significant phenomenon. But he did not interpret its significance in precisely the same manner as did the populists; nor did he share their tendency to attribute the commune to the peculiar character of the Russian people. For him the commune is not the expression of the Russian people *per se*, but of the Russian people insofar as they are permeated by the church idea: ''*Essentially*, save for this 'idea' there dwells no other in our people; everything is derived from it. . . .'' This idea, according to Dostoyevsky, was not spontaneously engendered by the Russian people; rather, it was absorbed by them through their contact with Orthodox Christianity. Although he concedes that the people do not possess a clear grasp of Orthodox doctrine—they could not pass an examination in the catechism, and no sermons are preached to

sky's Grand Inquisitor (Baton Rouge, 1971), pp. 31-34, 86-88, 140, 210; R. Peace, *Dostoyevsky* (Cambridge, 1971), pp. 303-304.

53 *DW*, pp. 1029-30 (Jan. 1881).

54 A. Herzen, ''The Russian People and Socialism,'' *Selected Philosophical Works* (Moscow, 1956).

55 Found in J. Pain, *Sobornost: A Study in Modern Russian Orthodox Theology* (unpublished D. Phil. dissertation, Oxford), pp. 124-25.

them—he nevertheless asserts that "the overwhelming mass of the Russian people is Orthodox."[56] The people's knowledge of Orthodoxy is derived from their familiarity with hymns and prayers which contain "the whole essence of Christianity," their acquaintance with certain biblical stories and lives of the saints and, above all, from their devotion to the image of Christ throughout centuries of suffering.[57]

While the manner in which the Orthodox teaching has been transmitted to the Russian people may be problematic, it is perfectly clear to Dostoyevsky what, principally, they grasped in this teaching. To the Russian people, Orthodoxy signifies, above all, the idea of the universal church. And, as Dostoyevsky is careful to note, this universal church is not to be identified simply with the ecclesiastical structure of Russian Orthodoxy, or with any other historical Orthodox church:

I am not speaking of church buildings, or the clergy. I am now referring to our Russian "socialism," the ultimate aim of which is the establishment of an oecumenical Church on earth in so far as the earth is capable of embracing it. I am speaking of the unquenchable . . . thirst in the Russian people for great, universal, brotherly fellowship in the name of Christ.

The brotherhood of the commune is rooted in a devotion to the higher order of the church, to "brotherly fellowship in the name of Christ" (*sobornost*).[58]

Yet, according to Dostoyevsky, it is not the Russian people but Russian Westernism which must take the active lead in making the new order of Russian socialism an historical reality. He thus affirms Versilov's contention that it is the uprooted gentry which is destined to bring the Russian idea onto the historical stage.[59] This brings us back to a final consideration of Dostoyevsky's view of the meaning and destiny of Russian Westernism.

We have noted Dostoyevsky's presentiment that the yearning of the uprooted Westernists for justice, to the point of self-sacrifice, would make them promising instruments for the builders of the universal state. For the same reason, Russian Westernism constituted a promise for those concerned with fostering a community which would point towards the universal church. Dostoyevsky's critique of the West was aimed chiefly at persuading Russian Westernism to find in Christianity the end of its yearning for the just order.

56 *DW*, p. 1028 (Jan. 1881). For an account of Dostoyevsky's relationship to the Russian "populism" of the 1870s, see G. Kabat, *Ideology and Imagination* (New York, 1978), pp. 6-8.

57 *PS*, p. 63; *DW*, pp. 802-804 (July-Aug. 1877).

58 *DW*, p. 1029 (Jan. 1881). The word *sobornost*, well-nigh untranslatable into English, is derived from the verb *sobirat*—"to assemble, gather, collect." The most etymologically correct translation of the noun, then, would be "the ingathering, convening, or assembling of people." The Russian church used the adjective *soborny* to translate the Greek *katholikos* (universal). The Slavophile theologian, Khomyakov, thus saw the catholicity of the church in the concord of those who are gathered together (*sobranye*) in the name of Christ. (See A. Khomyakov, *The Church is One*.) Dostoyevsky once remarked that his understanding of the church is essentially that of Khomyakov. See *UD*, III, p. 158.

59 *The Adolescent*, pp. 468-70 (III,7,ii,iii).

While attempting to educate Russian Westernists to the "first step," he directed them at the same time towards the task of forming the new community of Russian socialism. This new community was to arise from the "spiritual communion" of Russian Westernism with the Russian people, a communion rooted in the common aspiration to a universal order of freedom, equality, and brotherhood.[60]

Dostoyevsky insisted that this "spiritual merger" had to be initiated by the deference of the uprooted intelligentsia to the people, for in the church idea the people possess the way to genuine freedom, equality, and brotherhood. The spiritual communion to which Dostoyevsky attempted to persuade Russian Westernism is expressed concretely in the "last pilgrimage" of that finest of Russian liberals, Stepan Verkhovensky.[61] Verkhovensky's pilgrimage is a return to the Russian soil which culminates in a return to Christianity. Yet his conversion subsequent to receiving the last sacrament does not entail the renunciation of that great idea of a just social order which he has served. He has been brought to an awareness, rather, that the great idea must be grounded in an orientation towards the eternal:

The mere presence of the everlasting idea of the existence of something infinitely more just and happy than I, already fills me with abiding tenderness and—glory—oh, whoever I may be and whatever I may have done! To know every moment, and to believe that somewhere there exists perfect peace and happiness for everyone and for everything, is much more important to a man than his own happiness. The whole law of human existence consists merely of making it possible for every man to bow down before what is infinitely great. If man were to be deprived of the infinitely great, he would refuse to go on living, and die of despair. The infinite and the immeasurable is as necessary to man as the little planet which he inhabits. My friends—all, all my friends: long live the Great Idea! The eternal, immeasurable Idea! Every man, whosoever he may be, must bow down before what is the Great Idea. Even the most stupid man must have something great. Peter, my boy—Oh, how I wish I could see them all again! They do not know—they do not know that the same eternal Great Idea dwells in them too![62]

Verkhovensky's "last pilgrimage" does not signify the self-annihilation of Russian Westernism before the Russian people. Dostoyevsky maintains that the merger with the people must be renounced unless Russian Westernism too can be a teacher: "We must bow [to the people] on one condition only, and this—*sine qua non*: that the people accept from us those numerous things which we have brought with us."[63] Of these "numerous things" which Russian Westernism brings to the people, the most important is "science"—the capacity for rational thought and discourse. Dostoyevsky does not, of course, imply that the church idea attains to its complete truth only when "elevated" to the plane of self-conscious rationality. He does maintain, however, that the

60 See, for instance, *DW*, pp. 1030, 204 (Jan. 1881; Feb. 1876).
61 *The Devils*, pp. 625-57 (III,7).
62 Ibid., p. 656 (III,7,iii).
63 *DW*, p. 204 (Feb. 1876).

work for the actualization of the church idea stands in need of reason.[64] For, in proper subordination to the heart, reason is able to speak the word of the God-man order in a language which is accessible to those who have not yet consented to that order. By its very nature reason speaks to all people, and is thus an indispensable instrument for the education of all to the "first step." Verkhovensky's *profession de foi* expresses the church idea of the Russian people in words which every person can hear. Russian Westernism, with its possession of science and its sense of universal mission, is the natural vehicle for the propagation of the church idea.

Dostoyevsky's final word, then, concerning the problem of Peter the Great is that Peter's turn towards the West has made possible the "universal service of mankind to which Orthodoxy is designated."[65] For the aspiration to a universal order, inherent in the Orthodox Christianity of the Russian people, had been obscured and distorted by the circumstances of history. This obfuscation began when, in the centuries prior to Peter, the identification of Orthodoxy with the Russian state came to serve as the ideological foundation for the expanding Muscovite Tsardom. In its close association with the emergence of Russia as a great political power, Orthodoxy had tended to become merely an attribute of the Russian particularity.[66] The needs and interests of this particularity had become, for many Russians, the ultimate criterion against which truth itself was measured. Through Peter's reforms, however, Russia had become reacquainted with its aspiration to universality:

With Peter's reform there ensued an unparalleled broadening of the view, and herein—I repeat—is Peter's whole exploit... Now, what is this "expansion of the view," what does it consist of, and what does it signify?... this is our acquired faculty of discovering and revealing in each one of the European civilizations—or, more correctly, in each of the European individualities—the truth contained in it, even though there be much with which it be impossible to agree. Finally, this is the longing, above all, to be just and to seek nothing but truth. Briefly, this is, perhaps, the beginning of that active application of our treasure—of Orthodoxy—to the universal service of mankind to which Orthodoxy is designated and which, in fact, constitutes its essence. Thus, through Peter's reform our former idea—the Russian Moscow idea—was broadened and its conception was magnified and strengthened. Thereby we got to understand our universal mission, our individuality and our role in humankind ....[67]

Dostoyevsky thus rejects the conservative longing for pre-Petrine order, and affirms the universal aspiration of Russian Westernism in words reminiscent of the liberal idealist, Versilov. But Dostoyevsky's great concern is that this aspiration be informed, not by the Geneva idea, but by that church idea which is still preserved among the Russian people.

64 Ibid., pp. 1035-36 (Jan. 1881). Cf. L. Strauss, *The City and Man* (Chicago, 1964), p. 1.
65 *DW*, p. 361 (June 1876).
66 See Shatov's exchange with Stavrogin in *The Devils*, pp. 255-58 (II,1,vii).
67 *DW*, p. 361 (June 1876).

Russia and the Modern Western Crisis

Russian Westernism's sense of universal mission was, as we have seen, directed particularly towards the West. Although Dostoyevsky did affirm this concern with the fate of the West, he maintained that Russia must first turn away from the West in order to become itself. In one of his last published articles he advocates that Russia relinquish its two hundred-year-old effort to be an accepted participant in Western civilization, and that it turn instead towards Asia. He calls for the overcoming of the "slavish fear" that the West will regard Russians as "Asiatic barbarians," for Asia may well be the principal outlet for Russia in its attempt to consolidate itself around its own idea of order.[68] Yet despite such assertions, the turn away from the West towards Asia is ultimately for Dostoyevsky no more than a preparation, a putting of one's house in order.

Such a preparation is necessary if Russia is to present itself to the West, not with the apish countenance acquired through decades of servile imitation of Western forms of life, but with the human countenance which it will recover by learning to become itself, for Dostoyevsky is certain that Russia will turn again to the West, that its destiny is ultimately inseparable from that of the West. Russia will inevitably be embroiled in the catastrophic conflicts which will arise from the Western crisis of order, and its involvement could be decisive. The nature of this involvement will depend on whether Russian Westernism has succeeded in shedding its apish countenance; if not, then Russia will come to the West only with "blood and iron."[69] The final object of Dostoyevsky's own "practical Christianity" was to inspire Russian Westernism to appear in the West, not with the sword, but with the word "of the great general harmony, of the final brotherly communion of all nations in accordance with the law of the gospel of Christ."[70]

The crisis of the modern West is most immediately present for Dostoyevsky, as we have seen, in the struggle between France and Germany. In the light of his account of Western history, it can be understood more clearly how this struggle signifies for him an "eternal" battle of "two civilizations very different from each other." The modern German rejection of French "freedom, equality, and brotherhood" is the contemporary form of the earlier Protestant rejection of the papal idea. And this rejection constitutes, in turn, a later historical form of the resistance of the Germanic peoples to the ancient Roman idea of universal unity:

> Germany's aim is one; it existed before, always. It is her *Protestantism*—not that single formula of Protestantism which was conceived in Luther's time, but her continual Protestantism, her continual protest against the Roman world . . .—against

68 *NP*, p. 251; *DW*, pp. 1043-52 (Jan. 1881).
69 *DW*, p. 259 (March 1876).
70 *PS*, pp. 57-58.

everything that was Rome and Roman in aim, and subsequently—against everything that was bequeathed by ancient Rome to the new Rome and to all those peoples who inherited from Rome her idea, her formula and element; against the heir of Rome and everything that constitutes this legacy.[71]

Although Dostoyevsky does tend to identify the resistance to the Roman idea of order with the German people, there is no justification for the claim that he reduces this resistance to a matter of race.[72] Protestantism—whether that of Luther or Bismarck—is for him a possibility which transcends any particular Western people.[73] Yet just as France must be regarded as a more historically significant bearer of the Roman idea than Italy, so Germany is for him the embodiment *par excellence* of the protest against Rome. Insofar, however, as the Inquisitor's social formula purports to encompass within itself the protest of individuality, the actualization of this formula in the West would not simply signify the triumph of French over German civilization. It would signify, rather, the reconciliation of the most profound aspirations of both nations.

For Dostoyevsky the advent of the final Western social formula implies the spiritual destruction of humanity. Yet the failure to realize this formula implies the more tangible destruction of those "immense cataclysms" which will attend future disorder in the West.[74] The crisis of the modern West is total. And it is a crisis which the West cannot resolve by itself, for it has lost the way to that church idea which alone can regenerate it.

Impinging on the horizon of the modern West, however, is Russia, destined by virtue of its latent material power to play a decisive role in shaping the future of the West. Dostoyevsky assumed that, despite its profound divisions, the West would be at one in its hostile suspicion of the emerging colossus.[75] His own account of the transformations undergone by the liberal idea within Russia would seem to justify this suspicion. A powerful nation in which the most tentative Western "hypotheses" immediately become "axioms" does indeed present an alarming aspect. As the public prosecutor in *The Brothers Karamazov* warns:

Our fateful *troika* dashes headlong on and, perhaps, to destruction. And for many, many years now the people of Russia have been stretching forth their hands and calling for a halt to its furious and reckless gallop. And if, for the time being, other nations stand aside from the *troika* galloping at breakneck speed, it may not be from respect, as the poet would have liked us to believe, but simply from horror. Remember that. From horror and perhaps also from disgust of her, and it is a good thing they stand aside, for one day perhaps they will no longer stand aside, but will

71 *DW*, pp. 727, 730 (May-June 1877).
72 Cf., for instance, *DE*, p. 24.
73 Dostoyevsky was well aware, for instance, that the English-speaking world has tended to refuse complete assimilation to the "Roman idea." See *PS*, p. 56.
74 *DW*, p. 908 (Oct. 1877).
75 *The Idiot*, p. 588 (IV,7); *DW*, pp. 351, 1044 (June 1876; Jan. 1881).

stand like a wall before the on-rushing apparition and will themselves halt the frenzied gallop of our unbridled passions for the sake of their own safety, enlightenment, and civilization! We have already heard those alarmed voices from Europe.
They begin to be heard already.[76]

Yet this galloping *troika* is no more than the distorted reflection of the dominant idea present at the heart of the West itself. The Western horror of the
"on-rushing apparition" is a horror of the future which it has been preparing
for itself. Dostoyevsky holds out the possibility, however, that the Geneva
idea within Russia might be redeemed by the church idea, that "the people
will meet the atheist and overcome him." If the universal aspiration of Russian Westernism were to be informed by the church idea of the Russian
people, then an "astonished" West would be confronted, not with a fearful
apparition, but with a "mighty, truthful, wise, and gentle giant."[77] The truth
which this giant would bear is that word of "final brotherly communion"
which alone can illumine the darkness descending upon the West.

Dostoyevsky's hope that Russia would bring this truth rather than the
sword to the West underlay his consuming concern with the "Eastern question" which was agitating the nations of late nineteenth-century Europe. For
him, the struggle itself between the Balkan Slavs and the decaying Ottoman
Empire was incidental. What was of genuine significance was the decisive
manner in which this struggle of obscure peoples in an obscure corner of
Europe raised the question of Russia and the West. The West was drawn into
the Eastern question for two principal reasons. First, the Austrian Empire had
a long-established interest in the Balkan Peninsula, and the European system
of alliances was such that the interests of Austria inevitably became the
interests of the rest of Europe. Dostoyevsky offers, in *The Diary of a Writer*
(the September 1877 issue, for instance), a highly detailed account of the
manner in which the "unnatural" political situation of Europe would make it
impossible for Germany and France to avoid embroilment in any serious
Balkan eruption. If the Eastern question were to become acute, then it would
become inextricably associated with the Franco-German question. The West
was drawn into the Eastern question, secondly, because of its suspicion of
Russia's intentions. The depth of Western fear and suspicion of Russia was
amply illustrated for Dostoyevsky by the Pope's open declaration of support
for Moslem Turkey against Orthodox Russia when Russian support for the
Balkan Slavs eventuated in the Russo-Turkish war of 1877.[78]

It was increasingly apparent to Dostoyevsky that the great questions
which had agitated the civilized world for centuries were rapidly approaching
a dénouement.[79] In its raising of the Franco-German question in conjunction
with the question of Russia and the West, the Balkan controversy hastened the

76 *BK*, p. 852 (XII,10).
77 Ibid., p. 370 (VI,3); *The Idiot*, p. 588 (IV,7).
78 *DW*, p. 696 (May-June 1877); *PS*, p. 87.
79 Ibid., pp. 720-22 (May-June 1877).

approach of this dénouement. For Dostoyevsky the most fundamental issue was this: What was the nature of that word which Russia was preparing to speak through its activity in the Balkan Peninsula? Dostoyevsky asserted that there could be only one justification for this activity: concern for the future of the church idea in the world. Dissociating himself from the aspiration to a "merely political" pan-Slav union under great Russian hegemony, he called for a disinterested involvement in the Eastern question. Insofar as he did support the notion of a pan-Slav union under Russian auspices, he envisaged a union which would be "spiritual" rather than "political." This union would serve as a model to the world of a common unity which is at the same time "the assurance to each of his independent personality."[80] Dostoyevsky discerned in the Russian people's concern with the Eastern question reason for hope, if not certainty, of their dawning consciousness of a mission of service to the church idea—a mission containing the possibility of a renewed life for the West. This mission and this mission alone would give Russia a "moral right" to the guardianship of Constantinople, the symbolic centre of Orthodox Christianity:

Briefly, this dreadful Eastern question constitutes almost our whole future fate. Therein lie, as it were, all our tasks, and what is most important—our only exit into the plenitude of history. In this question is also our final conflict with Europe and our ultimate communion with her but only upon new, mighty and fertile foundations. Oh, how can Europe at this time grasp the fatal and vital importance to ourselves of the solution to this question?—In a word, no matter what may be the outcome of the present, perhaps quite indispensable diplomatic agreements and negotiations, nevertheless, sooner or later, *Constantinople must be ours*, let it be only in the future, in a century![81]

80 Ibid., pp. 360-65, 667-68 (June 1876; April 1877); *UD*, III, pp. 31, 123: "In the Slavic question neither Slavdom, nor Slavism is the essence, but Orthodoxy." Dostoyevsky's support for Russian intervention on behalf of the Balkan Slavs raises decisively the question of his attitude towards the Russian state. He tended to accept the Slavophile insistence on a radical distinction between the Russian *state* and the Russian *people*. The modern Russian state was for him essentially an artificial construction imposed upon the Russian people from without by Peter the Great and his successors. Yet he does concede that the state can, in some instances, express the aspirations of the people; and this is especially so insofar as the state understands itself according to the centuries-old symbolism of the Tsar who is the father of all Russians. This self-articulation of the political structure in terms of the father-child symbolism is, for Dostoyevsky, intimately related to the tendency of the Russian people to organize themselves into the *obschina*, or "brotherhood"—a manifestation, in turn, of *sobornost*. (See *DW*, pp. 1032-33 [Jan. 1881].) Because Dostoyevsky upheld the legitimacy of the Russian state only insofar as its activity manifested the spontaneous union of the Tsar with the aspiration of the people towards *sobornost*, it was crucial to him that this aspiration be evident in the undertakings of the state. He was convinced that the Russian intervention in the Balkans was not merely the product of the desire for conquest on the part of the St. Petersburg military and bureaucratic establishment, but was a genuine expression of the best aspirations of the Russian people as a whole. (For his disagreement with Tolstoy over this issue, see *DW*, pp. 793-813 [July-Aug. 1877].)

81 *DW*, pp. 636-37 (March 1877).

Concluding Remarks

The call for the liberation of Constantinople from Ottoman rule marks the disturbing culmination of Dostoyevsky's attempt to bridge the gap between the church idea and its realization. It is the last consequence of his effort to develop a "theory of practical Christianity" in response to the imminent presence of the final Western social formula within the world. Even the most sympathetic interpreters of Dostoyevsky's thought must find this sort of response to the Inquisitor's social formula objectionable—for it appears to constitute an acquiescence in that formula.

It must be assumed that Dostoyevsky did not think the Turks would voluntarily relinquish control of Constantinople, and that he therefore envisaged the necessity of compelling such a surrender—and not merely by diplomatic means. The compulsion would presumably be applied by the armies of the Russian state, and his acquiescence in this would certainly appear to constitute acquiescence in the adoption of "Caesar's sword" as a means of resolving the problem of human order. Yet it is precisely this offer of "Caesar's sword" which is the meaning of the third temptation rejected by the God-man. Dostoyevsky's own apparent weakness in the face of this temptation is often attributed to an atavistic Russian nationalism which tended to erupt in him from time to time, and which he fortunately managed to confine largely to his journalistic writings.[82] More attentive interpreters of his thought have explained his call for the liberation of Constantinople in terms of a distinction between his exoteric and his esoteric teachings (or between his journalism and his art). According to this latter view, his teaching about Russia's mission to the West should be regarded as an exoteric doctrine aimed at reuniting an increasingly fragmented Russian culture around a superior "magnanimous idea"—and thereby staving off the worst consequences of Westernization.[83] His esoteric teaching, on the other hand, points towards a personal spirituality which transcends the realm of history or politics.

Neither of the preceding explanations of Dostoyevsky's words about Constantinople is satisfactory. As I have attempted to demonstrate throughout this study, Dostoyevsky's concern with the practical political question of Russia and the West is intimately related to his most profound thought. To dismiss his teaching about Russia and the West as the expression of an unthinking, xenophobic nationalism is to renounce the attempt at a genuine explanation, and hence to renounce the possibility of a more complete understanding of his whole teaching about human order. The more thoughtful distinction between his exoteric and his esoteric teachings also avoids a genuine explanation, for it implies that his idea of Russia's mission to the West

---

82 See I. Howe, *Politics and the Novel* (London, 1961), pp. 54-55; H. Kohn, "Dostoevsky and Danilevsky: Nationalist Messianism," *Occidente* (1954), pp. 349-66.

83 See E. Sandoz, *Political Apocalypse, a Study of Dostoevsky's Grand Inquisitor* (Baton Rouge, 1971), pp. 231-33; *DW*, pp. 665-68 (April 1877).

ultimately need not be taken seriously, at least by Westerners. This is not to deny that he took care to present his teaching in the manner most appropriate both to the teaching itself and to those receiving it. There is undoubtedly a vast difference between the artistic and the journalistic presentation of his ideas; but there seems to be no justification for perceiving this difference as indicative of two different teachings intended for two sorts of people. While Dostoyevsky certainly employed journalism as a means of speaking to the Russian people at large, a careful study of both his journalism and his art reveals no significant difference in thought between them. His most cherished ideas are present in both.[84] The diminished expression which these ideas receive in the journalism must be attributed more to the exigencies of the medium itself than to any fundamental distinction made by Dostoyevsky in regard to his readers. (He considered human beings to be equal in the most important respect, and therefore equally capable of openness to the most important questions.) In a letter to Pobedonostsev, Dostoyevsky says that his appeal for a Russian mission of renewal to the West is the public expression of his most "intimate convictions." He also states, however, that this appeal is made in the "most extreme spirit" of his convictions.[85]

There may be little doubt that the notion of Russia's mission to the West is *too* "extreme" to be consistent with Dostoyevsky's own thought as a whole. It is important, however, to discover the precise point at which his teaching about Russia and the West becomes too "extreme." It could be said that this extremity appears at the very point where Dostoyevsky brings the church idea into alliance with the Russian sword. Yet although the call for the liberation of Constantinople would appear to entail such an alliance, note must be taken of Dostoyevsky's explicit and repeated denial that the church idea would be borne to the West by Russian arms. He insists, for instance, that "our destiny is universality, won not by the sword but by the strength of brotherhood and our fraternal aspiration to reunite mankind"; Russia is not to conquer the West, but to "stand before" the West as a light, to allow the God-man to "shine forth in opposition to the ideas of the West."[86]

Notwithstanding these protestations, the words about Constantinople indicate that Dostoyevsky was unwilling to eschew the use of the sword altogether, and this unwillingness may be responsible for much of the confusion concerning his teaching about Russia and the West. In opposition to the pacifism of writers such as Tolstoy he does justify the use of the sword, but only to protect the innocent from the sufferings inflicted upon them by injustice. Ivan's description of the suffering of the innocent includes an account of

---

84 This is not to say, of course, that there is an exact correspondence between Dostoyevsky's journalism and his art. Obviously some ideas are present in one group of writings, while not being represented in the other. Nevertheless, his journalism does seem to constitute a "laboratory" or "testing-ground" for most of the fundamental ideas present in his art. See, in this regard, his letter of 9 April 1876 to Mrs. Altaschevsky.

85 Letters of 19 May and 16 Aug. 1880 to K. Pobedonostsev.

86 *PS*, p. 58; *The Idiot*, p. 586 (IV,7).

unspeakable atrocities committed by the Turks against Bulgarian women and children. Dostoyevsky, who derived this account from his own reading of the newspapers, maintained that such evil must be forcibly resisted—not for the sake of "mere vengeance," but in order to protect the innocent. According to his own testimony, it is for this reason only that he would countenance the use of the sword against the Ottoman Empire.[87] The argument that Dostoyevsky's teaching becomes too extreme wherever it countenances force presupposes that the use of force, even to defend the innocent, is contrary to true justice. This is a presupposition which is far from self-evident.

The charge that Dostoyevsky conceived a universal Russian military conquest as the precondition for the actualization of the church idea[88] cannot find support in any careful study of his writings. Indeed, this sort of charge must be made in the face of explicit evidence to the contrary. Yet even if the suspicion concerning his attitude towards the sword can be dispelled, the extremity of his teaching about Russia and the West continues to obtrude itself. The source of this extremity would seem to be his tendency to associate the church idea with a particular nation, and to seek signs of its actualization in those events which constitute the history of that nation. A central concern of this chapter was to show that Dostoyevsky's close association of the church with Russia and the state with the West cannot be dismissed simply as unthinking and arbitrary. Yet the very tendency to make such associations undoubtedly exposes Dostoyevsky's thought to the possibility of that same confusion of God with nationality which Stavrogin detects in the following words of Shatov (in *The Devils*):

"The purpose of the whole evolution of a nation, in every people and at every period of its existence, is solely the pursuit of God, their God, their very own God, and faith in Him as in the only true one. God is the synthetic personality of the whole people, taken from its beginning to its end.
    ... If a great people does not believe that truth resides in it alone (in itself alone and in it exclusively), if it does not believe that it alone is able and has been chosen to raise up and save everybody by its own truth, it is at once transformed into ethnographical material, and not into a great people.... But there is only one truth, and therefore there is only one nation among all the nations that can have the true God, even though other nations may have their own particular great gods. And the only 'god-bearing' people is the Russian people...."
    ... Stavrogin said, looking sternly at him, "All I wanted to know is whether you believe in God yourself."
    "I believe in Russia. I believe in the Greek Orthodox Church. I—I believe in the body of Christ—I believe that the second coming will take place in Russia—I believe—" Shatov murmured in a frenzy.
    "But in God? In God?"
    "I—I shall believe in God."[89]

87 *DW*, pp. 806-13 (July-Aug. 1877).
88 See E. Voegelin, *The New Science of Politics* (Chicago, 1952), p. 117.
89 *The Devils*, pp. 256-59 (II,1,vii).

Shatov's contention that the Russian god is the "true God" rather than merely a "particular great god" can be demonstrated only through the historical success of the Russian people, for he is unable to affirm any truth beyond history, beyond the "synthetic personality of the whole people, taken from its beginning to its end." This confusion of God with history, of the good with the necessary, makes Shatov a proponent of the state idea (presumably in its Russian expression of Moscow as the "Third Rome"). Dostoyevsky's own search for historical evidence to buttress his hope that the Russian people is a "god-bearing" people\implies the possibility of a similar confusion. The tendency to look to history for hope, if not certainty, concerning the realization of the church idea inevitably exposes Dostoyevsky's thought in some measure to the judgment of history. This judgment can be particularly damaging when, for instance, the declaration that the Russian people "will meet the atheist and overcome him" is regarded in the light of subsequent Russian history. Why, then, did Dostoyevsky risk such a judgment? And more fundamentally, why did he risk that confusion of historical necessity with God which characterizes Shatov's messianic nationalism?

A passage in "The Grand Inquisitor" may point towards the answer which we seek. Subsequent to the confession that "we are . . . with *him*," the Inquisitor makes this declaration:

It is said that the whore, who sits upon the beast and holds in her hands the *mystery*, will be put to shame, that the weak will rise up again, that they will rend her purple and strip naked her "vile" body. But then I will rise and point out to you the thousands of millions of happy babes who have known no sin. And we who, for their happiness, have taken their sins upon ourselves, we shall stand before you and say, "Judge us if you can and if you dare."[90]

In his unpublished writings Dostoyevsky makes even more explicit this association of the Antichrist with the final Western social formula. And at one point in his rough notes for *The Devils* the Russian mission to the West is characterized as follows:

We are bringing the world the first paradise of the millennium.—And from amongst us, there will appear Elias... and Enoch, who will give battle to the Antichrist, i.e., the spirit of the West which will become incarnate in the West.[91]

These words are attributed to the character who was to become Stavrogin in the final published version of the novel; indeed, such allusions to the Book of Revelation are seldom voiced by Dostoyevsky as his own, even in his unpublished writings. Yet while he was evidently reluctant to commit himself fully to such apocalyptic speculation, he was deeply interested in it. This interest

90 *BK*, p. 305 (V,5).
91 *NP*, p. 226. See also V. Solovyov, "Tri rechi v pamyat Dostoyevskago," *Sobranie sochinenii* (Brussels, 1966), III-IV, p. 223. Solovyov states that Dostoyevsky laid most emphasis upon the following passages from the Book of Revelation: 12:1-2, 19:6-8, 21:1-4. According to Solovyov, he identified Russia with the "woman clothed with the sun" who is "with child and she cried out in her pangs of birth, in anguish for delivery."

stemmed ultimately from his effort to comprehend and affirm the statement attributed to Christ in the Gospel of John: "In the world you have tribulation; but be of good cheer, I have overcome the world." In this effort Dostoyevsky looked to history for "signs" and "portents" that the darkness of the modern world would indeed be overcome by the church idea. If he became too extreme in this, then this extremity must be attributed to the seriousness with which he approached the Revelation to John as an explanation of the overcoming of the world expressed in the Gospel of John.[92]

Dostoyevsky—as few other thinkers—has revealed the danger of confusing heaven and earth, and of holding them utterly apart. Yet his writing also demonstrates that such a two-fold danger is inescapably present in that delicate balance between transcendence and immanence at the centre of the Christian idea of the divine. Dostoyevsky's effort to bridge the gulf between the church idea and its realization may have led him to risk an improper identification of God with historical necessity in his teaching about Russia's mission to the West. But a truly adequate judgment of Dostoyevsky in this matter would presuppose a final answer concerning the extent to which the temptation to such a risk may be fundamentally inherent in Christianity itself.

It must be emphasized, further, that although Dostoyevsky risks that confusion of the good with the necessary which he discerns at the centre of the Western solution to the problem of order, he does not finally succumb to such a confusion. There is no solid evidence in his writings of a tendency to immanentize the "last things." The church on earth remains in his thought merely the entry to human participation in an eternal order, in a kingdom not of this world, but of a "new heaven and a new earth." As for the question of when the universal church will be realized on earth, Father Zosima renounces any attempt to penetrate the "secret of times and fixed dates":

This will be, it will be, even though at the end of time, for this alone has been ordained to come to pass! And one should not be troubled about times and fixed dates, for the secret of times and fixed dates is in the wisdom of God and in his foresight and his love.[93]

Zosima's words express Dostoyevsky's clear recognition of the limits inherent in the attempt to discern in history evidence of the overcoming of the final Western social formula by the church idea. The first and the last word of his "theory of practical Christianity," therefore, is his appeal to each to work "without ceasing" for the true order—even if the whole world should refuse it.[94] For Dostoyevsky, this work is undertaken in the conviction that the world is overcome by the truth, whether individuals happen to recognize it or not.

92 These two writings, more than any others, stand at the centre of Dostoyevsky's Christianity. See his letter of 1 Jan. 1868 to his niece, Sofya Ivanova. See also *BK*, pp. 422-27 (VII,4); V. Solovyov, "Tri rechi v pamyat Dostoyevskago," *Sobranie sochinenii* (Brussels, 1966), III-IV, p. 223.

93 *BK*, p. 73 (II,5).

94 Ibid., pp. 378-79 (VI,3); *PS*, p. 82; *NRY*, p. 450. See *NBK*: "the clever Pilate... had reflected on truth... What is the Truth? It stood before him, Truth itself" (p. 102).

APPENDIX

Although Dostoyevsky does not enter directly into the *filioque* issue in his writings, his account of the historical relationship between the "church idea" and the "state idea" clearly points towards this issue. I think it important therefore to offer a brief elucidation of it. For our purposes it is appropriate to approach the issue from the perspective of the Eastern church.

The Eastern church has always maintained that the *filioque* clause betrays a misapprehension of the ultimate principle of Christianity. This principle is, for Eastern theology, that of the simultaneous transcendence and immanence of God—a principle which is ultimately inaccessible to reason. We have noted Dostoyevsky's teaching that the merely "material" faculty of reason is prone to over-reach itself, to "demand a chapter for itself." The formulation of the Trinitarian principle in the Nicene Creed was intended to preclude the intrusion of reason into a realm of apprehension open only to the higher spiritual faculty within human beings. This became necessary when its new role under Constantine as the civil theology of the Empire compelled Christianity to formulate its truth conceptually, in a creed which could be professed by all, regardless of whether or not they had realized the spiritual principle within themselves. An attempt to explain fully how the Nicene Creed renders the Christian truth conceptually explicit for all, without subjecting it to the reason of all, would be far beyond the scope of this study.[1] It must suffice to state here that, according to the Eastern church, the original Nicene formulation preserves the paradox of the simultaneous transcendence and immanence of the Divine by means of a clear distinction. It distinguishes between the absolutely unqualified, unknowable, and incommunicable Essence of the Triune God, and the hypostatic powers of each Person of the Trinity whereby God manifests himself in such a way that he is said to be present in all created being. In this formulation the unity of the Triune God has its source, not in the Essence which transcends any of the finite determinations inherent to reason or speech, but in the Person of the Father. This Person

---

1 For a lucid discussion of this question, see P. Sherrard, *The Greek East and the Latin West* (London, 1959), chap. 2.

191

is the sole creative principle within the Trinity, and hence the source of the other two hypostases—of the Son by "begetting" and of the Spirit by "procession."

The Western church was concerned that the original formulation of the Trinitarian principle did not assert the unity of God with sufficient force and clarity. This concern can be attributed to the threat posed to Christianity in the West by the Arianism of the Goths and the polytheism of pagan Gaul; and it can be attributed to the relative lack of philosophical sophistication within the Western church at the time.[2] The Latin theologians thus sought a more solid basis for the unity of the Triune God than that provided by the Person of the Father. This unity they found in the Essence common to the three Persons of the Trinity. Their desire to establish the unity of God in evident and unmistakable terms, and to do so with reference to the Divine Essence, resulted in a de-emphasizing of the hypostatic powers and energies whereby God can be "present in, sustain, and save the living, multiple, and changing world of known and perishable things." The theological divergence between the Latin West and the Greek East, which eventuated in the Western addition of the *filioque* clause to the Creed, has been summarized as follows:

In effect, what Western theologians tended increasingly to stress was the idea of the *Summum Ens*, of the absolute One in whom no distinctions of any kind may be admitted. Indeed, one may go further and say that a certain restriction of spiritual understanding took place, in the sense that a perspective which envisaged in God both an unqualified Essence, a 'Divine Darkness' of an absolute and infinite potentiality, and a real distinction of hypostases, gave way to a perspective which tended to envisage the essential nature alone, and this considered, not as a pre-ontological, but as a purely ontological, reality—as, in fact, Being Itself.

  ... The Essence, according to the tradition accepted by the Greeks, is, although entirely simple and unknowable, neither Being Itself, nor the cause of being in others. Further, there can be no causal, principial or other relationship either between the Essence and something else, or of the Essence with Itself, for the Essence is both prior to, and cannot enter into, any relationship of whatsoever kind. It was on this account that the Greeks maintained that the cause and principle of being in the Trinity is not the Essence, but the hypostasis of the Father. If, however, Essence and Being describe one and the same reality, as they tended to do for the Latins, then it becomes meaningless to say that the hypostasis, and not the Essence, of the Father is the cause and principle of being in the Trinity. On the contrary, it must now be maintained that the cause and principle of being in the Trinity is the entirely simple Essence, and it is from this that both the Son and the Spirit derive their being. But as the Son is identical in Essence with the Father, and the cause and principle of being in the Trinity is the Essence, it follows that it must be in, or through, a single essential act that the Father and Son together 'project' the Spirit.[3]

In the view of the Eastern church, the *filioque* clause constitutes a rationalization of the Trinitarian principle because it implies the overcoming of that

2 Ibid., p. 67. See also S. Runciman, *The Eastern Schism* (Oxford, 1955), pp. 11, 109.
3 P. Sherrard, *The Greek East and the Latin West* (London, 1959), pp. 67-69.

paradox or contradiction which signifies the ultimate inaccessibility of Christian truth to reason. The paradox is overcome, however, only through the exclusion of one of its poles. The tendency to emphasize the simple and indivisible Essence of God, to the point of disregarding the multiple and communicable powers and energies of the three Persons, finally implies the exclusion of God from the world.

So fundamental an alteration in the understanding of the supreme principle of Christianity was bound to have far-reaching implications for other aspects of Christian doctrine and practice. One such implication, which manifested itself immediately, was a different conception of ecclesiastical organization. For Dostoyevsky, the papal claim to primacy within the church—a primacy not only of honour but of rights and powers—was the first and most significant practical manifestation of the Western rationalizing tendency.[4] It has been noted that for Dostoyevsky the church constitutes the reconciliation of personal freedom with unity, in that individuals find themselves in themselves through common participation in the God-man. This participation depends on the presence of the God-man in the church—and not in one part of the church only, but wherever two or three are gathered together. The acknowledgment of God's complete and undivided presence in each of the many local churches is rooted in the paradoxical conception of God as absolutely transcendent of all created being and yet at the same time fully present within the multiplicity of created things. The unity of the local churches is derived from their common participation in God, as is the unity of all creation. Such was the manner in which, at least theoretically, Eastern Christianity understood Christ to be the Head of the church. A consequence of this understanding was the Eastern insistence upon the equality of rights and powers of all bishops within the church. For the bishop is the visible image of the presence of Christ within each local church, and Christ cannot be more or less present at one church than at another because he cannot be more or less than himself.[5] The Western tendency to rationalize the Christian paradox entailed a changed conception of the church, a change which has been expressed as follows:

Yet if the full reality of the idea of participation, according to which Christ may be recognized as without mediation the head and unifying principle of the local churches, ceases, as it did for the Latins, to have that effective vitality it had for the Greeks, while, on the contrary, what becomes an over-riding consideration, as it did for the Latins, is the totally transcendent and non-participable nature of God, then, to that extent, Christ cannot be recognized as the actual head and unifying principle of the local churches in *His own Person*. Thus, to that extent, this head and unifying principle must be sought for elsewhere, in another head and unifying principle which in a certain sense replaces the absent Person of Christ, and is the visible representation of His invisible, and totally transcendent, unity. One might say that the emphasizing in a somewhat exclusive manner of the transcendent and

4 *BK*, p. 302 (V,5); *PS*, p. 89; *DW*, pp. 728-29 (May-June 1877).
5 V. Lossky, *The Mystical Theology of the Eastern Church* (London, 1957), chap. 9;
  P. Sherrard, *The Greek East and the Latin West* (London, 1959), pp. 74-75.

indivisible nature of God, of the conception of God as the *Summum Ens*, leads to the notion of a 'real absence' of God from the world, and hence to the idea that until His 'coming again' His place on earth must be taken by a visible head who claims His titles and powers and unites the visible and multiple local centres of the Church into a single organization under his directing leadership. Once such an understanding of things had become sufficiently general in Western Christendom to have practical effect, it was more or less inevitable that the Bishop of Rome would be regarded as possessing this divine controlling authority: the Roman See is the one Apostolic See of Western Christendom, while Rome itself was the scene of the martyrdom of two Apostles, St. Peter and St. Paul, the ancient imperial capital, and the place where ideals of an absolutism similar to that of the Caesars would naturally tend to focus.[6]

6 P. Sherrard, *The Greek East and the Latin West* (London, 1959), pp. 85-86.

SELECTED BIBLIOGRAPHY

A complete bibliography of writings concerned with Dostoyevsky would represent a major undertaking in itself. What follows, therefore, is a highly selective list of those books and articles which I consider to be most pertinent to this study of Dostoyevsky, and hence most likely to be of use to the interested reader.

The bibliography is divided into three sections: Section A lists writings by Dostoyevsky, both in the Russian edition and in the English and French translations referred to in the notes; Section B cites books and articles about Dostoyevsky; and Section C contains writings which, though not directly or exclusively concerned with Dostoyevsky, are highly relevant to the themes arising out of this study.

Section A

Dostoyevsky, F. M. *Polnoye sobranie sochinenii v tridsati tomakh*. Leningrad: Nauka, 1966-1977.

_____ . *Pisma*. 4 vols. Ed. by A. S. Dolinin. Moscow: State Publishers, 1928, 1930, 1934, 1959.

_____ . *The Gambler, Bobok, A Nasty Story*. Trans. by J. Coulson. Harmondsworth, Eng.: Penguin Books, 1966.

_____ . *The House of the Dead*. Trans. by C. Garnett. New York: Dell, 1959.

_____ . *Winter Notes on Summer Impressions*. Trans. by R. L. Renfield. Criterion Books, 1955.

_____ . *Notes from Underground, White Nights, The Dream of a Ridiculous Man, and Selections from The House of the Dead*. Trans. by A. R. MacAndrew. New York: New American Library, 1961.

_____ . *Crime and Punishment*. Trans. by D. Magarshack. Harmondsworth, Eng.: Penguin Books, 1966.

_____ . *The Notebooks for Crime and Punishment*. Trans. by E. Wasiolek. Chicago: Univ. of Chicago Press, 1967.

_____ . *The Idiot*. Trans. by D. Magarshack. Harmondsworth, Eng.: Penguin Books, 1955.

_____ . *The Notebooks for The Idiot*. Ed. by E. Wasiolek and trans. by K. Strelsky. Chicago: Univ. of Chicago Press, 1967.

————. *The Devils*. Trans. by D. Magarshack. Harmondsworth, Eng.: Penguin Books, 1953.

————. *The Notebooks for The Possessed*. Ed. by E. Wasiolek and trans. by V. Terras. Chicago: Univ. of Chicago Press, 1968.

————. *The Adolescent*. Trans. by A. R. MacAndrew. New York: Doubleday, 1972.

————. *The Notebooks for A Raw Youth*. Ed. by E. Wasiolek and trans. by V. Terras. Chicago: Univ. of Chicago Press, 1969.

————. *The Brothers Karamazov*. Trans. by D. Magarshack. Harmondsworth, Eng.: Penguin Books, 1958.

————. *The Notebooks for The Brothers Karamazov*. Ed. and trans. by E. Wasiolek. Chicago: Univ. of Chicago Press, 1971.

————. *The Diary of a Writer*. 2 vols. Trans. by B. Brasol. New York: Charles Scribner's Sons, 1949.

————. *The Dream of a Queer Fellow and The Pushkin Speech*. Trans. by S. S. Koteliansky and J. M. Murry. London: Allen and Unwin, 1972.

————. *Occasional Writings*. Ed. and trans. by D. Magarshack. New York: Random House, 1963.

————. *Dostoïevski et l'Europe en 1873*. Ed. and trans. by J. Drouilly. Montreal: Leméac, 1969.

————. *Correspondance de Dostoïevski*. 4 vols. Trans. by D. Arban, N. Gourfinkel. Paris: Calmann-Lévy, 1949, 1959, 1960, 1961.

————. *Letters of Fyodor Michailovich Dostoevsky*. Trans. by E. C. Mayne. New York: Horizon Press, 1961.

————. *Letters and Reminiscences*. Trans. by S. S. Koteliansky and J. M. Murry. New York: Books for Libraries Press, 1971.

————. *New Dostoevsky Letters*. Trans. by S. S. Koteliansky. New York: Haskell House, 1974.

————. *The Unpublished Dostoevsky*. 3 vols. Ed. by C. R. Proffer and trans. by T. S. Berczynski, B. H. Montu, A. Boyer, E. Proffer. Ann Arbor: Ardis, 1973.

Section B

Bakhtin, M. *Problems of Dostoevsky's Poetics*. Trans. by R. W. Rotsel. Ann Arbor: Ardis, 1973.

Berdyaev, N. *Dostoevsky*. Trans. by D. Attwater. New York: Meridian Books, 1957.

Carr, E. H. *Dostoevsky*. London: Allen and Unwin, 1962.

Cox, R. L. "Dostoevsky's Grand Inquisitor," *Cross Currents*, Fall 1967, 427-44.

Dolenc, I. *Dostoevsky and Christ, a Study of Dostoevsky's Rebellion Against Belinsky*. Toronto: York Publishing, 1978.

Dolinin, A. S. (ed.). *F. M. Dostoyevsky v vospominaniyakh sovremennikov*. 2 vols. Moscow, 1964.

Dostoyevsky, Anna. *Reminiscences*. Ed. and trans. by B. Stillman. New York: Liveright, 1975.

Fanger, D. *Dostoevsky and Romantic Realism*. Cambridge, Mass.: Harvard Univ. Press, 1965.

Frank, J. "Notes from the Underground," *Sewanee Review*, lxix, 1961.

————. *Dostoevsky, the Seeds of Revolt 1821-1849*. Princeton: Princeton Univ. Press, 1976.

Gibson, A. B. *The Religion of Dostoevsky*. London: S.C.M. Press, 1973.

Golosovker, E. *Dostoyevsky i Kant*. Moscow: Nauka, 1963.

Grossman, L. *Dostoevsky*. Trans. by M. Mackler. London: Allen Lane, 1974.

Guardini, R. "The Legend of the Grand Inquisitor," trans. by S. Cunneen. *Cross Currents*, Fall 1952, 58-86.

Jones, M. V. *Dostoyevsky*. London: Paul Elek, 1976.

_____ . "Dostoyevsky's Conception of the Idea," *Renaissance and Modern Studies*, xiii, 1969, 106-31.

de Jonge, A. *Dostoevsky and the Age of Intensity*. London: Secker & Warburg, 1975.

Kabat, G. *Ideology and Imagination, the Image of Society in Dostoevsky*. New York: Columbia Univ. Press, 1978.

Lawrence, D. H. "The Grand Inquisitor," in *Selected Literary Criticism*, ed. by A. Beal. New York: Viking Press, 1956.

Lord, R. *Dostoevsky, essays and perspectives*. London: Chatto & Windus, 1970.

Lossky, N. *Dostoyevsky i ego khristianskoe miroponimanie*. New York: Chekhov Publishing House, 1953.

Mochulsky, K. *Dostoevsky, his Life and Work*. Trans. by M. A. Minihan. Princeton: Princeton Univ. Press, 1967.

Panichas, G. A. *The Burden of Vision, Dostoevsky's Spiritual Art*. Michigan: W. B. Eerdmans, 1977.

_____ . "Fyodor Dostoevsky and Roman Catholicism," *The Greek Orthodox Theological Review*, Summer 1959, 16-34.

Peace, R. *Dostoevsky, an Examination of the Major Novels*. Cambridge: Cambridge Univ. Press, 1971.

Ramsey, P. "No Morality without Immortality: Dostoevsky and the Meaning of Atheism," *Journal of Religion*, April 1956, 90-108.

Rozanov, V. *Dostoevsky and the Legend of the Grand Inquisitor*. Trans. by J. E. Roberts. New York: Cornell Univ. Press, 1972.

Sandoz, E. *Political Apocalypse, a Study of Dostoevsky's Grand Inquisitor*. Baton Rouge: Louisiana State Univ. Press, 1971.

Shestov, L. *Dostoevsky, Tolstoy, and Nietzsche*. Trans. by B. Martin and S. Roberts. Athens: Ohio Univ. Press, 1969.

Solovyov, V. "Tri rechi v pamyat Dostoyevskago," *Sobranie sochinenii* III-IV. Brussels, 1966.

Steinberg, A. Z. *Dostoievsky*. London: Bowes, 1966.

Wasiolek, E. *Dostoevsky, the Major Fiction*. Cambridge, Mass.: M.I.T. Press, 1964.

Wellek, R. (ed.). *Dostoevsky, a collection of critical essays*. Englewood Cliffs, N.J.: Prentice-Hall, 1962.

Section C

Berdyaev, N. *The Russian Idea*. Trans. by R. M. French. New York: Macmillan, 1948.

Bulgakov, S. *The Orthodox Church*. Trans. by E. S. Cram. London: Centenary Press, 1935.

Camus, A. *The Rebel, an Essay on Man in Revolt*. Trans. by A. Bower. New York: Alfred A. Knopf, 1954.

Christoff, P. K. *An Introduction to 19th Century Slavophilism*. 3 vols. Paris: Mouton, 1972.

Cohn, N. *The Pursuit of the Millennium*. New York: Harper & Row, 1961.

Khomyakov, A. *The Church is One*. [n.p., n.d.].

————— . *L'Eglise Latine et le Protestantisme*. Lausanne, 1872.

Koyré, A. *La philosophie et le problème national en Russie au début du XIX siècle*. Paris, 1929.

Lossky, N. *History of Russian Philosophy*. London: Allen and Unwin, 1952.

Lossky, V. *The Mystical Theology of the Eastern Church*. London: James Clarke, 1957.

Löwith, K. *Meaning in History*. Chicago: Univ. of Chicago Press, 1949.

de Lubac, H. *The Drama of Atheist Humanism*. Trans. by E. M. Riley. Cleveland: World Publishing, 1963.

Planty-Bonjour, G. *Hegel et la pensée philosophique en Russie*. The Hague: Nijhoff, 1974.

Sherrard, P. *The Greek East and the Latin West*. London: Oxford Univ. Press, 1959.

Solovyov, V. *Lectures on Godmanhood*. Trans. by P. Zouboff. London: Dobson, 1948.

————— . *The Meaning of Love*. Trans. by J. Marshall. London: Beks, 1945.

Strauss, L. *On Tyranny*. New York: Glencoe Press, 1967.

Voegelin, E. *The New Science of Politics*. Chicago: Univ. of Chicago Press, 1952.

————— . *From Enlightenment to Revolution*. North Carolina: Duke Univ. Press, 1975.

Weil, S. *The Need for Roots*. Trans. by A. Wills. New York: Harper & Row, 1971.

Zernov, N. *The Russians and their Church*. London: S.P.C.K., 1945.

INDEX

199